Language, Culture and the Law

Linguistic Insights

Studies in Language and Communication

Edited by Maurizio Gotti,
University of Bergamo

Volume 111

PETER LANG
Bern · Berlin · Bruxelles · Frankfurt am Main · New York · Oxford · Wien

Vijay K. Bhatia, Christopher N. Candlin &
Paola Evangelisti Allori (eds)

Language, Culture and the Law

The Formulation of Legal Concepts across Systems and Cultures

PETER LANG
Bern · Berlin · Bruxelles · Frankfurt am Main · New York · Oxford · Wien

Bibliographic information published by Die Deutsche Bibliothek
Die Deutsche Bibliothek lists this publication in the Deutsche Nationalbibliografie; detailed bibliographic data is available on the Internet at ‹http://dnb.ddb.de›.

British Library Cataloguing-in-Publication Data:
A catalogue record for this book is available from *The British Library*, Great Britain.

Library of Congress Cataloging-in-Publication Data

Language, Culture and the Law : the Formulation of Legal Concepts Across Systems and Cultures / Vijay K. Bhatia, Christopher N. Candlin & Paola Evangelisti Allori (eds).
p. cm. – (Linguistic insights, 1424-8689 ; v. 64)
Includes bibliographical references.
ISBN 978-3-03911-470-2 (alk. paper)
1. Legal polycentricity–Language. 2. English language–Foreign countries
I. Bhatia, V. K. (Vijay Kumar), 1942- II. Candlin, Christopher
III. Evangelisti Allori, Paola.
K236.L36 2008
340'.14–dc22

2008041441

Published with a grant from MIUR COFIN Project n.2002104353.

ISSN 1424-8689
ISBN 978-3-03911-470-2

Contents

Part 2: European Legal and Institutional Language

Part 3:
Translating Legal Discourse

VIJAY BHATIA / CHRISTOPHER N. CANDLIN /
PAOLA EVANGELISTI ALLORI

Introduction

Legal language has been the focus of analysis for a long time. Jurists themselves have traditionally regarded language as the primary means for the formulation and interpretation of legal concepts. In the philosophy of law (Bobbio 1997; Lazzaro 1997; Pintore/Jori 1997) and in legal semiotics (Jackson 1995), there has been a longstanding debate about important issues such as the role of language in the 'science of law', the use and interpretation of specific terms/concepts, and the definition and analysis of legal 'acts'. Legal discourse has also been studied from the standpoint of legal anthropology where close (careful) analysis of legal events and legal settings has been carried out from an anthropological and ethnographic point of view (Conley/O'Barr [1]1998, [2]2005). At the same time, language has itself been the object of legislation and legal debate, as in the case of the rules for the choice of language of the procedure in international arbitration. Indeed, it is in the context of international exchanges and interaction, whether business, institutional or political, that interlinguistic and intercultural issues most evidently affect legal action and praxis.

Much of the published work on legal discourse, however, has been devoted either to specific linguistic features of legal language or to the analysis of legal discourse in different courtroom situations or other legal contexts especially in the field of forensic linguistics. All of these studies have been rooted in a specific language and context, usually English in English-speaking legal contexts (Bowers 1989; Gibbons 1994; Tiersma 1999). In recent times, two major socio-political events and processes have contributed enormously to the spread of multicultural studies of legal discourse. The process of politically merging the different European countries into a single European Union has involved much effort at harmonizing legislation and procedures within the Union. The effort of creating a common

European legal framework while preserving the different member states' cultural and legal traditions and identities has required and initiated close comparison of the different national legal systems, norms, concepts and terminology.

Total harmonization, nonetheless, has proven difficult to achieve. The process of creating a single corpus of European Law has witnessed much negotiation and compromise on the nature of the language and terminology within which the EU norms are worded, in order to avoid culture-loaded terms which, in turn, might induce culture-bound interpretations. The resulting language, referred to as Eurolanguage, Eurolect (Goffin 1994), or European legalese (Mariani Sacerdoti, this volume), is a symbol of intercultural, inter-linguistic mediation. As such, it is often a hybrid concept resulting from negotiation among different cultural, legal and linguistic traditions.

Important side effects of the legal situation specific to the European context have been a greater awareness by continental European linguists of the importance of multicultural, multilingual studies and comparisons of legal discourses across cultures (Bouglak 2001, Robertson, 2001, Salmi-Tolonen 2001, Simonnœs, 2001) and the great importance given to legal translation and the training of translators in this specific field (Sarcevič [1]1997, [2]2000, 2001; Chroma 2004).

The second major process worldwide is the rapid spread of globalization which, although affecting all walks of life, has had its primary and most noticeable effects in the world of international commercial transactions, on their regulation, as in international contract law, and on dispute resolution through international arbitration. The latter, in particular, has produced an important corpus of linguistic analyses across multicultural and socio-political contexts spanning over different continents (Bhatia/Candlin/Engberg/Trosborg 2003; Bhatia/Candlin/Gotti 2003; Bhatia/Engberg 2004; Bhatia/Engberg/Gotti/Heller 2005; Bhatia/Candlin/Engberg 2008). These studies have been primarily inspired by a multinational effort in which more than twenty countries have collaborated to explore the complexities of arbitration discourses and practices. This international project, entitled *Generic Integrity in Legislative Discourse in Multilingual and Multi-*

cultural Contexts,[1] has investigated the generic integrity of legislative discourse by analysing the linguistic and discoursal properties of a multilingual corpus of international arbitration laws drawn from a number of different countries, cultures, and socio-political backgrounds, written in different languages, and used within and across a variety of legal systems.

The project, focusing on the discourse of arbitration in use in different countries, written in distinct languages, each with its own distinctive legal culture and system, has investigated legal discourse in a number of different languages, such as Chinese, Czech, Danish, English, Finnish, French, German, Hindi, Italian, Japanese, Malaysian, Portuguese, Spanish and Swedish in order to draw upon and reference a number of distinct legal systems, including Brazilian, Chinese (PRC, i.e. People's Republic of China), Czech, Danish, English, Finnish, French, German, Indian, Italian, Japanese, Malaysian and Spanish.

The second project on which this volume especially draws is an internationally refereed Italian project, *Interculturality in Domain-specific English*,[2] aiming to identify the cultural and linguistic traits responsible for intercultural diversity in different areas of social practice. Legal discourse, both within the context of the evolving European political and juridical context and directed at international arbitration, was one of the areas of social practice on which this latter project especially focused its attention.

This volume presents a set of invited and commissioned papers, many of which inspired by the two projects discussed above, based on analyses of legal discourse drawn from a number of international contexts where often the English language and legal culture have had to adjust to legal concepts very different from those of the Common Law system. The various chapters address a number of key questions among which are:

---

1 The project entitled *Generic Integrity in Legislative Discourse in Multilingual and Multicultural Contexts* (No. 9040474) was supported by a Competitive Earmarked Research Grant awarded by the Hong Kong UGC Research Grant Council.

2 The project, supported by a Research Grant from the Italian Ministry for Higher Education and Research (project N° 2002/104353), involved research units from five Italian universities: Bergamo, Turin, Milan, Rome-IUSM and Naples.

- How does the socio-political and cultural context affect the use of language in the formulation of legal discourse?
- How are the meanings of language choices made within the framework of one juridical tradition modified when the same language is put to use in a different context and tradition?
- How does the resulting, hybrid 'Eurolanguage' reflect the amount of negotiation and compromise needed to reach agreement on fundamental political issues?

In the present context of globalization these issues are of great relevance, particularly in contexts of commercial contracting and international arbitration where legal discourse has become the international instrument for guaranteeing agreements or resolving disagreements across borders and systems. They are also extremely relevant in legal and institutional discourse, particularly within the recently changed European context, where the process of political unification has given rise to a number of related juridical, linguistic and ideological issues.

The contents of the volume

The volume is divided into three sections. The first section deals with issues related to the impact of culture on the legal discourse of international arbitration and trade. The discourse of arbitration is analysed in two specific fields of professional action, commercial and sport-related. In both cases, there exist an international code in English and local, national codes usually modelled on the international one but where local, socio-cultural undertones can be detected. The commercial international context is also evoked in two chapters on contracting and insurance. The second section deals with issues related to specific European socio-political and juridical contexts where the variety of linguistic and cultural issues at stake also have political implications at different levels of actuation. Legal translation is specifically dealt with in the third section, although the concept of translation, or of transposition of legal concepts from one system to the other, runs through most of the papers in various forms.

International arbitration and trade law

In the first section, Maurizio Gotti's chapter, in examining and discussing the kinds of discrepancies found in the formulation of normative texts (re)produced in different contexts, also sets the scene for many of the chapters to follow. His study analyses the main linguistic differences found in the regulations for international arbitration produced in English by three important Italian chambers of commerce on the blueprint of the UNCITRAL model and concludes that local constraints constitute an important conditioning factor in the formulation of legal concepts.

The chapter by Giuliana Garzone explores some English versions of international arbitration rules issued by institutions having their seat in non-English speaking countries, namely Italy and France, comparing and contrasting them with their original Italian and French source texts. As a subsidiary source of information, further comparison is also carried out between the Italian and French versions of rules originally formulated in English in an attempt to ascertain whether translated legal texts present any of the peculiar discoursal features, e.g. *simplification* and *explicitation*, which according to translators, characterize translated texts. Garzone concludes that some of the procedures routinely performed by translators may have a negative impact on the rendering of the meaning and effects of legal texts.

In her chapter, Paola Evangelisti Allori examines the way in which relations of power among the various participants in the arbitration procedure are expressed linguistically in international and Italian national rules for arbitration in sport. By looking at the pragmatic functions in the two sets of rules and at the modals used to express them in the two languages, she is able to point to a basic ambiguity in the use of the English modal system, in particular by *shall* and *may* which, in this kind of legal discourse, are also used to carry the function of 'attribution of power or of authority'. On the basis of this distinction she finds that the kinds of acts attributed to each category of participants are indicative of the level of power assigned to the various participant categories. The differences in the degree of power, obligation or prohibition attributed to different categories in the two regulations are not due to differences in the linguistic systems alone, but are indicative of different socio-cultural attitudes towards the participants on the part of the two drafting authorities.

Again in the field of sports arbitration, Michela Menghini's chapter looks at the linguistic correspondences – and discrepancies – found in the linguistic comparison of international and Italian regulations, which may lead to conceptual misunderstanding. She then describes the approach adopted in the construction of a multilayered electronic bilingual glossary in which such linguistic constructions are listed for each language; the glossary provides the possibility of comparing each construction with its equivalent in the other language and of reintegrating it in the original co-text (sentence) and context (the whole regulation), thus providing a tool for a quick and efficient comparison of single constructions and of the same constructions in larger units, for use by practitioners, legal translators and students of law.

Salmi-Tolonen's and Solly's chapters deal with intercultural issues in trade contracting and insurance law. Salmi-Tolonen approaches the issue of negotiated meaning in business-to-business contracting within a framework of *proactive* law, a movement promoted by a group of researchers and practicing contract lawyers in Finland, which has presently spread all over the Nordic countries, particularly in the field of international commercial contracting, to prevent litigation at later stages. Against this legal backdrop, she discusses some of the basic concepts used in the international sale of goods showing what conceptual and terminological problems may occur in international commercial contracting. She argues for negotiation to be understood as a methodological concept for describing and explaining interaction between legal and business professionals in this delicate field of action and suggests more awareness of the linguistic aspects likely to give rise to legal problems in cross-border transactions.

Solly examines the influence, both linguistic and cultural, that the language of the United Kingdom Marine Insurance Act of 1906 has had on the language choice in some of the marine insurance statutes of other English-speaking countries, which, have become in time more and more removed from their original legal, cultural and linguistic frameworks.

European legal and institutional language

The chapters in the second section address the role played by language in the construction of Europe as a new political and legal entity, and the consequent forging of a new legal language resulting from a process of negotiation and compromise in order to accommodate concepts and terms from one culture into a common system suited to, and accepted by, a commonality of cultures and systems. In many cases, it is the English language, legal culture and tradition that have been adapted to serve the linguistic needs of the political and juridical unification of a cohort of non-English speaking countries and cultures. In other cases, it is English which has to translate back into its own system terms and legal concepts which in the process of consensus building in Europe have acquired a new meaning borrowed from other cultures.

The section opens with the chapter by Gigliola Sacerdoti Mariani who analyses some of the key terms and expressions in the text of the Draft EU Constitution as rendered in the English, French and Italian versions. The comparative analysis shows translational imprecision and questionable choices as well as different world views reflected in the three versions. On the basis of her detailed comparative analysis of language(s) and concepts, Sacerdoti Mariani maintains that the inaccurate, imprecise, or even deceptive translations of that fundamental EU legislative text, at least in the languages analysed, reveal evident traces of the consensus-building effort and of the compromises incurred in the laborious drafting process.

Marina Dossena, in the next chapter, examines the different linguistic strategies used in various Scottish sites to make the text of the 'The Abolition of Feudal Tenure (Scotland) Act 2000' more accessible to the general public. In all cases, the process of popularization adopted has involved stylistic and linguistic choices, discussed comparatively by Dossena, who shows how, in each case, the process has been influenced by the different encoders' stance about the reform.

In their chapter, Giuditta Caliendo and Marco Venuti show a further illustration of skilful use of language in the negotiation of meaning as it appears in the EU documents on the acceptance of new member states. They examine the thorny issue of Turkey's membership through the documents issued by the two bodies overseeing acceptance: the EU Commission on enlargement and the European Council. Their linguistic analysis of the 'Annual Reports of the Commission' and of the 'Conclusions' of the European Council shows the strategic way in which the EU attempted to maintain diplomatic and economic relations with Turkey without officially committing itself to opening accession negotiations while also indicating the different roles and attitudes of the EU Commission and the European Council.

The chapter by Cristina Pennarola, analyses the language in the provision of humanitarian aids as it appears in EU legal documents published in the Official Journal of the European Union. The aim is to verify whether such documents comply with the impersonal traits typical of legal discourse or whether, given the topic, they present a more personal, 'human touch'. Applying the tools of Critical Discourse Analysis, she finds that the highly loaded lexicalizations found in the distinction between home disasters and third-country catastrophes points to a deeper, hidden distinction made between home and third-countries. The linguistic analysis thus shows an implied political and economical asymmetry together with geographical and cultural distance which characterise the EU aid to third countries as a benevolent, if not patronizing, concession.

The next chapter by Marchilia Volini analyses the 'phrasemes' characterising the discourse of EU Framework Decisions, a legislative instrument introduced by the Amsterdam Treaty to approximate the laws and regulations of the Member States on matters of Police and Judicial Cooperation in Criminal Matters. Legally, Framework Decisions are binding on the Member States as to the result to be achieved but leave the choice of form and method to national authorities. Such flexibility is reflected in the wording which is flexible enough to be adjusted to different national contexts and systems. In line with the view that sees terminological phrasemes as indicators of conceptual meaning, Volini looks at different kinds of phrasemes which appear to be typical of Framework Decisions as against other EU secondary legislation texts. She then compares the English phrasemes with their rendering in the Italian version of the same texts, finding that in many cases the Italian texts adopt literal translations or calques from English. Such calques also tend to be overused thus causing possible misinterpretations or over- generalisations.

The chapter by Paola Catenaccio looks at the debate surrounding the implementation of Council Directive 1993/13/EEU on Unfair Terms in Consumer Contracts in Britain from a linguistic perspective with a view to assessing the impact of European legal language on this area of English law. The discussion is framed within the wider context of the development of a European contract law designed to gradually replace national legislations and investigates the articulation of resistant discourses within official English documents.

Translating legal discourse

The chapters in the third section deal specifically with issues in translating legal discourse. In this section, Girolamo Tessuto approaches legal concepts both from semantic and socio-cultural perspectives as these help explain the close connection between language and conceptual structure on the one hand, and the constraints posed on legal concepts by the law system within which they are formulated on the other. He therefore advocates the need for a basic knowledge of legal concepts and terms through a comparative method of descriptive terminography for use by anyone involved in cross-cultural, cross-linguistic situations requiring awareness of the implications and pitfalls lying behind the legal import of concepts.

Marta Chromá explores the intricacies of legal translation in view of the training of translators. She suggests that legal translation requires knowledge and expertise at different levels, linguistic, cultural and legal. Not only does it require basic knowledge of the respective legal systems, familiarity with the relevant terminology and competence in the target language's specific legal style of writing, but also an extensive knowledge of the respective legal topic in both source and target language. She further illustrates how knowledge of the law of the target system helps in avoiding linguistic pitfalls which may lead to ambiguous or erroneous interpretation of the target text by analyzing some elements of legal English which might cause problems to a Czech legal audience if only translational equivalents are used. She finally describes a course for legal translators, based on the principles expounded, held at the School of Law of Charles University in Prague.

In the final chapter of the volume, Stefano Marrone offers a hands-on description of the hard task faced by his team of in-house Parliamentary interpreters and translators in the translation of the *Regolamento* of Italy's Lower House of Parliament into English in view of its need for diffusion both in print and on the Internet. The source text is a legal text regulating the interplay of relations between parliamentary authorities and parliament's administration as well as between parliament and other state organs; it is the result of culture- and system-bound legislative, political and administrative concepts, formulated over the years in one and a half centuries of national political history. Its transferral to the de-materialised time and space of the Internet for an undefined audience, possibly made of mostly non-English speaking readers but certainly including both specialists and non-specialists, has required a deep understanding of politically- and historically-bound legal concepts whose translation required reference to the legal and political discourse of different English-speaking countries and systems.

As can be seen from this overview, the volume presents a wide range of issues within different international legal and juridical contexts emanating from a variety of approaches to legal discourse. As such it provides a rich and multifaceted picture of the impact of issues of culture on the formulation of legal concepts for international, cross-system contexts.

References

Bhatia, Vijay K / Candlin, Christopher N. / Gotti, Maurizio (eds) 2003. *Arbitration in Europe: Legal discourse in a Multilingual and Multicultural Context.* Bern: Peter Lang.

Bhatia, Vijay K. / Candlin, Christopher N. / Engberg, Jan / Trosborg, Anna (eds) 2003. *Multilingual and Multicultural Contexts of Legislation: An International Perspective.* Frankfurt am Main: Peter Lang.

Bhatia, Vijay K. / Candlin, Christopher N. / Engberg, Jan 2008. *Legal Discourse across Cultures and Systems.* Hong Kong: Hong Kong University Press.

Bhatia, Vijay K. / Engberg, Jan 2004. Generic Integrity in International Commercial Arbitration. *HERMES* 32, thematic issue.

Bhatia, Vijay K./ Gotti, Maurizio / Engberg, Jan / Heller, Dorothee (eds) 2005. *Vagueness in Normative Texts.* Bern: Peter Lang.

Bobbio, Norberto, 1997. The Science of Law and the Analysis of Language. In Pintore, Anna / Jori Mario (eds) *Law and Language. The Italian Analytical School.* Liverpool: Deborah Charles Publications. 25-50.

Bouglak, Valentina 2001. A Comparative Study of Several Law Languages. In Meyer Felix (ed.) *Languages for Special Purposes: Perspectives for the New Millennium.* Tübingen: Gunther Narr. Vol. 2. 704-710.

Bowers, Frederick 1989. *Linguistic Aspects of Legislative Expression.* Vancouver: University of British Columbia Press.

Chroma, Marta 2004. Cross-cultural Traps in Legal Translation. In Christopher N. Candlin / Maurizio Gotti (eds) *Intercultural Aspects of Specialized Communication.* Bern: Peter Lang, 197-221.

Conley, John M. / O'Barr, William M. ^{1}1998, ^{2}2005. *Just Words. Law, Language and Power.* Chicago: University of Chicago Press.

Galanes Santos, Iolanda 2001. La qualité linguistique de la Langue Spécialisée du droit : Le cas des langues moins répandues. In: Meyer Felix (ed.) *Languages for Special Purposes: Perspectives for the New Millennium.* Tübingen: Gunther Narr. Vol. 2. 728-734.

Gibbons, John 1994. *Language and the Law.* New York: Longman.

Goffin, Roger 1994. L'Eurolecte: Oui, Jargon Communautaire: non. *Meta* 39/4, 636-642.

Jackson, Bernard S. 1995. *Making Sense in Law. Linguistic, Psychological and Semiotic Perspectives.* Liverpool: Deborah Charles Publications.

Lazzaro, Giorgio 1997. Law and Ordinary Language. In Pintore, Anna / Jori Mario (eds) *Law and Language. The Italian Analytical School.* Liverpool: Deborah Charles Publications, 175-209.

Robertson, Colin D. 2001. Multilingual Law: a Framework for Understanding. In: Meyer Felix (ed.) *Languages for Special Purposes: Perspectives for the New Millennium.* Tübingen: Gunther Narr. Vol. 2. 697-703.

Salmi-Tolonen, Tarja 2001. Legal Language in National and Supranational Contexts; Law, Ideology, Power and Language. In: Meyer Felix (ed.) *Languages for Special Purposes: Perspectives for the New Millennium.* Tübingen: Gunther Narr. Vol. 2. 594-602.

Sarcevič, Susan [1]1997, [2]2000. *New Approaches to Legal Translation.* The Hague: Kluwer Law International.

Sarcevič, Susan 2001. Problems of Interpretation in an Enlarged European Union. In R. Sacco (ed.) *L'Interprétation des Textes juridiques rédigés dans plus d'une langue.* Torino, Paris: L'Harmattan Isaidat, 239-272.

Simmonœs, Ingrid 2001. Rechtskulturelle Unübersetzbarkeit? Ein Vergleich zwischen Norwegen und Deutschland. In: Meyer Felix (ed.) *Languages for Special Purposes: Perspectives for the New Millennium.* Tübingen: Gunther Narr. Vol. 2. 759-766.

Tiersma, Peter M. 1999. *Legal Language.* Chicago: The University of Chicago Press.

Part 1:
International Arbitration and Trade Law

MAURIZIO GOTTI

The Formulation of Legal Concepts in Arbitration Normative Texts in a Multilingual, Multicultural Context

1. Introduction

Recent trends in the context of co-operation in international trade have accelerated moves towards the globalisation of business practices and communication issues. This globalising trend has also affected the legal field, where an international perspective is becoming more and more widespread. However, in spite of the growing efforts of the international community to guarantee greater and greater harmonisation in legislation and procedures, the normative texts in use in the various contexts often show significant discrepancies in their formulations. This is due to the fact that legal terminology is so culture-bound (the reasons being at the same time historical, sociological, political and jurisprudential) that a satisfactory translation of all the legal terms of a text from one context to another is at times impossible.[1] David underlines this difficulty with a few examples:

> To translate into English technical words used by lawyers in France, in Spain, or in Germany is in many cases an impossible task, and conversely there are no words in the languages of the continent to express the most elementary notions of English law. The words *common law* and *equity* are the best examples

1 This also applies to different contexts using the same language. As Nadelmann and Mehren rightly exemplify, "Even in the same language the meaning of a legal term may differ from system to system. Thus, 'domicile' has one meaning in English law and quite different meanings in American jurisdictions." (1967: 195). As Nida aptly remarks, "competent translators are always aware that ultimately words only have meaning in terms of the corresponding culture" (Nida 2001: 13).

> thereof; we have to keep the English words [...] because no words in French or in any other language are adequate to convey the meaning of these words, clearly linked as they are to the specific history of English law alone. (David 1980: 39)

The adoption of a particular term instead of another may give rise to ambiguity and misinterpretation. Several examples of this are given by Fletcher (1999), who examines the translation into various languages of the English text of the European Convention on Human Rights. For instance, the translation provided for the expression *fair and regular trial* into *juicio justo y imparcial* (Spanish) and *procès juste et équitable* (French) is not satisfactory, as the use of the non-equivalent adjectives *regular* (English) / *imparcial* (Spanish) / *équitable* (French) can easily show. The same could be said for the rendering of the concept of *reasonableness*, basic in common law systems, where expressions such as *reasonable steps*, *reasonable measures*, *reasonable person* and *proof beyond a reasonable doubt* frequently occur. This concept, instead, when translated into languages spoken in countries adopting a civil law system is considered too vague and its rendering as *ragionevole*, *raisonnable* or *vernünftig* often gives rise to criticism and dissatisfaction.

Other excellent examples of translation discrepancies can easily be found in texts relating to the process of building a common European legal framework, a task which is much more complex than the simple rendering of common normative documents in all the languages of the European Union, because this newly created framework is meant to be interpreted within the contexts of a diversity of individual legal systems and tongues. For example, translators into English find it difficult to express such culturally-specific French collocations as *acteurs sociaux, acteurs économiques, acteurs institutionnels, acteurs publics, acteurs politiques*, which have no direct equivalent in the target language (Salmasi 2003: 117), and they sometimes transliterate terms or create calques from one language into another, relying on the false premise of a very close relationship between similar lexemes in different languages (see the examples of *transmettre/transmit* and *prévoir/foresee* in Seymour 2002). Indeed, in Europe the legal drafting issue has become extremely important with the elaboration of a multilingual legislation concerning the European Union. This depends on the fact that the official languages of the European Union are those of its Member States, and as new countries join the Union, their languages are added to the number. This is part of a precise policy aiming to build a community of peoples respecting and safeguarding at the same time the existing variety of customs and cultural identities, a principle based on the conviction that the languages of Europe are part of its immense and diverse cultural heritage, and therefore it is considered the duty of the Union to guarantee their preservation.

As European Union legislation must be published in all Member States' official languages in order to be valid also at a national level, in the elaboration of European legislation and its introduction into the various national contexts a fundamental role is played by legal drafting and translation. As regards the former, the elaboration of the texts is carried out in a parallel fashion by the various teams, making use of a common multilingual terminological database and relying on shared Community concepts and institutions. This procedure, however, encounters problems mainly due to the presence of different legal systems in the various countries and the existence of a specific tradition of the legal register in each Member State. Indeed, closer co-operation between the various legal systems of the EU members has not been achieved through creation of a new legislative framework to replace the existing one. Such systems are still in use and only in a very few cases have the more evident discrepancies been eliminated.

The European authorities are aware of these problems and greater and greater emphasis is being laid on the quality of legislation drafting at supranational level. An example of this is the 'Declaration on the Quality of the Drafting of Community Legislation' which is an important part of the Treaty of Amsterdam (1998); this document explicitly states that "the quality of the drafting of Community legislation is crucial if it is to be properly implemented by the competent national authorities and better understood by the public and in business circles". This has led to much greater uniformity in the translation of European directives into the various languages of the Union and to more marked homogeneity and interdependence of the resulting texts. Translators work in single-language units of approximately twenty people and translate, almost without exception, into their mother tongue. Their command of foreign languages is expected to be backed up by a good general knowledge and some competence in at least one specialised area such as law, technology, economics, etc. Translators are also assumed to possess word processing and other computer skills such as database interrogation, as they frequently rely on terminology and documentation available in electronic versions.

This new approach to the translation of European directives has also served a harmonising function, in the sense that from the adoption of the texts of the European Union greater uniformity has been achieved in the use of terminology as well as a higher degree of conceptual homogeneity, which is then transferred into local legal practices. A typical example of this influence of European legislation on the local legal language is the frequent adoption of equivalent definitions of legal concepts deriving directly from European regulations and directives (Cassese 1992: 325, Dibattista 1998: 168).

However, these efforts and initiatives in better drafting procedures have not solved all discrepancy problems, as the final texts are also conditioned by the different rhetorical traditions pertaining to the cultural systems involved, thus often leading to diverging constructions and therefore to conflictual interpretations, with the risk of raising legal controversies. Moreover, in the translation process there is often an addition to and/or alteration of the semantic value of the original, due to the fact that the interpreter brings his/her own experience, knowledge and attitude to the text he/she is translating into another language. For this reason it is commonly suggested that translators working in this field should have two different types of competence: not only linguistic but also legal.[2]

1.1. Globalising trends

Issues like these are crucial for the construction, interpretation and use of legal language across languages and legal systems. They are especially relevant in international trade, which often involves contracts written in English but incorporating statutes and regulations issued by

---

2 For example, the Court of First Instance and the Court of Justice of the European Communities have eleven translation divisions (one for each of the Community languages) averaging fifteen 'lawyer/linguists' each. (cf. Weston 1995).

a third country. Indeed, in the great, rapid changes taking place all over the world, there is a tendency for a single global standard to evolve and dominate over all others – i.e., English. The position of English as the language for international communication is a very strong one and is to become even stronger, due to the need for a common global language. However, it has often been remarked that the adoption of a *lingua franca* may have important consequences on the approach adopted locally. Indeed, when the language chosen for the international arbitration procedure is English, there is a tendency to adopt procedures typical of common law countries:

> Frequently the presence of American (or British) lawyers in a procedure normally leads to the de facto use of US (or English) procedures. (Lazareff 1999: 37)

The influential role played by this language is much more significant now that English is so frequently used also in cases in which no native English-speaking party is involved. The frequency of this situation is confirmed by Taniguchi's testimony:

> There are very many different arbitral practices associated with different legal and commercial cultures. However, the world has been unmistakingly proceeding toward a single commercial culture. Japanese businessmen, for example, are negotiating business in the English language not only with English speaking businessmen but also Korean, European and middle eastern businessmen. This is one of the realities of international trade today. (Taniguchi 1998: 39)

In this way, English terms are creeping into local legal terminologies. For example, over the last two decades, because of the rapid internationalisation of commerce, an increasing number of English legal terms (such as *leasing*, *factoring*, and *franchising*) has been introduced into Italian legal language. Legislators often attempt to translate some of these terms, as for example the term *antitrust rules*, which has been adopted by Parliament using the expression *leggi per la tutela della competizione e del mercato* ('rules in order to safeguard competition and market'); the original English term avoided by Parliament has recently been reintroduced by the Government in a few legislative decrees (Belotti/Facchinetti/Giannoni 2003: 214). In some cases the original word has been maintained as the concept itself did not exist in that context; this is the case of the term *joint venture*, the English expression commonly in use also because of the inaccuracy of the numerous translations that have been proposed.

2. Aims and background

It is the aim of this chapter to investigate the ways in which normative discourse (statutes and regulations) is formulated in different cultural, linguistic and legal environments to express similar legal concepts.[3] To illustrate this phenomenon, examples will be drawn from legislation on international arbitration based on the Model Law on International Commercial Arbitration (ML) and the UNCITRAL Arbitration Rules (UAR) issued by the United Nations and later integrated into the laws of several countries with varying constitutional, sociocultural and economic conditions. In particular, a comparison will be made with Italian arbitration law from the Code of Civil Procedure (arts. 806-840) and with regulations drafted by the arbitration chambers of Milan, Bergamo and Venice.[4] Specific samples taken from arbitration

3 The analysis presented in this chapter is one of the results of an international research project entitled *Generic Integrity in Legislative Discourse in Multilingual and Multicultural Contexts* (http://gild. mmc.cityu.edu.hk/). This project – which is linked to the national research programme funded by the Italian Ministry of Research on *Intercultural Discourse in Domain-specific English* (http://www.unibg.it/cerlis/projects.htm) – investigates the generic integrity of legislative discourse by analysing the linguistic and discoursal properties of a multilingual corpus of international arbitration laws drawn from a number of different countries, cultures, and socio-political backgrounds, written in different languages, and now used within and across a variety of legal systems. Some of the results of the project are presented in Bhatia/Candlin/Engberg (2008), Bhatia/Candlin/Engberg/Trosborg (2003) and Bhatia/Candlin/Gotti (2003).

4 The texts taken into particular consideration are: articles 806-840 of the Code of Civil Procedure (CCP, available at <http://www.camera-arbitrale.com/ codice.htm>; an English translation, offered by the Milan Chamber of National and International Arbitration, is available from <http://www.camera-arbitrale>. <com/eng/rifarb.htm>; it is the version referred to in this article),

discourse in the two languages will be analysed so as to point out how the linguistic choices adopted in them have been greatly influenced by the legal, cultural and linguistic environment in which these texts have been produced, and thus offer a more detailed understanding of linguistic and textual phenomena closely linked to cross-cultural traits. Such matters will be discussed in the light of sociocultural factors within common law systems on the one hand and civil law systems on the other. It is likely that such a focus will be illuminating in integrating language and law where translation across languages and cultures is the issue.

The field of international commercial arbitration constitutes an excellent case in point for the analysis aimed at here. Indeed, the high recourse to this mediating procedure has given rise to a widely felt need for greater harmonisation of the procedures followed, which has led to the elaboration of the ML and UAR documents to be used as models by most United Nations member countries in the construction of their own individual statutory provisions for commercial arbitration.[5] However, this process of harmonisation has been very hard to carry out, and even if all the procedures were to be unified, some differences would still remain in their perception at a local level. The reason for this is to be found in the underlying professional background. As Lazareff aptly remarks:

UNCITRAL Arbitration Rules (UAR, available at <http://www.uncitral.org/english/texts/arbitration/arbitrul.htm>), the United Nations Model Law on International Commercial Arbitration (ML, available at <http://www.uncitral.org/english/texts/arbitration/ml-arb.htm>), the regulations enacted by the Milan Arbitration Chamber (CONAIAM, available at <http://www.mi.camcom.it/eng/arbitration-chamber/reging.htm>), the regulations enacted by the Bergamo Arbitration Chamber (ACOB, available at <http://www.bg.camcom.it/camera_arbitrale>), and the regulations enacted by the Venice Arbitration Chamber (VENCA, available at <http://www.venca.it/rules.htm>).

5 Legislation based on the UNCITRAL text has been enacted in many countries, such as Australia, Bahrain, Belarus, Bermuda, Bulgaria, Canada, Croatia, Cyprus, Egypt, Germany, Greece, Guatemala, Hong Kong Special Administrative Region of China, Hungary, India, Iran, Ireland, Kenya, Lithuania, Macau Special Administrative Region of China, Madagascar, Malta, Mexico, New Zealand, Nigeria, Oman, Peru, Republic of Korea, Russian Federation, Scotland, Singapore, Sri Lanka, Tunisia, Ukraine, Zimbabwe and some of the states in the USA (California, Connecticut, Florida, Oregon and Texas).

> Our own legal cultures remain, for the time being, in certain areas, an important limiting factor to harmonisation because [...] the application of the same rule may lead, despite all good intentions, to strikingly different results. (Lazareff 1999: 36)

One of the great problems in the attainment of this process of harmonisation is constituted by the formulation of legal concepts. Indeed, in the process of adoption of the UNCITRAL model, the English language text of the original has often had to be translated into the local languages, a procedure which has implied not only the adaptation of the original discourse to the typical features and resources of the national tongues, but also its adjustment to the cultural needs and legal constraints of each specific country. It is the aim of the following sections to point out examples of discrepancy in the formulation of arbitration concepts in the two languages taken into consideration and to identify the various motivations that have determined such diverging outcomes.

3. The formulation of arbitration concepts across languages and cultures

3.1. Drafting conventions

Important elements of a particular legal system are its drafting tradition and stylistic conventions. These may influence arbitration discourse significantly, as can be seen in the differentiation between civil law and common law texts: the former are mainly characterised by generality, while the latter prefer particularity. Indeed, it is commonly asserted that civil law statutes are written in terms of principle, whereas common law statutes are written in detail as "the civil code draftsman is eager to be widely understood by the ordinary readership, whereas the common law draftsman seems to be more worried about not being misunderstood by the specialist community" (Bhatia 1993: 137). This conceptual differentiation is reflected in the drafters' stylistic choices: in common law legislation sentences are very long, consisting of three or more main clauses, each modified by many subordinate clauses; this remarkable sentence length depends on the great number of details to be inserted and the need that specifications should be precise and clear (Mellinkoff 1963, Gustafsson 1975, Tiersma 1999, Gotti 2005). Civil law sentences are shorter, with a less strict use of paragraphing; this makes the understanding of the sentences easier, but renders the reconstruction of the relationship between the various sentences more complex. The same stylistic difference may be seen as regards contract drafting techniques:

> Parties with a Common Law background usually prefer long and detailed contracts, eager to mention and list expressly each and every contingency that could possibly become a subject of dispute under the agreement. This may be explained by their assumption and expectation that a contract can only be relied on to the extent it is expressly so worded. Parties with a Civil Law background, in contrast, find it often acceptable not to mention every detail because they expect that a court or an arbitral tribunal in interpreting the contract would not only look at the actual wording but also consider what the parties actually had intended to agree upon taking into account the circumstances surrounding the negotiations. (Borris 1994: 84)

The different legal systems thus determine the adoption of different textual strategies on the drafter's part. For example, common law legislation is usually associated with particular emphasis on precision and detail for action in specific circumstances (Campbell 1996). As regards arbitration legislation, this feature is confirmed by the frequent use of explicit textual schematisation in ML and its major concern for clarity of expression and for conceptual and terminological unambiguity.

3.1.1. Textual schematization

The different degree of textual schematization can be seen, for example, in the comparison of ML with the Italian legislative provisions on arbitration contained in articles 806-840 of the Code of Civil Procedure (CCP). The Italian text displays a high degree of intertextual linking as this new law is embedded in the extant body of legislation, and therefore has to be interpreted in the light of hundreds of other texts of greater or equal authority. The sources of some of these references are explicitly mentioned in the text (cf. (1)), but in other cases the links to other documents remain implicit, as in (2), where references to other parts of the Civil Code (c.c.) or Penal Code (c.p.) are given in brackets:

(1) La clausola compromissoria contenuta in condizioni generali di contratto oppure in moduli o formulari non è soggetta alla approvazione specifica prevista dagli *artt.1341 e 1342 del Codice civile*. (CCP 833; emphasis added, as in all quotations in this chapter)
[An arbitration clause contained in general conditions of contract or standard forms shall not be subject to the specific approval provided for in *Arts. 1341 and 1342 of the Civil Code*]

(2) Gli arbitri possono essere sia cittadini italiani sia stranieri. Non possono essere arbitri i minori (*2 c.c.*), gli interdetti (*414 c.c.*; *32 c.p.*), gli inabilitati (*415 c.c.*), i falliti (*50.1 fall.*), e coloro che sono sottoposti a interdizione dai pubblici uffici (*829 n. 3*; *28, 23, 31 c.p.*). (CCP 812)
[The arbitrators may be Italian or foreign nationals. Minors (*2 c.c*), persons under a legal incapacity (*414 c.c.*; *32 c.p., 415 c.c.*), bankrupts (*50.1 fall.*) and those who have been disqualified from holding a public office (*829 n. 3*; *28, 23, 31 c.p.*) may not act as arbitrators]

In ML, instead, reference is usually internal and has the function of facilitating 'textual mapping' (Bhatia 1987). Intra-textual links also occur in CCP, as can be seen in (3). However, these devices are less frequent in the Italian text, this being probably linked to the fact that this law is firmly embedded within the Code of Civil Procedure and its authority, whereas ML is a stand-alone law with no inherent intertextual linking.

(3) La clausola compromissoria deve risultare da atto avente la forma richiesta per il compromesso *ai sensi dell'articolo 807*, commi primo e secondo. Le controversie *di cui all'art. 409* possono essere decise da arbitri solo se ciò sia previsto nei contratti e accordi collettivi di lavoro purché ciò avvenga, a pena di nullità, senza pregiudizio della facoltà delle parti di adire l'autorità giudiziaria. (CCP 808)

[The arbitration clause shall be contained in a document meeting the formal requirements for an arbitration agreement *according to Art. 807*, first and second paragraphs. Dispute *ex Art. 409* may be decided by arbitrators only if this is provided for in collective labour contracts and agreements and if, under penalty of nullity, the parties' right to have recourse to the courts is not affected.]

Another relevant aspect of common law legal drafting tradition is the use of coordination to provide a great degree of textual cohesion; ML frequently adopts *and/or* to express both parallel and alternative coordination, as can be seen in the frequent use of multinomials joined by alternative/complementary coordination. Also a civil law text such as CCP uses similar expressions, but mainly with parallel coordination; indeed, the two texts have a comparable amount of parallel coordination (with 55 *e(d)* in CCP, 59 *and* in ML), while alternative coordination is considerably more frequent in the UNCITRAL text, with 172 occurrences of *or* as compared to 70 of *o/oppure* (Giannoni 2003: 231). Also Garzone's (2003: 202) analysis of the set of rules of the London Court of International Arbitration shows a prevalent use of alternative coordination, with *or* being the fourth most frequent word in the text after *the*, *of* and *to*. The pervasiveness in ML of this second type of binomial is particularly evident inasmuch as it links whole paragraphs rather than single words. Alternative/complementary options with *or* are frequently used in the UNCITRAL text, and the way in which they are usually punctuated and set out emphasizes their function of making the provisions both more inclusive and semantically transparent. Here is a particularly striking example:

(4) Grounds for refusing recognition *or* enforcement

(1) Recognition *or* enforcement of an arbitral award, irrespective of the country in which it was made, may be refused only:

(a) at the request of the party against whom it is invoked, if that party furnishes to the competent court where recognition *or* enforcement is sought proof that:

(i) a party to the arbitration agreement referred to in article 7 was under some incapacity; *or* the said agreement is not valid under the law to which the parties have subjected it *or*, failing any indication thereon, under the law of the country where the award was made; *or*

(ii) the party against whom the award is invoked was not given proper notice of the appointment of an arbitrator *or* of the arbitral proceedings *or* was otherwise unable to present his case; *or*

(iii) the award deals with a dispute not contemplated by *or* not falling within the terms of the submission to arbitration, *or* it contains decisions on matters beyond the scope of the submission to arbitration, provided that, if the decisions on matters submitted to arbitration can be separated from those not so submitted, that part of the award which contains decisions on

matters submitted to arbitration may be recognized and enforced; *or*
(iv) the composition of the arbitral tribunal *or* the arbitral procedure was not in accordance with the agreement of the parties *or*, failing such agreement, was not in accordance with the law of the country where the arbitration took place; *or*
(v) the award has not yet become binding on the parties *or* has been set aside *or* suspended by a court of the country in which, *or* under the law of which, that award was made; *or*
(b) if the court finds that:
(i) the subject-matter of the dispute is not capable of settlement by arbitration under the law of this State; *or*
(ii) the recognition *or* enforcement of the award would be contrary to the public policy of this State. (ML 36)

By arranging content schematically, the drafter can construct a denser, more cognitively demanding text such as the one cited above. The prevailing pattern in Italian is simply coordination with *or* at word level:

(5) La parte che intende far eseguire il lodo nel territorio della Repubblica è tenuta a depositarlo in originale *o* in copia conforme, insieme con l'atto di compromesso *o* con l'atto contenente la clausola compromissoria *o* con documento equipollente, in originale *o* in copia conforme, nella cancelleria della pretura nella cui circoscrizione è la sede dell'arbitrato. (CCP 825)
[The party intending to have the award enforced in the territory of the Republic shall file the original award *or* a certified copy thereof, together with the original arbitration agreement *or* document containing the arbitration clause *or* an equivalent document, *or* a certified copy thereof, with the Registry of the Magistrate's Court [Pretura] of the district in which the arbitrator has its seat]

3.1.2. Clarity of expression

As has already been pointed out in several preceding studies (Mellinkoff 1963, Bhatia 1993, Solan 1993, Tiersma 1999), normative texts have to be very precise in defining the obligations they are meant to impose or the rights they confer; this is why permission and prohibitions must be stated in a clear and unambiguous way. As regards arbitration legislation, this feature is confirmed by its major concern for terminological unambiguity. This explains why the Model Law devotes various parts of its text to very detailed terminological explanations, particularly in Articles 2 and 7:

(6) For the purposes of this Law:
(a) 'arbitration' *means* any arbitration whether or not administered by a permanent arbitral institution;
(b) 'arbitral tribunal' *means* a sole arbitrator or a panel of arbitrators;
(c) 'court' *means* a body or organ of the judicial system of a State; (ML 2)

This concern for clarity can also be found in the many cases in which the ML reader is required to understand an expression in the light of a given text by means of the verb phrase *refers to*:

(7) (f) where a provision of this Law, other than in articles 25 (a) and 32 (2) (a), *refers to* a claim, it also applies to a counter-claim, and where it *refers to* a defence, it also applies to a defence to such counter-claim. (ML 2)

Another way of enhancing precision is the use of past-participle clauses to state clearly the source of the qualification of a term, as can be seen in the following quotation:

(8) any party may request the court or other authority *specified in article 6* to take the necessary measure, unless the agreement on the appointment procedure provides other means for securing the appointment. (ML 11.4.c)

These forms also occur in civil law texts, but in general there is less marked emphasis on precision. In the Italian text, for example, there are also cases in which the link remains implicit or refers vaguely to law in general:

(9) Gli arbitri debbono pronunciare il lodo entro il termine *stabilito* [...] *dalla legge*; (CCP 813)
[The arbitrators shall render their award within the time limit *set* [...] *by law*]

(10) se nel procedimento non sono state osservate le forme *prescritte per i giudizi sotto pena di nullità*. (CCP 829.7)
[where the formalities *laid down for proceedings under penalty of nullity* have not been observed]

Different degrees of precision are also visible in the lexis found in the two texts, the Italian one employing a wider range of words. Indeed, types in CCP account for 20 per cent of tokens, as compared to 14 per cent in ML (Giannoni 2003: 229). Moreover, the great lexical variety of CCP also means a higher proportion of polysemous items in its specialized lexis. This evidence suggests that English legal discourse is more lexically restricted and specific than Italian, which results from the layering of the formal, specialized and bureaucratic registers of language (Petta 1994).

3.2. Linguistic constraints

The analysis of arbitration texts has also shown examples of discrepancy due to variations in legal discourse features in different languages. This can be seen, for example, in the way juridical obligation is signalled. This concept is traditionally expressed by the modal *shall* in English legal discourse. Italian legal discourse, instead, often adopts the present indicative to state legal provisions, thus emphasising the actuality and applicability of the legal provision and also implying that the law draws its force from the natural order of things rather than an order imposed by human agents:

(11) Gli arbitri, sentite le parti, *provvedono* entro venti giorni. (CPC 826.2)
[The arbitrators *take* the necessary action within twenty days, after hearing the parties]

(12) In the event the Parties have not appointed the Arbitrator/s and not designated a different appointing authority within the applicable terms, the arbitrator/s *is/are appointed* by the Court within 30 (thirty) days from when the Court is noticed by the most diligent Party. (VENCA 10)

This preference for the present tense[6] is also part of the drafting tradition of another country belonging to the civil law system, that is, France. As Garzone's (2003: 206) analysis shows, the simple present indicative – rather than the deontic modal *devoir* – is the form customarily used to convey both the prescriptive and the performative functions of normative and legislative texts.

6 Further examples from legal texts in Italian can be found in Caliendo (2004) and Williams (2004, 2005).

3.3. Socio-cultural constraints

Differentiation in the formulation of legal concepts may also depend on diverging socio-cultural implications involved in dispute resolution. One of the main features of the common law system is the greater degree of autonomy enjoyed by the judge (cf. Borris 1994). Similarly, in the arbitration process the arbitrator plays a very active role due to the fact that no jury is involved in the proceedings and that the majority of the disputes in international commercial arbitration are of a technical and complicated nature. Moreover, the arbitrator often makes proposals for an amicable settlement of the dispute if he sees any feasible solutions. It is important, therefore, that the decision-making process should be totally transparent and that the arbitrator should be impartial and independent. This need is particularly felt in the Italian context, where the custom of non-standard arbitration has often been regarded as too sensitive to the parties' interests and pressures (Ceccon 2000: 12), and provides an explanation for the specific rules that several Italian arbitration chambers have laid down to regulate the conduct of appointed arbitrators (cf. Bartolini/Delconte 2001). In particular, the regulations laid down by a few arbitration chambers contain specific codes of conduct concerning such important issues as the arbitrator's competence, impartiality and independence, which are largely modelled on the Criteria of Arbitral Ethics *(Criteri di Deontologia Arbitrale)* enacted by the Italian Arbitration Association in 1999 (cf. Bartolini/Delconte 2001). In the UNCITRAL text, instead, this issue is considered in very general terms.

Also in the Arbitration Law of the People's Republic of China the grounds for challenging the appointment of arbitrators are stated in very specific terms, and are exemplified in the mention of a close relationship with any "one litigant" or "the attorney", "private meetings with the litigants or with their attorneys" or acceptance of "invitation of the litigants or their attorneys to dine" or acceptance of "gifts" (Bhatia/Candlin/Wei 2001: 10). This implication of possibilities of bribery or influence may be prompted by particular socio-cultural factors specific to that country, a hypothesis which finds confirmation in the words of an expert on Chinese law, Professor Jerome Cohen from New York University, quoted by Jane Moir in an article in the *South China Morning Post* (5 October 2001):

> The longer my experience as either an advocate or an arbitrator in disputes presented to Cietac [China International Economic and Trade Arbitration Commission], the graver my doubts have become about its independence and impartiality. […] At a minimum, I would surely no longer advise clients to accept Cietac jurisdiction unless the contract's arbitration clause required the appointment of a third country national as presiding arbitrator. (Quoted in Bhatia/Candlin/Wei 2001: 8)

The socio-economic environment in which legal provisions are introduced may also influence the style adopted in drafting the normative texts. An example can be seen in the regulations enacted in the Italian context by the Milan, Bergamo and Venice Arbitration Chambers. These institutions are situated in one of the most highly industrialized areas in Northern Italy, where a large number of small enterprises operate successfully on foreign markets. Their sets of rules are intended for a number of business people running small and medium-sized companies and wanting clear indications on how to resolve commercial disputes without recourse to ordinary justice. This explains the higher degree of user-friendliness encountered in their texts, which can be noted in several cases. One instance is the fact that two of them (ACOB and CONAIAM) include standard arbitration clauses – such as the clauses for a sole arbitrator, for an arbitral tribunal and for a multi-party arbitration – which can be adopted verbatim and completed easily by the reader, as can be seen from the following examples:

(13) *Arbitration agreement* [(a)]

The undersigned [(b)] ....and .... considering that a dispute has arisen on the subject [(c)] .... agree to defer this dispute to the decision of [(d)] ....
to be appointed in accordance with the Rules of the National and International Arbitration Chamber of Bergamo, which the parties expressly declare they know and which they accept in full.
The arbitrators / the sole arbitrator shall decide according to the rules and regulations .... / fairness (specify what is relevant).
The language of the arbitration shall be ....

Notes

[(a)] The arbitration agreement is a document that is stipulated when the dispute has already arisen between the parties and in the absence of a precautionary arbitration clause.

[(b)] Specification of the name and residence, or in the case of companies, the head offices of the parties.

[c] Reference, also expressed in general terms, of the subject under dispute, with possible reference to the contract out of which the dispute originated.
[d] Specification of the number of arbitrators (one or three). (ACOB, Arbitration agreement)

(14) *Clause for Sole Arbitrator*
All disputes arising out of the present contract [1], including those concerning its validity, interpretation, performance and termination, shall be referred to a sole arbitrator according to the International Arbitration Rules of the Chamber of National and International Arbitration of Milan, which the parties declare that they know and accept in their entirety.
The sole arbitrator shall decide according to the norms ... [2].
The language of the arbitration shall be ...
Notes
[1] Where the arbitration clause is contained in a document other than the contract to which it pertains, the contract referred to shall be indicated.
[2] The parties may indicate the norms applicable to the merits of the dispute; alternatively, they may provide that the arbitrator decide ex aequo et bono. (CONAIAM, Clause for Sole Arbitrator)

The texts above have the form of ready-to-use specimens and are thus very easy to copy and complete. Instead, the UNCITRAL arbitration rules, on which the Italian texts are modelled, are mainly informative and imply some sort of adaptation on the part of the user of the clauses presented:

(15) *Model arbitration clause*
Any dispute, controversy or claim arising out of or relating to this contract, or the breach, termination or invalidity thereof, shall be settled by arbitration in accordance with the UNCITRAL Arbitration Rules as at present in force.

Note
Parties may wish to consider adding:
(a) The appointing authority shall be ... (name of institution or person);
(b) The number of arbitrators shall be ... (one or three);
(c) The place of arbitration shall be ... (town or country);
(d) The language(s) to be used in the arbitral proceedings shall be … (UAR 1)

UAR's adherence to a more traditional legal style is also demonstrated by the lengthy and complex structure of most of its sentences, in line with the features of legal discourse (Mellinkoff 1963, Gustafsson 1975, Tiersma 1999, Gotti 2005). As can be seen from Table 1, the average sentence length is higher in UAR than in the other three texts:

	Average sentence length
UAR	43.1
CONAIAM	37.0
ACOB	34.4
VENCA	29.8

Table 1. Average sentence length in the corpus analysed. (From Belotti 2003: 33)

The more complex structure of legal discourse in UAR is confirmed by the data concerning sentence types. As Table 2 shows, UAR has more complex sentences than the Italian texts; CONAIAM, ACOB and VENCA, on the contrary, contain more simple and compound sentences.

	UAR		CONAIAM		ACOB		VENCA	
Simple	5	17%	9	19%	15	28%	4	33%
Compound	1	3%			2	4%	5	42%
Complex	24	80%	36	77%	37	68%	3	25%
Complex-compound			2	4%				

Table 2. Distribution of sentence types. (From Belotti 2003: 34)

The shorter length of sentences together with the lower number of complex sentences have a positive impact on readability thus making the Italian texts easier to process and adding to their user-friendliness This greater attention to reader's competence and expectations is confirmed by the use of lexis. Indeed, UAR contains many Latinate and French forms, some of which already found in ML: *ex aequo et bono, amiable compositeur, de iure, de facto, ipso iure, in camera*. These, in contrast, do not occur at all in some of the Italian arbitration rules (such as ACOB) or are very rare in others (CONAIAM and VENCA). The same can be said for archaic words, as can be seen in Table 3:

	UAR	CONAIAM	ACOB	VENCA
Forthwith		1		
Hereinafter	1			
Such (used as adjective)				
Therefore	2	2		
Therefor	2	2		
Therein		1		
Thereof	2	3		3
Thereon	2			
Thereto	2			
Total	*11*	*9*	*0*	*3*

Table 3. Type and number of occurrences of archaic words. (From Belotti 2002:132)

4. Conclusion

As can be seen from the analysis carried out in this chapter, the formulation of legal concepts in normative texts in a multilingual/multicultural context is greatly conditioned by specific socio-cultural and economic factors strictly depending on the different cultural, linguistic and legal environments in which it takes place. The investigation of the process of adaptation of the UN Model Law to different national realities has pointed out several cases in which the source text offers the input on the basis of which new autonomous texts are created taking into consideration the needs of the final users, a result in line with the findings of other scholars (e.g. Vermeer 1996). Indeed, the discussion of certain linguistic and textual features has provided interesting insights into how drafting procedures may be influenced by different target readers with their own legal culture and professional expectations, and has demonstrated that variations in the formulation of legal concepts in normative texts are mainly to be attributed to the different cultural traits and legal traditions of the communities for which they are meant.

In spite of the growing globalisation of arbitration culture, the elaboration of the UN Model Law has not guaranteed complete uniformity among the various national legislations, as the single countries have used this model in different ways, depending upon their national requirements, concerns, cultures, legal systems, languages, and other constraints. Being the result of a translation or a re-writing process, the local texts thus possess clear features of 'hybrid' (Trosborg 1997: 146) discourse and show significant traces of the adjustment and adaptation of the text issued by an international organisation to the legal and socio-cultural traits of the various national target users. In spite of the desire to make international arbitration texts 'unbound' (Paulsson 1981), the existing differentiations in the construction of legal discourse derive from conscious and deliberate decisions by national drafters, thus confirming the important conditioning factor that local constraints play in the formulation of legal concepts.

References

Bartolini, Francesco / Delconte, Roberto C. (eds) 2001. *Il codice dell'arbitrato* [The Arbitration Code]. Piacenza: La Tribuna.

Belotti, Ulisse / Facchinetti, Roberta / Giannoni, Davide S. 2003. An Introduction to the Legal System in Italy. In Bhatia/Candlin/Engberg/Trosborg (eds), 193-224.

Belotti, Ulisse 2002. The Language of Italian Arbitration Rules in English: Some Measurable Aspects. *Linguistica e Filologia* 15, 113-141.

Belotti, Ulisse 2003. Generic Integrity in Italian Arbitration Rules. In Bhatia/Candlin/Gotti (eds), 19-40.

Bhatia, Vijay K. 1987. Textual-Mapping in British Legislative Writing. *World Englishes* 1/1, 1-10.

Bhatia, Vijay K. 1993. *Analysing Genre: Language Use in Professional Settings*. London: Longman.

Bhatia, Vijay / Candlin, Christopher N. / Engberg, Jan (eds) 2008. *Legal Discourse across Cultures and Systems.* Hong Kong: Hong Kong University Press, 221-252.

Bhatia, Vijay K. / Candlin, Christopher N. / Engberg, Jan / Trosborg, Anna (eds) 2003. *Multilingual and Multicultural Contexts of Legislation*, Frankfurt am Main: Peter Lang.

Bhatia, Vijay K. / Candlin, Christopher N. / Gotti, Maurizio (eds) 2003. *Legal Discourse in Multilingual and Multicultural Contexts: Arbitration Texts in Europe.* Bern: Peter Lang.

Bhatia, Vijay K. / Candlin, Christopher N. / Wei, Sandy 2001. *Legal Discourse in Multilingual and Multicultural Contexts: A Preliminary Study.* Research Group Report. Hong Kong: City University of Hong Kong.

Borris, Christian 1994. Common Law and Civil Law: Fundamental Differences and their Impact on Arbitration. *Arbitration* 60/2, 78-85.

Caliendo, Giuditta 2004. Modality and Communicative Interaction in EU Law. In Candlin, Christopher N. / Gotti, Maurizio (eds) *Intercultural Aspects of Specialized Communication.* Bern: Peter Lang, 241-259.

Campbell, Lisbeth 1996. Drafting Styles: Fuzzy or Fussy? *ELaw. Murdoch University Electronic Journal of Law* 3/2. Available at <http://www.murdoch.edu.au/elaw/issues/v3n2/campbell.html>.

Cassese, Sabino 1992. Introduzione allo studio della normazione [Introduction to the study of normative drafting]. *Rivista trimestrale di diritto pubblico* 2, 307-330.

Ceccon, Roberto 2000. "La Corte Arbitrale di Venezia, una nuova istituzione per attrarre l'arbitrato internazionale in Italia" [The Venice Arbitration Chamber, a new institution to attract international arbitration to Italy]. In *Le prospettive dell'arbitrato interno ed internazionale: il Regolamento della Corte Arbitrale di Venezia*. Turin: Giappichelli, 7-12.

David, René 1980. *English Law and French Law*. London: Stevens.

Dibattista, Denise 1998. Osservazioni in tema di plurilinguismo nel diritto comunitario. In Bayley, Paul / San Vicente, Félix (eds) *In una Europa plurilingue: Culture in transizione.* Bologna: CLUEB, 159-169.

Fletcher, G.P. 1999. Fair and Reasonable: A Linguistic Glimpse into the American Legal Mind. In Sacco, Rodolfo / Castellani, Luca (eds) *Les multiples langues du droit européen uniforme*. Turin: L'Harmattan Italia, 57-70.

Garzone, Giuliana 2003. Arbitration Rules across Legal Cultures: An Intercultural Approach. In Bhatia/Candlin/Gotti (eds), 177-220.

Giannoni, Davide S. 2003. The UNCITRAL Model and Italian Statute Law: A Linguistic and Topical Description. In Bhatia/Candlin/ Gotti (eds), 221-246.

Gotti, Maurizio 2005. *Investigating Specialized Discourse.* Bern: Peter Lang.

Gustafsson, Marita 1975. *Some Syntactic Properties of English Law Language.* Turku: University of Turku, Department of English.

Lazareff, Serge 1999. International Arbitration: Towards a Common Procedural Approach. In Frommel, Stefan N. / Rider, Barry, A.K. (eds) *Conflicting Legal Cultures in Commercial Arbitration: Old Issues and New Trends.* The Hague: Kluwer Law International, 31-38.

Mellinkoff, David 1963. *The Language of the Law.* Boston: Little, Brown & Co.

Nadelmann, Kurt H. / von Mehren, Arthur T. 1967. Equivalences in Treaties in the Conflicts Field, *The American Journal of Comparative Law* 15, 195-203.

Nida, Eugene A. 2001. *Context in Translating.* Amsterdam: Benjamins.

Paulsson, Jan 1981. Arbitration Unbound: Award Detached from the Law of its Country of Origin. *International and Comparative Law Quarterly* 30, 358-387.

Petta, Paolo (1994). Il linguaggio del legislatore [The legislator's language]. *Quaderni Regionali*, 1303-1316.

Salmasi, Stefano 2003. English as a *Lingua Franca* at the European Union: The Undertakings of Pride?. *Recherches Anglaises et Nord-Américaines* 36, 113-120.

Seymour, Edward 2002. Euro-English: The New Pidgin?. *Terminologie et traduction* 3, 22-32.

Solan, Lawrence M. 1993. *The Language of Judges.* Chicago: The University of Chicago Press.

Taniguchi, Yasuhei 1998. Is There a Growing International Arbitration Culture? An Observation from Asia. In ICCA (International Council for Commercial Arbitration). *International Dispute Resolution: Towards an International Arbitration Culture.*

Albert Jan van den Berg (Gen. ed.). Dordrecht: Kluwer Law International, 31-40.

Tiersma, Peter M. 1999. *Legal Language*. Chicago: The University of Chicago Press.

Trosborg, Anna 1997. Translating Hybrid Political Texts. In Trosborg, Anna (ed.) *Text Typology and Translation*. Amsterdam: Benjamins, 145-158.

Vermeer, Hans J. 1996. *A Skopos Theory of Translation (Some Arguments For and Against)*. Heidelberg: Textcontext Wissenschaft.

Weston, Martin 1995. Translating at the European Court of Human Rights. *Terminologie et traduction* 3, 121-134.

Williams, Christopher 2004. Pragmatic and Cross-cultural Considerations in Translating Verbal Constructions in Prescriptive Legal Texts in English and Italian. In Candlin, Christopher N. / Gotti, Maurizio (eds) *Intercultural Discourse in Domain-specific English,* monographic issue of *Textus: English Studies in Italy* 17/1, 217-245.

Williams, Christopher 2005. *Tradition and Change in Legal English: Verbal Constructions in Prescriptive Texts*. Bern: Peter Lang.

GIULIANA GARZONE

International Commercial Arbitration Rules as Translated/Re-written Texts: An Intercultural Perspective

1. Background and study design

1.1. Introduction

In the last few years international commercial arbitration texts have attracted increasing attention by scholars of linguistics. Amongst them, arbitration rules are particularly interesting as – although generated within the framework of the legal system of the country where the issuing institution has its seat – they are conceived for application in an international context. Thus, they qualify as typically hybrid texts (Trosborg 1997: 145-146), representing a sort of interface between the national dimension and the sphere of international commercial relations.

Research conducted so far on arbitration texts in English (e.g. within the framework of the LLC project and the Italian project 'Intercultural discourse in domain-specific English' – cf. Bhatia/Candlin/Gotti 2003) has studied such texts in terms of lexico-grammatical and discoursal features, use of terminology, relation with the legal culture of the home countries of the issuing arbitration institution, similarities and differences with respect to the UNCITRAL Model Law, etc. However, hardly any attention has been given so far to the fact that all arbitration rules exist in different language versions, and for every set of rules at least two of such versions are considered official and authoritative, one of them – often the most widely used – being in English. This obviously relies on the presumption of the equal authenticity of the different language versions, a principle which is widely accepted in international law, being set out in Art. 33 of the Vienna Convention of the Law of Treaties 1969 (cf. Šarčević 1997: 198-200; Garzone 2002: 39-40). All these factors make the analysis of the different versions of sets of arbitration rules as translated texts particularly interesting.

This chapter focuses on the English versions of arbitration rules issued by some major institutions having their seats in non-English speaking countries (see 1.2 below) and analyses them as translated/re-written texts (Lefevere 1992), comparing and contrasting them with their Italian and French source texts and with versions – if any – in other languages; as a subsidiary source of information, it also looks at the Italian and French versions of arbitration rules originally generated in English.

1.2. Theoretical premises and corpus description

This study does not question the findings and conclusions of previous linguistic studies which have analysed the same texts without giving any attention to their translated nature: as the approach adopted here is essentially descriptive, it considers not only legitimate, but highly recommendable the analysis of translated/re-written texts as autonomous texts destined to function in the context of the target culture without regard for their relation to the source text and the evaluation of their 'correctness' (cf. Toury 1995). Considerations concerning their relation to the source text – like those put forth in this paper – come at a later stage and can help explain characteristic features and/ or problems identified in the target-culture perspective.

Within this descriptive theoretical framework the present study looks at a representative sample of translated arbitration rules, accompanied by the parallel corpus of their STs[1] and by a corpus of comparable 'native' English texts,[2] in order to ascertain whether the trans-

1 As is customary in the literature on translation, here the abbreviations ST for Source Text and TT for Target Text will be used.

2 The terms 'parallel corpus' and 'comparable corpus' are used here according to the definition given in Picchi/Peters 1997. In this case the parallel corpus consists of sets of arbitration rules issued by arbitral institutions in English-speaking countries or issued in English for international use.

lated texts present any peculiar features that characterize them as a distinctive group of texts, while at the same time trying to identify any regularities in translators' behaviour that may yield indications on the 'norms' (Toury 1980: 57) that today translators customarily apply in their re-writing of arbitration rules. Incidentally, it should be remembered that in descriptive translation studies norms are not pre-established rules, but rather "a category for descriptive analysis of translation phenomena" (Toury 1980: 57), which are inferred by means of generalisation from the analysis of a representative sample of texts and have no permanent or definitive value, as it is now fully recognised that the concept of translation itself is culture-specific, varying in different cultures and in different historical periods. Therefore this study concentrates on recurrent features in translated arbitration texts, also trying to highlight possible interferences on the part of their original drafting in the source languages, both in terms of legal formulation and of linguistic form. This will also provide some more general insight into the 'norms' followed by translators of legal texts from Latinate languages into English.

A further aim is to verify whether the so-called 'universals of translation' apply also to legal translations, in other words if it is possible to identify some of the linguistic and discoursal features that translation scholars hypothesize translated texts have in common, whatever the pair of languages involved. While previous research (Garzone 2003), although not specifically focussed on universals, has found that in translated arbitration texts there is evidence of one of such universals, i.e. *discourse transfer* from the original legal cultures of the institutions issuing them, the phenomena investigated here are *simplification*, i.e. the tendency on the part of the translator to simplify the language and the message or both, accompanied by avoidance of repetition, and *explicitation*, i.e. the tendency to 'spell things out' in translation rather than leaving them implicit (cf. Laviosa-Braithwaite 1997: 288-291; Bassnett *et al.* 1999: 235).

The corpus analysed consists of four sets of international commercial arbitration rules originally drafted respectively in Italian and French: the Arbitration Rules of the Chamber of National and International Arbitration of Milan (CNIAM), of the Venice Court of National and International Arbitration (VENCA), the Rules of Arbitration of the International Chamber of Commerce of Paris (ICC) and the International Arbitration Rules of the Canadian Commercial Arbitration Centre (CCAC). This small corpus is analysed together with the parallel corpus of their English translations, i.e. the versions most frequently relied on in international arbitration proceedings, and with a comparable corpus of texts originally drafted in English, consisting of the Rules of the London Court of International Arbitration (LCIA), the International Arbitration Rules of the American Arbitration Association (AAA) and UNCITRAL Rules.

Some research work has already been done on the English versions of Italian arbitration texts, although not in a translational perspective. Comparing Italian arbitration rules[3] in their English version with UNCITRAL Rules Belotti found that the former are syntactically less complex as they have shorter and less elaborate sentences, with a higher frequency of simple sentences and a lower occurrence of embedded clauses, an aspect which is enhanced by typographical devices aimed at making the text more reader-friendly (Belotti 2003). This characteristic is all the more evident in VENCA rules, which are characterised by an evident effort to avoid 'legalese', i.e. technical or archaic expressions (Belotti 2002).

2. The translation of arbitration rules: textual evidence

2.1. Criteria generally adopted in legal translation

In history[4] the practice of legal translation was characterised by the unquestioned predominance of the kind of approach that Šarčević, (1997: 24) calls 'strict literal', being oriented towards the preservation of the letter rather than the effective rendering in the target language.

3 In addition to CNIAM and VENCA, Belotti (2003) – as well as Belotti (2002) – has also analysed the Rules of the Arbitration Chamber of Bergamo. As concerns CNIAM, although a new edition of the Rules, with the relative English version, was introduced in January 2004, Belotti's findings can still be considered valid.

4 For a detailed history of legal translation from Justinian to the present day see Šarčević (1997: 23ff.).

It was only in the XIX century that the introduction of multilingual legislation in some multi-ethnic countries (Austria, Switzerland, Belgium) paved the way to a change in perspective with a gradual shift towards a more flexible attitude, leading in time to the definition of a criterion of equivalence which is specific to legal translation, that of *legal equivalence* (Beaupré 1986: 179; Herbots 1987). This new criterion adds the consideration of the legal effects that a translated text will have in the target culture (Gémar 1997: 81-85) to other criteria of equivalence[5] (e.g. Pigeon 1995; Gémar 1995, I: 148ff.; Scarpa 1997: 103), seeking to achieve identity of meaning between original and translation, i.e. identity of propositional content as well as identity of legal effects (Sager 1993: 180). This in linguistic terms corresponds to identity of propositional content, illocutionary and perlocutionary force, and intentionality (de Beaugrande/Dressler 1981: 3-11; 113ff.) or 'author intent' (Neubert/Shreve 1992: 70-72).

The advent of target-oriented, functional approaches to translation (e.g. Reiss/Vermeer 1984; Nord 1991, 1997; Vermeer 1996) re-contextualised these concepts. While confirming the theoretical viability of the principle of legal equivalence, the new conceptual framework brought home the idea that such a principle is not universally applicable, thus redeeming the strict-literal approach which is considered to be suitable for certain legal texts under certain circumstances at the translator's discretion, depending first and foremost on the intended function of the TT as well as on the nature of the ST.

However, in spite of the opening to functionalism, ultimately in the overwhelming majority of cases legal translation still takes the source text as its main yardstick against which the standard of a translation is assessed, being guided mainly by a criterion of *interlingual concordance*, i.e. *intertextual symmetry* or *intertextual correspondence* (Šarčević 1997: 202 ff.).

5 Of course, the concept of equivalence is as vague as it is controversial and would need some discussion; since this falls beyond the scope of this paper, reference is made to Garzone (1999 and 2000) where this concept is discussed specifically for the legal field.

2.2. Approach adopted in the translation of arbitration rules

In line with this notion, a brief examination of the translated arbitration texts in the corpus under discussion shows that in general the translator follows the ST closely as far as possible, shifting to an interpretive approach whenever the circumstances so require. This approach is hardly possible in the translation of texts which are situated in a specific legal culture, but is adopted in the translation of many international instruments, e.g. international conventions (cf. Garzone 2002), and is viable in this case because international arbitration texts are conceived for international use and are typically 'hybrid'. In the whole corpus there is hardly any example of the expression of a legal concept belonging to one specific national legal system for which *transpostion juridique* would be necessary. Neither are there any culturally-connotated terms requiring the use of a 'legal equivalent', the only exception being possibly the word *domicile* in CNIAM which, although it has a specific meaning in common law legal systems (cf. De Franchis 1984: *ad vocem*), is used to translate the Italian *domicilio*, instead of the more common English word (*place of*) *residence*, which has a more general meaning. How hard the translator tries to render the ST as closely as possible is evident in the following examples:

(1) Il Tribunale Arbitrale decide il merito della controversia secondo diritto se le parti non hanno espressamente previsto che decida secondo equità. (CNIAM 3.1)
The Arbitral Tribunal shall decide on the merits of the dispute in accordance with the rules of law unless the parties expressly provided that the Tribunal decide ex aequo et bono.

(2) Lorsqu'une partie introduit une demande relative à une relation juridique faisant déjà l'objet d'une procédure d'arbitrage entre les mêmes parties conformément au Règlement, le Centre peut, à la demande d'une partie, à la condition qu'il se satisfasse de la compatibilité des conventions d'arbitrage et qu'il le juge opportun, décider d'intégrer les chefs de demande sur lesquels elle porte à la procédure déjà pendante. (CCAC 13)
When a party submits a Request in connection with a legal relationship in respect of which an arbitral procedure between the same parties is already pending under the Rules, the Centre may, at the request of a party, decide to include the claims contained in the Request in the pending arbitral procedure if it is satisfied that the arbitration agreements are compatible and that consolidation would be appropriate.

Here it is obvious that the translator relies on a strategy of close rendering of the source text, with only minor changes. As shall be seen shortly, only occasionally, and in most cases out of necessity, the text is treated more freely. These considerations are corroborated by quantitative analysis, which confirms that in all the cases examined the translators have proceeded by rendering sentence by sentence. Data obtained with the Wordlist/Statistics Tool of Wordsmith Tools 3.0 (see Table 1) confirm this impression as the number of sentences in the translated texts is virtually the same as that in the STs, with the exception of ICC where it is about 28% higher (139 in French, 177 in English), which means that in the English version some sentences have been re-organised or broken down into two.

	nr. words (tokens)	Length Variation	nr. types	st.type / token ratio	nr. of sentences	average sentence length
LCIA	8,266	=	953	26.98	180	45.92
AAA	4,446	=	752	29.13	132	32.95
UNCITRAL	6,026	=	782	26.42	161	37.42
CNIAM Italian	5,556	=	1,116	35.14	229	24.50
CNIAM English	5,896	+4.24	732	25.7	232	25.16
VENCA Italian	4,668	=	984	37.33	146	28.79
VENCAEnglish	4,929	+10.72	796	29.10	144	33.97
ICC French	6,628	=	1,231	34.05	139	42.75
ICC English	6,997	+6.37%	962	27.95	177	38.30
CCAC French	5,328	=	1,031	33.10	172	30.66
CCAC English	5,908	+10.88%	877	27.62	161	36.38

Table 1. Basic quantitative analysis of texts in the corpus.

It is interesting to note that the data provide evidence that in all cases the English text is longer than the Italian or French ST, which – considering that the number of sentences remains practically unvaried – entails that there are more words in each sentence. This is an unusual characteristic in texts translated from Latinate languages, and in particular from Italian, into English as in most of its varieties and genres English tends to be more concise. An explanation could possibly be found in the complexity and prolixity of legal English, which is more marked in the case of native texts, but evidently influences drafting practices also in 'hybrid' documents drawn up in English (cf. Garzone 2003).

Another interesting finding is that in the translated versions the number of types decreases regularly by as much as 25% (in CNIAM), thus generating a lower standardized type/token ratio, which is an indicator of a lower degree of linguistic variety and a higher frequency of repetitions. This seems to contradict the results of researches in translation studies which have found that in general repetitions are less frequent in translated texts (Blum Kulka/Levenston 1986; Toury 1991). As anticipated above, this tendency to omit in the TT the repetitions contained in the ST, which according to Toury is "one of the most persistent, unbending norms in translation in all languages studied so far" (Toury 1991: 188), is classified by translation scholars within the framework of the universal of 'simplification'. Our data regarding arbitration texts seem to falsify the validity of this theory for legal texts, where evidently the aspiration to clarity weighs more than stylistic considerations. This same aspiration underlies other recurrent aspects of translators' behaviour broadly falling within the scope of another translation universal, explicitation, of which many examples can be found in the texts under discussion here. Some of them will be analysed in the following paragraphs.

2.3. Explicitation

Explicitation, i.e. the tendency – either conscious or unconscious – to make texts more comprehensible to the target audience is one of the most widely recognised traits of translated texts in all languages (Baker 1996; Laviosa/Braithwaite 1998; Ulrych/Bollettieri Bosinelli 1999: 235). The elements that have emerged in this research confirm that re-written arbitration texts are no exception. In many cases, explicitation is in the service of cohesion consisting in the replacement of a pronoun present in the ST with the noun it refers to, for purposes of clarity and avoidance of ambiguity:

(3) Il lodo sia esso parziale o definitivo, è sottoscritto dagli Arbitri e contiene la data ed il luogo in cui esso è reso. (VENCA 27.2)
The final or partial award is signed by the Arbitrators and it contains the date on which and the place where the award is made.

(4) Il Tribunale Arbitrale investito di più procedimenti pendenti può disporre la loro riunione, se li ritiene oggettivamente connessi. (CNIAM 25.3)
Where multiple proceedings are pending before the Arbitral Tribunal, the Tribunal may order that they be consolidated, if it deems them to be objectively connected.

(5) Avant d'accepter sa mission, l'arbitre pressenti signe une déclaration d'indépendance et d'impartialité suivant une formule prescrite par le Centre. Il déclare par écrit au Centre les faits ou circonstances susceptibles de susciter un doute raisonnable quant à son indépendance ou son impartialité. (CCAC 18.2)
Before he agrees to serve, a prospective arbitrator shall sign a statement of independence and impartiality. The arbitrator shall disclose in writing to the Centre any facts or circumstances which might be of such a nature as to raise a reasonable doubt with regard to his independence or impartiality.

(6) Toutes les notifications ou communications du Secrétariat et du tribunal arbitral sont faites à la dernière adresse de la partie qui en est le destinataire ou de son représentant, telle que communiquée par celle-ci ou par l'autre partie le cas échéant. (ICC 3.2)
All notifications or communications from the Secretariat and the Arbitral Tribunal shall be made to the last address of the party or its representative for whom the same are intended, as notified either by the party in question or by the other party. (ICC 3.2)

This kind of behaviour is more frequent in ICC rules, also on account of the fact that in French drafting practice pronouns are preferred to the repetition of the noun more often than in Italian, probably also because of the availability in that language of distal and proximal pronouns (e.g. *celui-ci*, *celle-la*) compatible with a formal register,[6] which combined with the use of morphemes selecting the gender and number of the element referred to makes pronominal reference clearer. In actual fact, the few cases where in the English translation repetition is

6 Distal and proximal demonstrative pronous are available also in Italian (e.g. *questo qui, quella là*), but they are typically deictic so their use is restricted to colloquial contexts; cf. in English: *this one here, that one there.*

avoided and a pronoun used instead are not totally unambiguous. See the following example:

(7) Après remise de la demande au tribunal arbitral, celui-ci accordera à l'autre partie un court délai […]. (ICC 29.2)
After transmittal of the application to the Arbitral Tribunal, it shall grant the other party a short time limit […].

But, of course, explicitation does not relate only to cohesive mechanisms, but also to the expression of concepts, i.e. by adding an element of explanation to a phrase which originally relied on the reader's decoding ability, so s/he is facilitated in her/his task, as in (8) and (9):

(8) Se la convenzione arbitrale prevede un numero pari di arbitri, il Tribunale Arbitrale è composto dal numero dispari di arbitri superiore. (CNIAM 14.4)
Where the arbitration agreement provides for an even number of arbitrators, the Arbitral Tribunal shall consist of that number of arbitrators plus one.

(9) La Segreteria Generale determina il valore della controversia sulla base degli atti introduttivi e sulla base delle ulteriori indicazioni delle parti e del Tribunale Arbitrale. (CNIAM 39.2)
The Secretariat shall determine the value of the dispute on the basis of the request for arbitration and statement of defence and all further indications of the parties and the Arbitral Tribunal.

Sometimes the process of explicitation requires a degree of interpretation on the part of the translator:

(10) Le comunicazioni scambiate tra le Parti sono inviate in copia alla Corte.(VENCA 5.1)
If exchanged between the Parties communications are copied to the Court.

In (10) the explicitation of the adverbial value of the participial finite clause goes well beyond a simple transposition and introduces an element which was not openly expressed in the ST, superimposing an interpretation which may be to some extent arbitrary.

(11) Dans le cas où un arbitre désigné par une partie est récusé ou relevé de ses fonctions, le Centre, tenant compte des circonstances de l'espèce et du principe d'égalité entre les parties, peut passer outre à la procédure initiale et procéder directement à la nomination de l'arbitre en remplacement. (CCAC 20.1)

In cases where an arbitrator designated by a party is successfully challenged or otherwise relieved of his duties, the Centre, taking into account the circumstances of the case and the principle of equality between the parties, may bypass the original procedure and proceed directly with the appointment of a substitute arbitrator.

In this case, although *récusé* and 'challenged' have exactly the same meaning, the English translator offers a helping hand to the reader, by specifying that the problem arises only if the challenge is successful.

In translation from French this procedure is more frequent in CCAC than it is in ICC, where the translator – as seen above – resorts to explicitation mainly to solve problems of cohesion but avoids doing so in other contexts. A comparison between similar cases in the two texts is meaningful. Where ICC translates "seulement sur pieces" as "solely on the documents (submitted)", CCAC has an explicative phrase: "on the basis of documents and materials alone", as follows:

(12) À défaut d'une telle demande, le tribunal décide s'il y a lieu d'organiser une audience ou de procéder uniquement sur pièces. (CCAC 291.)
In the absence of such a request, the Tribunal shall decide whether to hold a hearing, or to conduct the proceedings on the basis of documents and other materials alone.

(13) Le tribunal arbitral peut décider de statuer sur le litige seulement sur pièces soumises par les parties, à moins que l'une des parties ne demande une audience. (ICC 20.6)
The Arbitral Tribunal may decide the case solely on the documents submitted by the parties unless any of the parties requests a hearing. (ICC 20.6).

2.4. Simplification

In (13) can also be found another trait which in translation studies has been recognised as typical of translated texts, the simplification of a linguistic expression, especially in those contexts where the rendering of complex structures generates problems in the drafting of the TT: for instance, lack of equivalence at word level is often overcome by making recourse to hyperonyms or approximate solutions or explicative paraphrases; excessive syntactic complexity is corrected by simply 'reducing' the elements in the sentence or omitting some of them. In (13) above, "Le tribunal arbitral peut décider de statuer sur le litige" becomes "may decide the case" with a reduction in the number of verb forms and a consequent syntactic simplification. Simplification is sometimes also used to reduce a partially redundant expression, as in (14):

(14) Se una parte contesta l'applicabilità del Regolamento, prima della costituzione del Tribunale Arbitrale, il Consiglio Arbitrale dichiara la procedibilità o l'improcedibilità dell'arbitrato (CNIAM, Art. 13.1)
Where a party objects to the application of these Rules before the Arbitral Tribunal is constituted, the Arbitral Council shall decide on the admissibility of the arbitration.

In other cases, one element of the ST is simply omitted, as in the following example, where the omission has the only effect of streamlining the noun groups in points *a* and *b* with no real consequences on the overall meaning:

(15) Il lodo è redatto per iscritto e contiene:
a. l'indicazione delle parti e dei loro difensori;
b. l'indicazione della convenzione arbitrale; (CNIAM 34.1)
The award shall be in writing and shall indicate:
a. Ø the parties and their counsel;
b. Ø the arbitration agreement

2.5. Nominalization and de-nominalization

Although, as illustrated in §2.2 above, the study of the translated texts shows that broadly speaking in all of them the approach adopted is basically one of close correspondence to the ST, often with one-to-one correspondence at sentence level, a detailed analysis within the boundaries of each sentence yields a number of indications of the strategies used by translators in organising clauses into sentences. This more detailed analysis is useful in that it provides clear indications of how the management of micro-structural elements in legal texts can be relevant to the overall process of meaning-generation.

Amongst the procedures which are found to have been enacted most consistently in the drafting of the four arbitration texts under discussion there are nominalization and de-nominalization. While legal language tends to resort to nominalization more than other non- specialized varieties of the language, it is often the case that the way this linguistic feature is used in Italian and French on the one hand and in English on the other is different, so the translator has the option of nominalizing or de-nominalizing in passing from the source language to the target language. In our case, de-nominalization procedures are especially frequent in translations from Italian and from French into English because, although legal English is characterised by a style which is potentially more nominal than other varieties of the language, the frequency of nominal constructions (noun phrases or nominal verb forms) in legal Italian and legal French tends to be higher than in legal English. In particular, in translation from Italian it is customary to make recourse to the shift from abstract deverbal nouns to non-nominal structures, as (16) and (17) show:

(16) Il Tribunale interpreta ed applica il Regolamento unicamente in relazione ai poteri ed ai doveri dell'Arbitro. (VENCA 35)
The Tribunal interprets and applies these Rules insofar as they relate to the Arbitrator's powers and duties.

(17) Il Regolamento è applicato se la convenzione arbitrale o altra convenzione tra le parti ne prevede l'applicazione (CNIAM 1.1)
These Rules shall apply where the arbitral clause or other agreement between the parties provides that they shall apply

Similar cases can be found in texts translated from French:

(18) En cas de remplacement d'un arbitre, la Cour décide, à sa discrétion, de suivre ou non la procédure initiale de nomination.(ICC 12.4)
When an arbitrator is to be replaced, the Court has discretion to decide whether or not to follow the original nominating process.

In translation from French the structures that are de-nominalized are often nominal verb forms, as in the following examples:

(19) La demande contient notamment:
a) une requête soumettant le différend à l'arbitrage conformément au Règlement; [...]
c) un exposé de la nature du différend et *des circonstances lui ayant donné naissance*; (CCAC 11.3)
In particular, the Request shall contain:

a) a request that the dispute be referred to arbitration in accordance with the Rules; [...]
c) a statement as to the nature of the dispute and the circumstances out of which it arose.

The recurrence of de-nominalization procedures is meaningful both from the point of view of legal formulation and from that of loyalty to the ST. In the examples discussed so far, the shift from nominal to verbal expression is relatively unproblematic and does not add anything to the meaning of the ST, but even in such straightforward cases the translator has to make explicit elements that were implicit in the Italian or French version. This requires a degree of interpretation on his/her part as in verbal expressions the subject as well as the mood and tense of action have to be specified, while nominal structures are indeterminate for all these elements. How this affects the rendering of meaning is evident in (21):

(21) Il lodo è sottoscritto da tutti i membri del Tribunale Arbitrale o dalla maggioranza di essi. In tale ultimo caso, il lodo deve dare atto dell'impedimento o del rifiuto degli arbitri che non sottoscrivono.
The award shall be signed by all the members of the Arbitral Tribunal or by a majority of them. In this latter case, the award shall state that the arbitrators who did not sign could not or did not wish to do so.

In this case the decision to de-nominalize has involved the specification of some elements which were not present in the ST, with the further complication that where the Italian text makes recourse to a simple present tense the English version prefers the use of the simple past, possibly on the grounds that if the award accounts for the arbitrator's failure to sign it then this implies that the arbitrator's refusal has already taken place. The Italian word *impedimento* is translated with the modal expression *could not* [*do so*] and *rifiuto* with *did not wish to do so*, which means that in the process of de-nominalization only one component of the meaning of the two original words is rendered: *impedimento* – like the English word *impediment* – refers not only to the impossibility of performing a given action but also to the fact that there may have been some hindrance or obstacles preventing its accomplishment; *rifiuto* means *refusal* and so does not only refer to a person's wish but also to his/her determination not to carry out a given action. However, fortunately this change does not really alter the effects of this clause in terms of actual application of this rule in arbitration proceedings.

Also the shift from a non-nominal form to a nominal one in English, only rarely found in the corpus, is potentially problematic in terms of the expression of meaning. This emerges clearly in the following example:

(22) Il Regolamento è applicato se la convenzione arbitrale o altra convenzione tra le parti ne prevede l'applicazione. Se la convenzione fa rinvio alla Camera Arbitrale di Milano o alla Camera di Commercio di Milano, tale rinvio è interpretato come previsione di applicazione del Regolamento. (CNIAM 1.1)
These Rules shall apply where the arbitral clause or other agreement between the parties provides that they shall apply. A reference in the agreement to the Chamber of Arbitration of Milan or to the Chamber of Commerce of Milan shall be deemed to provide for the application of these Rules

While in the Italian text the expression 'fare rinvio' really means that it is to the Milan Arbitration Chamber that any possible controversy arising from the contract should be referred, in English the noun 'reference' is much weaker as it simply means 'mention' or 'allusion',[7] while obviously the condition for applicability of the rules under discussion is subordinate to a specific statement that controversies should be handled by the Milan Court. In the light of these observations one can conclude that, although frequent recourse to nominalization/denominalization procedures is amongst the 'norms' customarily followed by legal translators in this field, it may have a critical impact on the rendering of the meaning and intentions of the ST, and therefore it requires special caution on the part of the translator.

2.6. Order of words / phrases / clauses and discontinuities

Another potentially critical set of procedures habitually enacted by translators in this field, often out of sheer necessity, is the reorganization of the order in which the different elements – nouns, adverbs,

7 While the verb *to refer* has the meaning "send sb/th to sb/sth for help, advice, action" (e.g. to refer sb to a specialist), this specific meaning is not present in the semantic coverage of the deverbal noun *reference* (cf. *referral*).

phrases, clauses – are arranged within the sentence. One of the problem areas in legal translation is the position of hypotheticals in the sentence, which is all the more critical on account of the high frequency and importance of hypothetical clauses in legal discourse. In particular, changes in the position of this type of clause from sentence-initial to sentence-final position may cause a shift in thematic focus and emphasis. For instance:

(22) Qualora le Parti non abbiano previsto un termine diverso nell'Accordo Arbitrale, il Convenuto invia all'Attore e alla Corte la Risposta alla Richiesta, entro 30 (trenta) giorni dalla data in cui il Convenuto ha ricevuto la Richiesta di Arbitrato. (VENCA 4.1)
The respondent addresses to the Claimant and to the Court the Answer to the Request within 30 (thirty) days from the date on which the Respondent has received the request for Arbitration from the Claimant, unless a different term is provided for in the Arbitration Agreement.

In the ST the hypothetical clause expresses a qualification and has the effect of restricting the validity of the rule that follows; instead, in the English translation the statement is introduced as general and only in the final part of the sentence is it indicated that it applies exclusively under certain circumstances. This kind of procedure is not unusual in the translations from French either:

(23) Lorsqu'il dispose du nombre suffisant de copies de la demande et que l'avance requise a été payée, le Secrétariat envoie à la partie défenderesse, pour réponse, une copie de la demande et des pièces annexes. (ICC 4.5)
The Secretariat shall send a copy of the Request and the documents annexed thereto to the Respondent for its Answer to the Request once the Secretariat has sufficient copies of the Request and the required advance payment.

Here not only does the postposition of the subordinate clause change the emphasis of the sentence, with a shift in thematic focus and a different relation between statement and qualification, but it also causes a problem of cohesion, leading to the repetition of the word *Secretariat*.

Sometimes the displacement of the subordinate clause is obviously due to the need to avoid syntactic discontinuity, as in (24) below, where nevertheless the English sentence would have been much clearer if the clause had been put in initial position:

(24) La Segreteria Generale segnala al Tribunale Arbitrale, che richieda l'esame di una bozza del lodo prima della sua sottoscrizione, l'eventuale mancanza dei requisiti formali richiesti da questo articolo. (CNIAM 34.4)
The Secretariat shall indicate any non-compliance with the formal requirements under this Article to the Arbitral Tribunal where the Tribunal submits a draft award for examination before signing it.

The attempt to eliminate discontinuities in passing from the source language to English is current practice and qualifies as one of the 'norms' consistently followed by translators, probably to make up for typological differences between the languages involved. English syntax is generally less tolerant towards syntactic discontinuities than are French or Italian and, although in legal drafting this restriction is largely disregarded, such general characteristic of English probably induces the translator to avoid discontinuities as far as possible, a behaviour which may also be classified as pertaining to the area of simplification.

Change in the order of words aimed at correcting syntactic discontinuities is quite frequent in the texts examined and in many cases it succeeds in making the sentence more linear and clearer than its source, without altering its original meaning, especially when – as in (25) and (26) below – it requires only a minor displacement and not the transfer of an element from the thematic to the rhematic part of a sentence:

(25) Il Tribunale, oltre ad emettere il lodo finale, è legittimato ad emettere lodi provvisori, non definitivi o parziali. (VENCA 7.1)
In addition to making the final award, the Tribunal is entitled to make interim, interlocutory, or partial awards.

(26) Le défendeur adresse, dans un délai de trente jours à compter de la réception de la demande d'arbitrage envoyée par le Secrétariat, une réponse (la « réponse ») contenant notamment les éléments suivants: [...] (ICC 5.1).
Within 30 days from the receipt of the Request from the Secretariat, the Respondent shall file an Answer (the "Answer") which shall, inter alia, contain the following information: [...]

However, in some cases the displacement of a clause or a phrase, while successfully correcting a syntactic discontinuity, does nevertheless raise problems in terms of clarity of meaning, thus providing evidence in favour of the need to tolerate discontinuity in legal discourse in order to avoid ambiguity; see the following example:

(27) Nel caso in cui l'Accordo Arbitrale non specifichi il numero degli Arbitri, la controversia è decisa da 3 (tre) Arbitri, a meno che la Corte, entro 30 (trenta) giorni dal ricevimento della Risposta alla Richiesta, non decida che venga nominato un solo Arbitro in considerazione del valore della controversia. (VENCA 12)
In the event the Arbitration Agreement does not specify the number of arbitrators, the dispute is decided by 3 (three) arbitrators, unless the Court directs that a sole Arbitrator is appointed in consideration of the importance of the dispute within 30 (thirty) days after receipt of the Answer to the Request.

Of course, the English version is more linear, but does not make it clear that the 30 days' term regards the Court's decision to appoint a sole Arbitrator and not the time period between the Court's decision and the actual appointment; this leaves the reader with two equally viable interpretations.

An even more misleading effect of the displacement of one element in the sentence is found in (28) where the shift of the Italian adjective *solo*, meaning 'on his/her own, exclusively' to the English adverb *only* yields a rendering which allows for two interpretations: a) only the President of the Tribunal may sign orders, and no one else; b) an order is valid even if it is signed only by the President; sense a), which is misleading, is the most readily available.

(28) Le ordinanze devono essere redatte per iscritto e possono essere sottoscritte anche dal solo presidente del Tribunale Arbitrale (CNIAM 26.3)
Orders shall be in writing and may be signed only by the President of the Arbitral Tribunal.

On the other hand, when the adjectives *solo*/*seul* are simply translated literally with *alone*, the problem does not appear to exist as shown in (29), (30) where a similar meaning has to be expressed in connection with the rendering of the award.[8]

---

8 It is to be noted that in the case of VENCA the relevant section – which is entitled 'Decisions' – concerns not only the award but also any other decision made by the Tribunal.

(29) Se il Tribunale è composto di tre Arbitri, il lodo e qualsiasi altra decisione è presa a maggioranza. Se non è possibile ottenere la maggioranza, la decisione viene presa dal solo Presidente del Tribunale. (VENCA 26.1)
When there are three Arbitrators, any award or other decision of the Tribunal is made by a majority of the Arbitrators. If there is no majority, the award is made by the presiding Arbitrator of the Tribunal alone.

(30) En cas de pluralité d'arbitres, la sentence est rendue à la majorité. A défaut de majorité, le président du tribunal arbitral statuera seul. (ICC 25)
When the Arbitral Tribunal is composed of more than one arbitrator, an Award is given by a majority decision. If there be no majority, the Award shall be made by the chairman of the Arbitral Tribunal alone.

2.7. Perfomativity and modality in the expression of rules

A further area which research on legal translation has found to be problematic and worthy of special attention is the translation of speech acts and modality (cf. Garzone 2002, 2003). A comparative analysis of the four sets of rules making up the corpus and of the comparable native texts shows that the use of modals in translations is quantitatively in line with their use in native texts (see Table 2).

	Shall	*May*	*must*	*should*	*will*
LCIA	150 = 1.78‰	66 = 0.78‰	0	13 = 0.50‰	3 = 0.04‰
AAA	94= 2.15‰	58 = 1.33‰	1 = 0.02‰	1 =0.02‰	1 = 0.02‰
UNCITRAL	125 = 2.05‰	64 = 1.06‰	2 = 0.06‰	3 = 0.05‰	5 = 0.08‰
CNIAM	156 = 2.65‰	58 = 0.98‰	1 = 0.01‰	0	0
VENCA	14 = *0.28‰*	31 = 0.63‰	0	3 = 0.06‰	2 = 0.04‰
ICC	142 = 2.02‰	55 = 0.78‰	10 =*0.14‰*	5 = 0.07‰	4 = 0.06‰
CCAC	133 = 2.25‰	56 = 0.95‰	4 = 0.07‰	1 = 0.02‰	1 = 0.02‰

Table 2. Use of modals in arbitration texts in the English text.

There are only two values (in italics in Table 2) that are abnormal in relative terms.[9] The first one concerns the VENCA text where the number of occurrences of *shall* is only 13% of the average of the other texts. This indicates that VENCA systematically expresses rules by

9 Here only variations exceeding 50% of the higher or lower value are considered abnormal.

means of the simple present indicative, while in all the other texts the *shall* form is prevalently used. A comparison of the rule concerning the Request for Arbitration in the four texts under discussion illustrates this divergence very well:

(31) 1) La sede dell'arbitrato è fissata dalle parti nella convenzione arbitrale. 2) In mancanza, la sede dell'arbitrato è Milano. (CNIAM 4.1-2)
1) The parties shall determine the seat of the arbitration in their arbitration agreement. 2) In the absence of such determination, the seat of the arbitration shall be Milan.

(32) La sede dell'arbitrato è fissata per accordo tra le Parti concluso al più tardi entro la data di presentazione della Risposta alla Richiesta. In assenza di tale accordo, la sede dell'arbitrato è la sede della Corte in Venezia o la diversa sede fissata dalla Corte. (VENCA 7.1)
In the absence of an agreement reached by the Parties within the date of submission of the Answer to the Request at the latest, the seat of the arbitration is the seat of the Court in Venice or a different seat fixed by the Court.

(34) La Cour fixe le lieu de l'arbitrage à moins que les parties ne soient convenues de celui-ci. (ICC 14.1)
The place of the arbitration shall be fixed by the Court unless agreed upon by the parties.

(35) À défaut d'accord entre les parties, le tribunal fixe le siège de l'arbitrage en tenant compte des circonstances de l'espèce et des observations des parties.
In the absence of an agreement between the parties, the Tribunal shall fix the seat of the arbitration taking into consideration the circumstances of the case and any observations of the parties. (CCAC 23.1)

This is in line with the formulation of this same rule in native-English arbitration texts:

(36) *The parties may agree in writing the seat (or legal place) of their arbitration. Failing such a choice, the seat of arbitration shall be London, [...] (LCIA 16.1)*

(37) *Unless the parties have agreed upon the place where the arbitration is to be held, such place shall be determined by the arbitral tribunal, having regard to the circumstances of the arbitration. (UNCITRAL 16.1)*[10]

10 The corresponding rule in AAA is not quoted as it is not relevant, being formulated with the modal *may*.

This comparison highlights the fact that in VENCA the approach to the translation of verb forms expressing rules is different, as *shall* forms are only rarely used (only 14 times, 0.08‰), in most cases with apparently no reason for this variation. The only exception is the following sentence, where the verb form – in Italian a gerund – is obviously interpreted as concessive and imperative in English; therefore *shall* is used instead of the simple present:

(38) Il Tribunale è legittimato a modificare tale procedura garantendo ad entrambe le Parti eguali opportunità di presentare qualunque tipo di documentazione e prova legittimamente acquisita. (VENCA 22.2)
The Tribunal is entitled to modify such procedure, but shall grant both Parties equal opportunities to present any kind of documentation and evidence lawfully acquired.

This draws attention to a potentially problematic area in the translation of legal and, more in general, of normative discourse from Latinate languages into English. In Italian and French, normative propositions are expressed mainly by means of the simple present indicative, which is used to convey both prescriptive and constitutive (performative) meaning. Resort to a deontic modal, *dovere* or *devoir*, is also possible, but more rare, because it sounds inevitably weaker in comparison with the imperative directness and unconditionality of the simple present tense (Carcaterra 1994: 220-223; Garzone 2001). In the ICC text 19 forms of *devoir* appear, in CCAC only 3; in CNIAM the forms of *dovere* are 18 and in VENCA only 1.

Also in English the present indicative is used in statutory provisions with a performative value, mostly in definition rules (95% to 100% of cases), in about a third of the cases in stipulation rules (from 29% to 36%) and only occasionally in action rules (from 6 to 10%) (Garzone 1999: 136-137):[11] overall, the simple present is used in 29 to 46% of cases. More frequently recourse is made to constructions with the modal *shall*, which can have either a prescriptive or a constitutive meaning, similarly to the present indicative in Italian and in French. In a quantitative analysis I conducted some time ago on English statutes

11 For the classification of legislative/normative rules into definition rules, stipulation rules and action rules cf. Gunnarsson (1984: 84). Cf. also Bhatia (1994: 138-140).

(reported in Garzone 1999: 139) I found that in the corpus examined *shall* was deontic in 42% to 46% of occurrences and performative in the remaining cases (54-58%).

As concerns international instruments in English, e.g. international treaties and conventions, it is customary to resort consistently to *shall* rather than to the simple present for the expression of all rules except definition rules, probably on account of the component of futurity present in the modal, in a context where the rules laid down do not get into effect immediately, but are subject to subsequent ratification at national level (cf. Garzone 2002) or, in the case of arbitration, to a private agreement which takes them as their legal frame of reference, thus fulfilling the felicity conditions for the rules to be valid.

The other abnormal value concerns *must* in ICC, with a percentage of 0.14‰ against an average of 0.026‰ for the other texts, and a difference of 50% with the highest value recorded (0.7‰). These figures become more interesting if the contexts where *must* is used in ICC are analysed, as in most of them a native English text would not use *must*. Neither is this justified in translational terms, as a comparison between the French and the English text shows that in most such contexts there is no coherent motivation for the use of *must* rather than *shall*. One might expect to find a consistent resort to *must* in positions where the French version has *devoir*, but this is so in only a few cases, while in others *shall* is mostly used, and *should* occurs in one case. Further, there seems to be no means of understanding why in contexts which are absolutely similar one or the other modal has been chosen. Only in one case is it really possible to see a rationale underlying the preference given to *must*, in Art. 7(1) ("Every arbitrator *must* be and remain independent of the parties involved in the arbitration"), where a moral duty is categorically imposed on the arbitrator, although the corresponding article in LCIA has *shall*.

On the whole, as I have already pointed out (Garzone 2003: 206-208), an analysis of how modals are used in translated arbitration texts shows that their use is less consistent than in the STs, particularly so in ICC. In the texts examined, forms of the verb *devoir* and Italian *dovere*, which introduce a strong imperative element in contrast with the constitutive or normative simple present, are not always translated with *must* (as in 38), but also with *shall* (39), (40) or *should* (41):

(38) Tout arbitre doit être et demeurer indépendant des parties en cause. (ICC 7).
Every arbitrator must be and remain independent of the parties involved in the arbitration.

(39) Toute demande reconventionnelle formée par un défendeur doit l'être avec sa réponse et contenir notamment : [...] (ICC 5.5).
Any counterclaim(s) made by the Respondent shall be filed with its Answer and shall provide:

(40) Il Tribunale Arbitrale deve depositare presso la Segreteria Generale il lodo definitivo entro sei mesi dalla sua costituzione, ponendo fine al procedimento.(CNIAM 36.1)
The Arbitral Tribunal shall file the final award with the Secretariat within six months of its being constituted, thereby closing the proceedings.

(41) Si le Secrétaire général estime qu'un coarbitre, un arbitre unique ou un président de tribunal arbitral ne doit pas être confirmé, cette question est soumise à la décision de la Cour. (9.2)
If the Secretary General considers that a co-arbitrator, sole arbitrator or chairman of an Arbitral Tribunal should not be confirmed, the matter shall be submitted to the Court.

In ICC *shall* is sometimes even used in rules where the French ST had *peut*, with an obvious alteration in meaning:

(42) Le demandeur peut présenter une note en réponse, dans un délai de trente jours à partir de la réception de la ou des demandes reconventionnelles, communiquées par le Secrétariat. (ICC 5.6)
The Claimant shall file a Reply to any counterclaim within 30 days from the date of receipt of the counterclaim(s) communicated by the Secretariat.

If this rule is interpreted literally, one may be led to understand that there is an obligation to file a Reply, while this is simply formulated as an option for the Claimant. In the light of these considerations, on the whole it can be concluded that in the translated versions the use of modality, and consequently the expression of performativity, seem to be less consistent than in native arbitration texts, with a degree of inconsistency in the criteria applied in their rendering. The hypothesis that this may be due to a difficulty in understanding the ST is highly improbable, so it could be reasonably speculated that such uncertainty may be due to the re-written nature of these texts. This would be in accordance with the idea which has emerged in translation studies (cf.

Garzone 2005: 52-53) that in the re-writing process the ability to tap the individual's intuitive and spontaneous competence of the language – which is available in first-time writing – seems to be partially impaired, giving sometimes rise to awkward choices and recourse to unnatural linguistic solutions.

3. Conclusions

The discussion has highlighted the impact that a number of procedures routinely performed by translators have on the rendering of the meaning and effects of legal texts. From the analysis of a number of examples of translated texts, it emerges that in the legal field any minor structural change, even if made necessary by structural (typological) differences between the languages involved, needs critical consideration as an apparently negligible syntactic modification can cause alterations of some importance. From the discussion there is also a lesson to be learnt about some aspects of legal drafting connected with the micro-structural organization of the text, which, however negligible they may seem, are crucial to the meaning-generation process.

The analysis also confirms that the process of re-writing itself confers certain characteristics on the translated text, such as inconsistency in the use of modality and in the expression of performativity. It also provides support to the applicability of the universals of discourse transfer, simplification and explicitation to the translation of legal texts, but does not confirm the presence of one of the elements usually associated with simplification, i.e. avoidance of repetition.

References

Baker, Mona 1996. Corpus-based translation studies: the challenges that lie ahead. In Somers, Harold (ed.) *Terminology, LSP and translation: studies in language engineering, in honour of Juan C. Sager*. Amsterdam/Philadelphia: John Benjamins, 175-186.

Beaugrande de, Robert Alain / Dressler, Wolfgang U. 1981. *Introduction to Text Linguistics*. London: Longman (*Einführung in die Textlinguistik*. Tübingen: Max Niemeyer Verlag, 1981).

Beaupré, Michael 1986. *Interpreting Bilingual Legislation*. Toronto: Carswell.

Belotti, Ulisse 2002. The language of Italian arbitration rules in English: some measurable aspects. *Linguistica e Filologia* 15, 113-138.

Belotti, Ulisse 2003. Generic integrity in Italian arbitration rules. In Bhatia/Candlin/Gotti (eds), 19-40.

Bhatia, Vijay K. 1994. Cognitive Structuring in Legislative Provisions. In J. Gibbons (ed.), *Language and the Law*, Longman, London & New York, 1994: 136-155.

Bhatia, Vijay K. / Candlin, Christopher N. / Gotti, Maurizio (eds) 2003. *Legal Discourse in Multilingual and Multicultural Contexts. Arbitration Texts in Europe*. Bern: Peter Lang.

Blum-Kulka, Shoshana / Levenston, Eddie (1983). Universals of Lexical Simplification. In Faerch, Claus / Casper, Gabriele (eds) *Strategies in Interlanguage Communication*, London & New York: Longman, 119-139.

De Franchis, Francesco 1984. *Law Dictionary. English-Italian*. Milan: Giuffré.

Garzone, Giuliana 2000. Legal Translation and Functional Approaches: a Contradiction in Terms?. In *Actes du Colloque International "La traduction juridique. Histoire, théorie(s) et pratique", 17–19.02.2000*. Genève: École de Traduction et d'Interprétation – Université de Genève, 395-414.

Garzone, Giuliana 2001. Deontic modality and performativity in English legal texts. In Gotti, Maurizio / Dossena, Marina (eds) *Modality in Specialized Texts*. Bern: Peter Lang, 153-174.

Garzone, Giuliana 2002. Tradurre la convenzione internazionale: aspetti testuali e pragmatici. In Schena, Leo / Snel Trampus, Rita D. (eds) *Traduttori e giuristi a confronto. Interpretazione traducente e comparazione del discorso giuridico*, Vol. II. Bologna: CLUEB, 37-72.

Garzone, Giuliana 2003. Arbitration Rules Across Legal Cultures: An Intercultural Approach. In Bhatia/Candlin/Gotti (eds), 177-220.

Garzone, Giuliana 2005. Osservazioni sull'assetto del testo italiano tradotto dall'inglese. In Cardinaletti, Anna / Garzone, Giuliana (eds) *L'italiano delle traduzioni*. Milano: FrancoAngeli, 35-57.

Gémar, Jean-Claude 1995. *Traduir ou l'art d'interpréter*. Presses de l'Université de Québec (I. tome 1: *Principes*).

Gémar, Jean-Claude 1997. Traduire le langage du droit en contexte bilingue et bijuridique. Le Canada: un cas d'espèce?. In Schena, Leo (ed.) *Atti del Convegno "La lingua del diritto. Difficoltà traduttive, applicazioni didattiche, Milano"*. Roma: CISU, 74-87.

Gunnarsson, Britt-Louise 1984. Functional Comprehensibility of Legislative Texts: Experiments with a Swedish Act of Parliament. *Text* 4/1-3, 71-105.

Herbots, Jacques H. 1987. La traduction juridique. Un point de vue belge. *Le Cahiers de Droit* 28, 813-844.

Laviosa-Braithwaite, Sara 1998. Universals of Translation. In Baker, Mona (ed.) *Routledge Encyclopedia of Translation Studies*. London/New York: Routledge, 288-291.

Lefevere, André 1992. *Translation, Rewriting and Manipulation of Literary Fame*. London: Routledge.

Neubert, Albrecht / Shreve, Gregory M. 1992. *Translation as Text*. Kent Ohio and London: The Kent State University Press.

Nord, Christiane 1991. Scopos, loyalty, and translational conventions. *Target* 3/1, 91-109.

Nord, Christiane 1997. *Translating as a Purposeful Activity. Functionalist Approaches Explained*. Manchester: St. Jerome Publishing.

Picchi, Eugenio / Peters, Carol 1997. Reference corpora and lexicons for translators and translation studies. In Trosborg, Anna (ed.) *Text Typology and Translation*. Amsterdam : Benjamins, 247-274.

Pigeon, Louis-Philippe 1982. La traduction juridique. L'équivalence fonctionelle. In Gémar, Jean Claude (ed.), *Langage du droit et traduction. Essai de jurilinguistique*. Montréal: Linguatech, 271-282.

Reiss, Katharina / Vermeer, Hans J. (1984). *Grundlegung einer allgemeinen Translationstheorie*. Tübingen: Niemeyer.

Sager, Juan C. 1993. *Language Engineering and Translation. Consequences of Automation*. Amsterdam: Benjamins.

Šarčević S. 1997. *New Approaches to Legal Translation*. The Hague: Kluwer Law International.

Scarpa, Federica 1997. Un esempio di traduzione giuridica dall'inglese in italiano: il contratto di compravendita immobiliare. In Schena (ed.), 93-116.

Toury, Gideon 1980. *In Search of a Theory of Translation*. Tel Aviv: The Porter Institute for Poetics and Semiotics.

Toury, Gideon 1991. What are Descriptive Studies into Translation Likely to Yield apart from Isolated Descriptions. In van Leuven-Zwart, Kitty / Naaijkens, Ton (eds) *Translation Studies: The State of the Art. Proceedings of the First James S. Holmes Symposium on Translation Studies*. Amsterdam: Rodopi, 179-192.

Toury, Gideon 1995. *Translation Studies and Beyond*. Amsterdam: Benjamins.

Trosborg, Anna 1997. Translating Hybrid Political Texts. In Anna Trasborg (ed.) *Text Typology and Translation*. Amsterdam: Benjamins, 145-157.

Ulrych, Margherita / Bollettieri Bosinelli, Rosa Maria (1999). The State of the Art in Translation Studies. In Bassnett, Susan / Bollettieri Bosinelli, Rosa Maria / Ulrych, Margherita (eds), *Translation Studies Revisited, TEXTUS Special Issue,* 12/2, 219-243.

Vermeer, Hans J. 1996. *A Skopos Theory of Translation (Some Arguments For and Against*). Heidelberg: TextContext Wissenschaft.

Paola Evangelisti Allori

The Linguistic Formulation of Power: Modality and Power Relations in Two Sets of Sports-related Arbitration Rules

1. Introduction

This chapter looks into the power relations holding between participants in a particular kind of arbitration procedure, the one obtaining in the solution of sports-related disputes. In particular, it looks into the ways in which the attribution of power is distributed among the various participants in the procedure in two sets of sports-related Arbitration Rules: the international regulation issued by the International Council for Arbitration in Sport (ICAS) and the Italian regulation issued by the Chamber for Conciliation and Arbitration in Sport (CCAS) established within the Italian National Olympic Committee (CONI).

The legal discourse of provision making in arbitration codes differs in many ways from other kinds of legal discourse, e.g. the provision making in statutes. One of the main reasons being the different status and position of the Senders and Receivers of the rules in arbitration and in statutory regulations. Statutes are generally meant to regulate social behaviour at large. Accordingly, the legal discourse they exhibit shows an asymmetrical relationship between Sender and Receiver of the rules, i.e. the legislative body and the citizens (Trosborg 1977) the latter being considered as one, undifferentiated, body. Power relations are realised in this case through the pragmatic actions of stating obligation and prohibition and of granting permission to the Receiver. The Sender is perceived as the Authority behind the scene, the 'Sovereign', who is the "source [of the norms] and simultaneously the guarantor of their autonomy, coherence and efficacy" (Tuori/

Bankowski/Uusitalo, 1997: 1-2) while the Receiver is any citizen; the style is impersonal in that no reference is made to the specific participants involved in the 'eventual' regulative situation.

Arbitration codes, on the other hand, are meant to regulate the procedure for the 'amicable' settlement of conflicts within specific fields of social action, i.e. business, sports, labour, etc. Although the general rules for arbitration are generally laid out in the individual country's private sector of the Law, the actual codes applicable in the specific field are issued by various authorities, recognized and authorised by the State legal system but different from it, e.g. Chambers of Commerce, in business. Further, differently from statutes where the participants can be identified in 'the authority' and 'the citizen' as an undifferentiated class, in the case of arbitration, the participants are clearly identified in specific categories of individuals according to their social role and function in the procedure. In the legal discourse of arbitration, therefore, the Sender, usually the institutional body offering the arbitration procedure, contemplates more than one Receiver. Receivers of the arbitration rules may be any of the various categories of participants in the procedure, including the Court and its President, the Court Office, besides the arbitrator or Panel of arbitrators and the parties seeking arbitration, as in the following example from the Italian Chamber for Conciliation and Arbitration in Sport (CCAS)

> *I componenti della Camera, il Segretario, il personale della Segreteria, i conciliatori, gli arbitri, i consulenti tecnici e le parti* sono obbligati a mantenere riservata qualsiasi notizia o informazione inerente agli argomenti trattati e alle procedure previste dal presente Regolamento. (27.1, emphasis added)
> *The members of the Chamber, the Secretary, the staff in the Secretariat, the conciliators, the arbitrators, the technical consultants and the parties*, are bound to the duty of confidentiality regarding any news or information about any issue dealt with and about the proceedings [carried out] according to the present Regulation. (my translation)

The issuing authority (Sender) can itself be the Receiver of the rules as in the following example from ICAS:

> *The ICAS or its Board* shall rule on the challenge […]. (Emphasis added)

Thus, each participant category, from the legislator to the parties seeking the amicable solution to a dispute, enters differing power relations with the other categories according to its role and function at different stages in the procedure and is seen as having varying degrees of obligation and of rights accordingly.

A further, consequent element of variation in the legal discourse of arbitration is the introduction of an additional pragmatic action, that is, explicitly entrusting some categories of participants, notably the issuing authority, the Court and the arbitrator or Panel of arbitrators, with varying degrees of power and authority at given stages in the procedure. This might seem obvious in a kind of legal discourse where rules have to be established for the smooth and equitable running of proceedings in dispute resolutions where much litigation among the parties might occur. The power assigned to the more 'powerful' participants in the arbitration context might be taken for granted by lay people. But, since the two regulations examined seemed to show some discrepancy in the degree of power and obligation assigned to the same categories of participants, it also seems to be the case that power and power relations among participants are perceived somewhat differently by the producers of the two texts. The issue of 'power' and power relations in arbitration rules is a relevant one, particularly so in sport-related arbitration, where the parties, usually élite athletes and federations, have much to lose from a negative award.

1.1. The nature of Arbitration / Power in Arbitration

Within the field of legal action, arbitration may be thought of, not only as a procedure to make the settlement of a controversy simpler and speedier than in traditional court proceedings, but also as a way to reach a settlement in more 'amicable' settings, in which the parties seeking arbitration are allowed some kind of 'say' in the process, therefore, some degree of power. Various definitions of arbitration point to this feature:

> The hearing and determination of a case in controversy *by a person chosen by the parties* or appointed under statutory authority (Webster, Seventh Collegiate)

> Submitting a controversy to an impartial person, the arbitrator, *chosen by the two parties* in the dispute to determine an *equitable settlement*. (Barron's Dictionary of Law, emphasis added)

This view is reinforced by the following note to the Model Arbitration Clause to be included in contracts present in the Arbitration Rules for international arbitration in trade, emanating from the United Nations Commission on International Trade Law (UNCITRAL), allowing some degree of power to the parties:

> *Note - Parties may wish to consider adding:*
> (a) The appointing authority shall be... (name of institution or Person);
> (b) The number of arbitrators shall be... (one or three);
> (c) The place of arbitration shall be... (town or country);
> (d) The language(s) to be used in the arbitral proceedings shall be…

In effect, though, the process of arbitration involves more than the two parties in the dispute and the arbitrator as one would expect from the definitions above. Usually, the parties apply to an arbitration authority, e.g. Chambers of Commerce in trade, the ICAS or one of the national Chambers in Sport. The arbitration authority is also the body issuing the regulation and overseeing the whole procedure, from the selection of the list of arbitrators to the issuing of the final award. The arbitration process also involves an arbitration structure, coordinated by a President who may have the power to select the arbitrator or arbitration tribunal out of a list of accredited arbitrators, and a Secretarial office which deals with the administrative aspects such as filing the case, keeping the connection between claimant and respondent, notifying time limits and so on.

Within this general framework, arbitration in sport differs from arbitration in other fields (Evangelisti Allori 2004) in that, in Sport Arbitration, there is only one recognized body providing international arbitration worldwide, the International Council for Arbitration in Sport (ICAS) with seat in Lausanne, Switzerland, and usually one body set up to provide arbitration on a national basis in single countries.[1] Such bodies are appointed respectively by the International Olympic Committee (IOC) and, regionally, by the individual National

1 There may be exceptions according to different NOCs. For instance, while the British Olympic Association has set up the Sports Dispute Resolution Panel (SDRP) to function as its national arbitration body, the American USOC refers any sports-related dispute to the external American Arbitration Association (AAA) as stated in the USOC Bylaws, § 220529.

Olympic Committees (NOCs). At the same time, the individual NOCs, as members of the International Olympic Committee, are closely tied to the IOC so that there are strong bonds between international and regional sport authorities. The resulting picture is one of a hierarchical structure firmly controlled by the issuing bodies both internationally and regionally. This may be one reason why authority is perceived as more dominant in the sport regulations than in other fields of arbitration practice. Also, the regulations for arbitration issued by the individual NOCs are generally modelled on the international regulation, although with variations probably due to the specific legal system and culture (Evangelisti Allori 2008).

Variation in arbitration regulations may also involve the structure of the power relations holding between participants. Such variation appears even in codes meant to serve the same purposes in the same field of action, as indicated in the previous comparison of two sports-related regulations (Evangelisti Allori 2008) where, for example, some imbalance in power relations was identified between the international and the Italian regulation for arbitration in sport. In the international regulation, some categories of participants, e.g. the parties seeking arbitration, seemed to be granted limited rights, while having quite a large number of obligations and prohibitions imposed upon them. The Italian regulation, on the other hand, seemed to allow slightly more rights to the parties while imposing statistically more obligations on to the 'more powerful' participant categories. The difference was attributed to variation in the issuing authorities' legal status and background and to the socio-cultural conditions in which the two institutions operate. It was therefore posited that the differing juridical position held by the two bodies within each system might also affect the power relations holding between the various participants in the arbitration procedure in terms of degree of power and obligation attributed to each.

The present study explores the issue further by analysing the linguistic strategies used to attribute power, grant permission, state obligation and prohibition in the two codes under consideration. This focus is further extended to the analysis of the distribution of the same acts among the various participants in the arbitration procedure to discover what degree of power is attributed in each regulation to the main agents of authority in the proceedings.

2. Modality and power

Modality and the system of modal auxiliaries have repeatedly been identified by critical linguists as the major grammatical tool for expressing ambiguity regarding authority and relations of power between participants, in particular as a means of an oblique affirmation of power on the part of the Sender. Kress and Hodge (1979: 123-24), in dealing with the role and features of modal auxiliaries in transactive vs non-transactive speech models, state that:

> The ambiguity about authority – power or knowledge – varies according to which speech model the auxiliary appears in. In the transactive speech model they are least ambiguous [...]. With the non-transactive speech model the *authority relation of the speaker is at its least clear.* 'He must come', as a command, makes no claims that the speaker is the source of the command. *The command is depersonalized and given an impersonal authority which is not specified and therefore is more difficult to challenge.* The third person non-transactive, then has clear advantages for an ideologue, who wishes *to mystify the basis of his authority and the fact that authority rather than reason is being appealed to.* [...] The non-transactive speech model conceals the force of the utterance. (Emphasis added)

More recently, Fairclough (2001: 106) takes up the issue again by pointing to the implicitness in power relations expressed by 'relational' modality as opposed to 'expressive' modality. He thus reiterates the inherent ambiguity of modals as 'disguisers' of power relations and, therefore, of ideology:

> the authority and power relations on the basis of which the producers [...] withhold permission from, or impose obligations upon, the people it is sent to, are not made explicit. *It is precisely implicit authority claims and implicit power relations [...] that make relational modality a matter of ideological interest.* (Emphasis added)

The ambiguity of modals as disguisers of power and power relations is particularly manifest in legal discourse which, although socially recognised and accepted as discourse meant to impose duties and obligations, is a clear example of 'dominant discourse' in Bourdieu's (1991) terms, that is, a 'symbolic system' not produced and appropriated by the social group as a whole but, rather, produced by "a body of *specialists* and, more precisely, by a relatively autonomous field of production and circulation" (1991: 168). As such, it is

> A structured and structuring medium tending to impose an apprehension of the established order as natural (orthodoxy) through the disguised (and misrecognized) imposition of systems of classification and of mental structures that are objectively adjusted to social structures. (1991: 169)

Further, power is created by a "*consensus* on the meaning of the social world" (1991: 166) and on the language used to structure it, so that words acquire their power through

> the belief in the legitimacy of words and of those who utter them [...]. Symbolic power [...] is a power that can be exercised *only if it is recognized* [...] it is defined in and through a given relation between those who exercise power and those who submit to it. (1991: 170)

Legal discourse is obviously a strong example of symbolic system where the use of modals is exploited to the full but where sources of ambiguity lie not so much in the features pointed to by critical linguists, i.e. the Sender disguising his/her authority, as in the English modality system itself and in the ambiguity in meaning of some of the modals, for example *shall*, as argued by Garzone (2001) among others. This becomes particularly evident when the English system is compared with other modality systems.

2.1. Modality in legal discourse

In legal discourse, modality appears both in 'constitutive' and 'regulative' provisions expressing either performative or directive/impositive acts. Constitutive rules "not only perform an act, but have the immediate effect of giving rise to a new state of things or a modification in the previous state of things", therefore bringing about "a change in reality" (Garzone 2001: 157-158) as in the following example:

> There *shall be* an Authority for Greater London, to be known as the Greater London Authority. (*Greater London Authority Act 1999*, 24: 2/5)

Regulation rules ('action' rules in Gunnarson 1984 and 'legislative provisions' in Bhatia 1993), on the other hand, are agent-oriented, i.e. they prescribe that the subject performs the action predicated in the verb form accompanying the modal. In Gunnarsson's words, they

> are meant to impose duties and obligations, to give rights, to prohibit actions, to assign power to certain members or bodies of the executive or other parties, or to state the law or just the penalties imposed on specific actions. (1984: 84)

Trosborg (1997), in her analysis of a substantial corpus of English statutes and contracts found that, in legal discourse in general, the pragmatic actions of stating obligation and prohibition and of granting permission are pre-eminently realised linguistically via the use of a specific set of modals. In the range of modal auxiliaries found to express 'regulative' or 'impositive'[2] acts, which accounted for 47.6% of the total 'regulative strategies', she found that *shall* (15.5%), *should/ ought to* (3.0%) and *is to* (1.2%) were used to express Obligation, *shall not* (3.6%) and *cannot* (8.3%) to express Prohibition and *may* (4.2%) to express Permission.

2.2. Directives in arbitration regulations

In a recent comparative study of regulative acts in two regulations for commercial arbitration and in English Contract Law, Trosborg, (2008) found evident variation in the relative frequency of the regulative acts appearing in the two arbitration regulations as compared with Contract Law. In particular, she found that Contract Law exhibited a higher percentage of Constitutive acts and of Prohibition counteracted by less Permission and less Obligation than the two regulations for commercial arbitration. At the same time, she found variation in the frequency and in the linguistic realisation of the different acts between the two arbitration regulations analysed, the Uncitral Model Law on interna-

---

2 Acts where the addresser imposes a certain behaviour on the addressee. They are defined by Haverkate (1984: 107) as "speech acts performed by the speaker to influence the intentional behaviour of the hearer in order to get the latter to perform [...] the action directly specified or indirectly suggested by the proposition".

tional commercial arbitration (UNCITRAL) and the Arbitration Law of the People's Republic of China (ALPRC). Of the two, ALPRC showed a higher proportion of Obligation (53.1% vs. 30.2%), Permission (22.8% vs. 21.8%) and Prohibition (2.5% vs. 2.0%) respectively. The modal forms used to express Permission in UNCITRAL were *be free to* (1.2%), *may* (19.8%), *need not* (0.4%), *could* (0.4%). Obligation was expressed by *oblige* (0.4%), *shall* (25.3%), *will* (1.2%), *would* (1.5%), *should* (1.1%), *must* (1.1%) and Prohibition by *shall not* (1.2%) and *may not* (0.8%). ALPRC made use of fewer modals, Permission being expressed only by *may* (22.2%) and *can* (0.6%), Obligation by *shall* (51.2%) and *should* (1.9%) and Prohibition by *shall not* (1.9%) and *may not* (0.6%). Her findings are summarised in Tables 1 and 2.

	Permission	Obligation	Prohibition
Contract Law	*may 4.2*	*shall 15.5*	*shall not 3.6*
		should/ought to 3.0	*cannot 8.3*
		is to 1.2	

Table 1. Modals used to express regulative acts in Contract Law.

	Permission / rights	Obligation	Prohibition
UNCITRAL	*may 19.8*	*shall 25.5*	*shall not 1.2*
	be free to 1.2	*would 1.5*	*may not 0.8*
	need not 0.4	*will 1.2*	
	could 0.4	*should 1.1*	
		must 1.1	
		oblige 0.4	
ALPRC	*may 22.2*	*shall 51.2*	*shall not 1.9*
	can 0.6	*should 1.9*	*may not 0.6*

Table 2. Modals used to express regulative acts in UNCITRAL and ALPRC.

In this categorization, no distinction is made between the acts of granting permission and attributing rights; the two are conflated into a single category realised linguistically by *may*, while *shall* is considered as expressing exclusively obligation. The analysis of the sport-related arbitration corpus, on the other hand, showed a fair amount of acts linguistically realised by both *shall* and *may*, clearly attributing rights, therefore power, rather than obligation or permission, to specific categories of participants as will be discussed later.

Nonetheless, Trosborg's findings, in particular the higher amount of Constitutive and Prohibition acts in Contract Law as against a higher percentage of Permission and Obligation in Arbitration Law, point to some aspects relevant to the present analysis, for one thing the different functions the two types of law are called to serve. Statutes in general focus on the regulation of (social) behaviour at large, whereas Arbitration codes focus on the regulation of a specific kind of activity carried out by specific categories of human participants in performing a specific social function. The code in this case has to specify the status of the various participants in the arbitration procedure and to state the rules of behaviour for each, i.e. state what kind of behaviour is allowed (permission) for, what is required of (obligation) and what is not allowed (prohibition) for each category of participants interacting in it.

The second aspect relates to the possibility of variation, in terms of frequency of acts and of their linguistic realisation, to be found in regulations emanating from different legal and socio-cultural contexts, although meant to serve the same legal purposes. Finally, we note the variation and relative frequency in the range of modal forms used to express the same acts in the two arbitration regulations analysed, as shown in Table 2, which makes evident the variation in terms of typology of modal forms and of statistical import of the regulative acts.

3. The study

The texts examined for the present study are the English version of the international regulation for sport-related arbitration (ICAS) and the Italian regulation (CCAS). The international regulation appears both in English and French; both the English text and the French text are considered authentic, i.e. not translated from one of the two languages into the other, as specified in Rules S24 and R68. CCAS appears only in Italian. The two regulations were issued at different points in time.

The international code was issued in 1994, when the ICAS was first created. The published second edition dates from January 2000. The Italian code was first issued in 2002, when the 'Camera di Conciliazione e Arbitrato per lo Sport' was established.[3]

The internal disposition of topics is somewhat different in the two documents; ICAS includes, as a first section (Rules S1-S26) 'Statutes of the Bodies working for the settlement of Sports-related issues', which includes both the ICAS and CAS statutory rules. Rules R27-R69 deal with the Procedural Rules proper. These are followed by a separate section on rules for Mediation (Articles 1-14). On the other hand, no mention about the statute of the CCAS is made in the Italian code, this being included as article 12 within the general CONI Statute.[4] Since the object of the present study were the 'regulative' strategies, 'constitutive' rules were not taken into consideration and only the rules dealing with the arbitration procedure proper were dealt with in the analysis. The portions of text dealing with 'regulative' strategies and related acts amount to 7,343 words in the international code and 6,314 in the Italian one.

4. Results

4.1. Modal forms in ICAS and CCAS

In the context of sport-related arbitration, the directives found fall into two main categories: the *attribution of rights* and the *granting of permission* (indirect strategies according to Trosborg 1997), on the one hand, and the *stating of obligation and prohibition* (direct strategies) on the other. The attribution of rights, therefore of power, to one participant over the other or over a situation, an act quite frequent in the

3 These are the versions on which the study is based. Both regulations have recently undergone slight revisions.

4 A detailed comparative analysis of the full contents of the two regulations can be found in Evangelisti Allori (2008).

two regulations examined, was not categorised in Trosborg's analysis of statutes. The act of attributing Power can therefore be considered as peculiar to arbitration regulations. The ICAS regulation has 245 modal forms realising directives. Their frequency and distribution in terms of the three categories identified by Trosborg according to the kind of modal used appear in Table 3.

	Permission / right	Obligation	Prohibition
ICAS	*may* 23.6	*shall* 65.7	*shall not* 1.6
	can 0.8	*is to* 4.4	*may not* 2.0
		should 1.2	
		must 0.8	
		to be bound to 0.4	

Table 3. Modal forms realising regulative acts in ICAS.

The Italian CCAS, on the other hand, presents only 78 modal forms distributed, according to the same categories, as shown in Table 4.

	Permission / right	Obligation	Prohibition
CCAS	*'potere'* 51.2%	*'dovere'* 43.5%	*'potere' neg* 5.1%

Table 4. Modal forms realising regulative acts in CCAS.

These forms represent 53.4% of the forms realising directives in the Italian text. They fall into the concepts of POTERE (*may*) and of DOVERE (*shall*). Differently from English, where Prohibition is realised by the negative form of either *shall* or *may*, in the Italian text only the negative form of 'potere', e.g. '*non può*', is found to express Prohibition; the negative form of DOVERE, which in other kinds of discourse also expresses Prohibition, is not found here. In addition to these true modals, the Italian regulation exhibits a large number (46.5%) of pro-modal forms, expressing either Permission/right or Obligation, the majority of which fall into the semantic area of DOVERE and express Obligation:

a. Passive form: E'/VIENE + Past Part.

(1) il lodo *è deliberato* dall'organo arbitrale – (the award *shall* be made by the Panel)
(2) l'accordo *viene* formalizz*ato* per iscritto – (the agreement *shall* be written);

b. DA + Inf.

(3) spese *da* corrispond*ere* – (expenses *to be paid);*
(4) [...] più uno *da* deposit*are* presso la Segreteria – ([...] and one *to be sent* to the Court Office)

c. ESSERE OBBLIGATI/TENUTI a + Inf.

(5) gli arbitri, i consulenti tecnici e le parti *sono obbligati a* manten*ere* riservata qualsiasi notizia – (the arbitrators, the technical consultants and the parties *are bound to* the duty of confidentiality)

d. Present Indicative

(6) la Segreteria [...] *provvede* ad informare la parte attrice – (the Court Office *shall* inform the Claimant)

Fewer forms fall into the semantic area of POTERE, in this case clearly expressing attribution of power:

e. AVERE COMPETENZA a + Inf.

(7) La Camera *ha competenza a* promuov*ere* la conciliazione di controversie. – (The Chamber *may* [is entitled to] seek to promote the conciliation of disputes).

f. ESSERE ABILITATA/O a + Inf.

(8) La Camera *è abilitata a* sostituirlo – (The Chamber *shall* [has the power to] substitute him).

When these are added to the true modal forms the resulting picture for the two regulations is the one shown in Table 5.

	Obligation	Permission / right	Prohibition
English	74	26	3.6
Italian	68.4	31.2	5.1

Table 5. Percentage and function of modal and pro-modal forms in the two regulations.

As the table shows, in this categorisation, the English international version has more modal and pro-modal forms than the Italian regulation. It also has a higher rate of Obligation versus Permission/Power.

4.2. Pragmatic functions in sports-related arbitration codes

Following Trosborg's categorization, in Table 5 obligation is given by the occurrences of *shall* and assimilated forms and permission/right by the occurrences of *may* and assimilated forms. This table, however, does not picture the real situation. The presence in the Italian text of forms such as (7) and (8), unambiguously expressing attribution of power and rendered in the corresponding English rules with *shall* or *may* shows that both these modals are also used to express power/ authority to carry out the stated actions. On the basis of these findings, the following distribution of acts and realising modals seems more appropriate for the English text under consideration:

1. Statement of Obligation: SHALL

(9) The CAS shall take all appropriate actions to set the arbitration in motion (R52)
(10) *Every arbitrator* shall be and remain independent of the parties and shall immediately disclose any circumstances likely to affect independence... (R33)
(11) *The claimant* shall pay the Court Office fee (R38)

2. Statement of Prohibition: SHALL / MAY negative

(12) *[...] the parties* shall not be authorised to produce any further written pleading (R44.2)
(13) *Such assignment* may not be contested *by the parties* (R20)
Thereafter, *no party* may raise any further claim […] (R44.1)

3. Granting Permission: MAY

(14) *The ICAS* may delegate this function to its Board (R35)
(15) *A party* may apply to the CAS for the interpretation of an award […] (R63)

4. Attribution of Power/Authority: SHALL / MAY

(a) SHALL
(16) *The ICAS or its Board* shall rule on the challenge of one of its members (R34)
(17) *The CAS* shall in any event keep this fee (R64.1)
(18) *The Panel* shall have full power to review the facts and the law (R57)

(b) MAY

(19) Challenges are in the exclusive power of *the ICAS* which may exercise such power through its Board (R34)

(20) *The President of the relevant Division* may make an order for [...] provisional or conservatory measures (R37)

(21) [...]*The Panel* may nevertheless proceed with the hearing (R44.5)

(22) *The President of the Appeals Arbitration Division* may decide to apply [...] either ex-officio or upon request of the President of the Panel (R65.4)

The Italian text basically uses the corresponding modals DOVERE and POTERE for the expression of Obligation, and Permission. POTERE is also used for the attribution of Power/Authority and, in its negative form, for statements of Prohibition. But, differently from English, Italian also adopts the simple present of the main verb as a parallel for *shall* in the meaning of 'is entitled to, has the power/ authority to'. The various acts are therefore expressed as follows:

1. Statement of Obligation: DOVERE

(21) *Le parti* debbono comparire personalmente o a mezzo di procuratori (5.4)
The parties shall appear in person or through their representatives;[5]

(22) Il presidente del collegio deve in ogni caso essere scelto tra i componenti in carica della Camera stessa (13.3)
The President of the Panel shall in any case be selected among the members of the Chamber;

(23) Ogni arbitro deve indicare il luogo e la data in cui la firma è stata apposta (20.2)
Each arbitrator shall state the place and date of signing.

2. Statement of Prohibition: POTERE negative

(24) La conciliazione non può essere richiesta *da soggetti* nei cui confronti sia stata irrogata una sanzione disciplinare. (3.4)
a request for conciliation may not be filed by subjects undergoing a disciplinary sanction.

(25) Non può essere nominato arbitro *chi* ha assunto la veste di conciliatore nella stessa controversia. (11.3)
[An arbitrator] who has acted as conciliator in the same litigation case may not be appointed as member of the arbitration panel.

---

5 Translations from Italian by the author. In them, the corresponding expressions from ICAS were used whenever possible.

3. Granting Permission: POTERE

(26) La parte convenuta <u>può</u> far pervenire alla Camera…. (9.1)
The respondent <u>may</u> send the Chamber…

(27) La conciliazione <u>può</u> essere richiesta *da una o entrambe le parti* interessate (3.2)
One or both the interested parties <u>may</u> apply for conciliation

4. Attribution of Power: POTERE / Present Indicative

a. POTERE

(28) *Il Presidente* <u>può</u>, in caso di urgenza, <u>adottare</u> provvedimenti di competenza della Camera (1.3)
The President <u>may</u>, in case of urgency, issue directions pertaining to the Chamber;

(29) *La parte* <u>può</u> <u>ricusare</u> un arbitro nei casi previsti dall'art. 51 del Codice di Procedura Civile (15.1)
A party <u>may</u> challenge an arbitrator in the cases provided for in art. 51 of the Civil Code.

b. Present Indicative

(30) La Giunta Nazionale <u>determina</u> l'importo dei diritti amministrativi… (25.3)
The Board <u>shall fix</u> the amount of the administrative dues;

(31) La Camera, dopo un primo richiamo scritto, <u>provvede a</u> rimuoverlo ed è abilitata a sostituirlo secondo quanto previsto dagli articoli 11 e seguenti del presente Regolamento (15.6)
After an initial written warning, the Chamber <u>shall remove</u> him and <u>shall replace</u> him according to the provisions in articles 11 and following of this Regulation.

Two points are to be made here: in this kind of legal text, both *shall* and *may* are used in English to cover the pragmatic function of attributing Power/Authority, thus differing from the canonical meanings of statement of Obligation and granting of Permission. In Italian, on the other hand, DOVERE (*shall*) expresses only Obligation while the attribution of Power is realised by a variety of forms among which the simple present and POTERE (*may*) are the most recurrent. The second point, stemming from the first, is that, in this case of legal discourse, the ambiguity carried by modals lies not so much in the disguising of the identity of the Sender, as pointed out by critical linguists, as in the value to be attributed to the modals themselves.[6]

Whether *shall* or *may* are used to attribute power rather than stating obligation or granting permission can only be disambiguated through the analysis of the wider arbitration context including the participant(s) involved, the process associated to the modal and the specific circumstances.[7] For instance, ICAS rule R54, 'Appointment of the sole arbitrator or of the President and Confirmation of the Arbitrators by the CAS', reads:

(32) If by virtue of the parties' agreement or of a decision of the President of a Division, a sole arbitrator is to be appointed, *the President of the Division* <u>shall appoint</u> the sole arbitrator upon receipt of the motion for appeal.

If three arbitrators are to be appointed, *the President of the Division* <u>shall appoint</u> the President of the Panel upon appointment of the arbitrator by the respondent. The arbitrators selected by the parties shall only be deemed appointed after confirmation by the President of the Division. Before proceeding to such confirmation, *the President of the Division* <u>shall ascertain</u> that the arbitrators fulfil the requirements of Article R33.

Here we find three instances of the same participant, *the President of the Division*, followed by the same modal *shall*, which might be interpreted as carrying the same value throughout. Yet, knowledge of this kind of arbitration context clarifies the value to be attributed to the different occurrences. As a general rule, arbitrators are appointed by the parties in the first instance and the President of the Panel is appointed by the two arbitrators selected by the parties; the President of the relevant Division is given the power/authority to appoint the arbitrators or the President of the Panel only in case of failure to reach an agree-

---

6 The intrinsic ambiguity, or 'fuzziness', of the English modals as a system has been pointed out by Coates (1983) who defines them as a 'fuzzy system' in which there is a gradual shift from one meaning to the other. The system is, thus, "characterized by a continuum of meanings, which favours the emergence of a certain degree of ambiguity and overlapping of semantic and pragmatic values" (Gotti/Dossena 2001:13).

7 The circumstances of the action, qualifications in Bhatia's terms, provide the immediate context for interpretation since they clarify "the nature and circumstances to which the main provisionary clause applies" (1993: 115).

ment. In the case of (32), on the other hand, it is evident that the first two instances of *shall* carry the pragmatic function of granting authority, i.e. in case of Appeal arbitration, it is only the President of the Division who appoints the sole arbitrator or the President of the Panel. The third instance, on the other hand, clearly indicates obligation to carry out a due action.

A similar kind of ambivalence is carried in the Italian text by the simple present which is used in place of modals to express the attribution of Power/Authority, in some cases of Obligation, a usage shared with French as revealed by a comparison with the French authentic version of the ICAS code (CIAS). Compare the following provisions on the ruling on the challenge of an arbitrator:

(33) Sulla richiesta di ricusazione [...] decide in via definitiva *la Camera* con provvedimento motivato. (CCAS 15.3)

The ICAS or its Board shall rule on the challenge [...] It shall give brief reasons for its decision (ICAS R34)

Le CIAS ou son Bureau tranche [...] Il rend une décision sommairement motivée (CIAS R34)

The resulting distribution of Power, Permission, Obligation and Prohibition among the different participants in the two codes for sport arbitration is shown in Table 6.

Issuing Body	PARTICIPANTS	Empowering	Permission	Obligation	Prohibition
ICAS	ICAS	14	0	2	0
CONI	CONI	0	0	1	0
ICAS	Tribunal: CAS	12	0	4	0
CONI	Tribunal: Chamber	7	0	3	1
ICAS	Court Office	3	0	8	0
CONI	Secretariat	1	2	10	0
ICAS	President of Division	20	0	4	0
CONI	President of Chamber	2	0	0	0
ICAS	President of Panel	10	0	1	0

CONI	President of Panel	1	0	1	0
ICAS	Panel/Arbitrator	16	4	11	0
CONI	Panel/Arbitrator	20	8	19	1
ICAS	Parties	1	12	28	6
CONI	Parties	3	15	21	4

Table 6. Comparative values per participant in the two regulations.

5. Discussion of results

The analysis of the pragmatic values carried by modal forms has revealed some interesting aspects about the power relations holding in sport-related arbitration, both general and specific, to each of the regulations examined. The kind of acts attributed to the different categories of participants are indicative of the status held by each category in the arbitration process as envisaged by the legislator. Common to both regulations is the place given to the different participants on the power scale. While the top ranking authorities – the executive – are, obviously, attributed a fair amount of Rights/Power and may undergo statements of Obligation, they are not recipients of acts of Permission and only very rarely of Prohibition. Among the participants involved in carrying out the arbitration procedure, the Court Office/Secretariat and the Arbitrators, on the other hand, seem to rank lowest in the central authority scale, being the recipients of a number of acts of Permission, and undergoing the highest degree of Obligation. The Parties, participants external to the arbitration structure, are placed at the lowest rank as recipients of Empowering acts and, at the same time, at the highest in terms of Permission, Obligation and Prohibition. The Arbitrator/Panel stands in a peculiar position in that it is the recipient of many acts attributing Power/Authority and of numerous statements of Obligation at the same time. In this, it stands between the executive and the parties. This seems to be due to its position and role in the procedure. The arbitrators share the authority of the structure in that they represent the executive and apply its norms in the carrying out of the arbitration process; they are therefore conferred the necessary power/authority to carry out given actions. At the same time, being external professionals designated – or directly appointed in some cases – by the relevant body of the executive, they are bound to a number of obligations towards the arbitration structure which also establishes norms for their professional behaviour in the form of obligation, permission and prohibition.

Such distribution of power and related acts of obligation, prohibition and permission confirms the fact that the participants involved in the arbitration procedure constitute a close set where roles are clearly defined and where the arbitration structure retains the power and the authority at strategic points in the process. This is particularly evident in sports-related arbitration where there is a single arbitration body both at international and at each regional level.

Within this general frame, the international regulation exhibits more empowering acts attributed to the top-ranking authorities – the executive and its members – paralleled by no Prohibitions and slightly more Obligations. The Italian regulation, on the other hand, seems to allow statistically more Power to the Panel and to the parties who are also granted more Permission while receiving fewer Obligations and fewer Prohibitions. The English version of the international regulation also sounds more categorical and exacting than the Italian regulation. This is probably due to the overarching use of *shall* where the Italian regulation, beside the deontic modals DOVERE and POTERE, makes use of differentiated forms which also help disambiguate the pragmatic meaning of the utterance. In addition, the use of the simple present, if compared with the English *shall,* tends to make the Italian normative statements somewhat more matter of fact to lay ears even though, in fact, in Italian legal discourse – and probably in French, as shown in example (33) – the simple present seems to carry "imperative directness and unconditionality" as expressed by Garzone (this volume) quoting the Italian jurist Carcaterra (1994).

The value and strength attached to such forms in Italian and French legal discourse as against the English *shall* could, no doubt, be ascertained through a further comparative analysis of the French version of the ICAS (CIAS) and the Italian CCAS regulations, a comparison outside the scope of this study.

6. Conclusions

The linguistic analysis of the ICAS and CCAS regulations for sports-related arbitration has highlighted some interesting points on the use of modals in establishing power relations among different categories of participants to the arbitration process. From the purely linguistic point of view, there appears to be a difference in the systems used to express regulative acts in the two languages. Whereas English uses essentially modal forms, Italian shows a balanced use of modals, pro-modal forms and of the present indicative. It has also revealed that, in this kind of discourse, ambiguity lies not so much in the identity of the Sender as in the pragmatic value to be attributed to the modals themselves and that a close analysis of the context, both within the sentence and the wider context of the arbitration practice, is in many cases the only way to disambiguate their meaning.

As for the quality of acts prevalent in arbitration legal discourse versus other kinds of legal discourse, this study has confirmed Trosborg's (2008) findings about the lesser proportion of prohibition counteracted by more obligation and permission/attribution of rights to be found in arbitration regulations. On the other hand, the search for the specific categories of participants to whom rights were attributed and permission granted has occasioned a necessary revision of Trosborg's categorization of acts. In the legal discourse analysed, Permission and Rights form two different classes of acts which are attributed to different categories of participants, placed at different levels on the scale of power relations. Further, the enquiry into the various categories of participants, their function and role in the arbitration procedure, has occasioned a redefinition of Rights as either attribution of Power or of Authority, according to the participant involved.

The picture resulting from the linguistic analysis also helps highlight the status of the various participants as set by the authority issuing the regulation. From the distribution of the various acts there emerges the picture of a kind of legal practice where its proclaimed flexibility lies probably in the speedier procedure which avoids all kinds of bureaucratic impediments but where the power stays, nonetheless, firmly with the executive.

References

Bhatia, Vijay K. 1993. *Analysing Genre: Language Use in Professional Settings*. London: Longman.

Bhatia, Vijay K. 1994. Cognitive Structuring in Legislative Provisions. In John Gibbons (ed.) *Language and the Law*. London: Pearson Education, 136-155.

Bourdieu, Pierre [2]1991/[1]1983. On Symbolic Power. In John B. Thompson (ed.) *Language and Symbolic Power. Pierre Bourdieu.* Cambridge: Polity Press, 163-170.

Carcaterra, Gaetano 1994. Norme costitutive. In Umberto Scarpelli / Paolo Di Lucia (eds) *Il Linguaggio del Diritto*. Milano: LED, 219-231.

Coates, Jennifer 1983. *The Semantics of the Modal Auxiliaries*. London: Croom Helm.

Evangelisti Allori, Paola 2004. International Arbitration in Different Settings: Same or Different Practice? In Christopher N.Candlin / Maurizio Gotti (eds) *Intercultural Aspects of Specialized Communication.* Bern: Peter Lang, 223-240.

Evangelisti Allori, Paola 2008. Arbitration in Sport: Rules and Legal Contexts. In Vijay K. Bhatia / Christopher N. Candlin / Jan Engberg (eds) *Legal Discourse across Cultures and Systems* Hong Kong: Hong Kong City University Press. 255-274.

Garzone, Giuliana 2001. Deontic Modality and Performativity in English Legal Texts. In Maurizio Gotti / Marina Dossena (eds) *Modality in Specialized Texts.* Bern: Peter Lang, 153-173.

Gotti, Maurizio / Dossena Marina 2001. Introduction. In Maurizio Gotti / Marina Dossena (eds) *Modality in Specialized Texts.* Bern: Peter Lang, 9-18.

Gunnarsson, Britt-Louise 1984. Functional Comprehensibility of Legislative texts. *Text* 4-1/3, 71-105.

Haverkate, Henk 1984. *Speech Acts, Speakers and Hearers*. Amsterdam: Benjamins.

Fairclough, Norman [1]1989/[2]2001. *Language and Power*. London: Longman.

Kress, Gunther / Hodge, Robert 1979. *Language as Ideology*. London: Routledge & Kegan Paul.

Trosborg, Anna 1997. *Rhetorical Strategies in Legal Language*. Tübingen: Gunter Narr.

Trosborg, Anna 2008. Rhetorical Strategies in Arbitration Law. In Vijay K. Bhatia / Christopher N. Candlin / Jan Engberg (eds) *Legal Discourse across Cultures and Systems* Hong Kong: University of Hong Kong Press. 199-220.

Tuori, Kaarlo / Bankowski, Zenon / Uusitalo Jyrki (eds) 1997. *Law and Power. Critical and Socio-Legal Essays*. Liverpool: Deborah Charles Publications.

MICHELA MENGHINI

Italian-English Correspondences in the Juridical Discourse of Sports Arbitration: An Electronic Glossary

1. Introduction

The main purpose of this chapter is to present a computer-assisted comparison of two codes of arbitration rules for sport, the *Code for Conciliation and Arbitration for Sport* (CCAS), issued in Italian by the Italian National Olympic Committee (CONI), and the *International Code of Arbitration for Sport* (ICAS), issued in English (and in French, both versions declared "authentic" in the Code) by the International Council of Arbitration for Sport. Following Bhatia (1993: 105-113), the analysis of the codes focuses particularly on the legislators' use of syntactic expressions especially relevant in juridical discourse to point out the similarities and, possibly even more interesting, the differences in their use between the two sets of rules. The expressions examined are the three main types of syntactic constructions identified by Bhatia: (a) *complex prepositional phrases*, namely complex constructions with a Preposition+Noun+Preposition structure (P+N+P from now on), (b) *binomial and multinomial expressions*, namely expressions sharing the same grammatical form and semantic area, connected by conjunctions such as *and* or *or* and (c) noun phrases, better known as *nominalizations*.

In order to detect such constructions in the two codes, specific tools for computerized corpus analysis were employed, mainly *WordSmith Tools* (Scott 2006). Since the two codes do not amount to a massive corpus, part of the study was also carried out manually when necessary. The results that surfaced from comparing the linguistic choices in the texts suggested the creation of a comparative glossary in electronic version, to show in a clear and efficient way the significant constructions and the correspondence – or the lack of correspondence – between them in the two codes, as well as their specific co-text and the wider context which they are placed in. The resulting CD-ROM allows faster searches of the relevant expressions and gives greater emphasis to their contexts and correspondences, thus helping further investigations of their role and importance.

2. Pivotal constructions in juridical discourse

Bhatia (1993: 103) sums up the outstanding characteristics of legal texts stating that their peculiarity is the result of the "seemingly impossible task of achieving the dual characteristic of clarity, precision and unambiguity on the one hand, and all-inclusiveness on the other hand […]." The need for clear, precise and at the same time exhaustive statements leads legislators to use a kind of language whose syntactic characteristics are deeply influenced by and connected to the semantic ones. Consequently, juridical discourse is characterized by manifest general complexity, mainly caused by compound and nominal constructions that make it possible to give even the smallest details of each and every aspect with the maximum of clarity. The following is an example of such complex constructions, binomials in this case, from ICAS:

(1) If, *by virtue of the arbitration agreement* <u>*or*</u> *of a decision of the President of the Division,* three arbitrators are to be appointed, *the claimant shall appoint its arbitrator in the request* <u>*or*</u> *within the time-limit set in the decision on the number of arbitrators* <u>and</u> the respondent shall appoint its arbitrator within the time-limit set by the Court Office upon receipt of the request. (R 40.2) [my italics and underlining]

(2) is a similar example from CCAS:

(2) Nell'ipotesi di arbitrato con più di due parti, *in assenza di previsioni specifiche nella clausola arbitrale circa il numero* <u>*o*</u> *le modalità di nomina degli arbitri* <u>*ovvero*</u> *in assenza di accordo sulla nomina di uno stesso arbitro tra le parti aventi posizioni coincidenti,* il Presidente della Camera nomina diretta-

> mente un Collegio di tre arbitri, uno dei quali con funzioni di presidente del collegio. (Art.11.2) [my italics and underlining][1]

Both these examples feature the three types of constructions which have been identified as the most relevant and frequent in juridical texts and are thus typical of juridical discourse:

- complex prepositional structures, these are more specific and thus more suitable than simple ones in order to avoid ambiguity. As Bhatia (1993: 107) points out:

> The use of complex prepositions rather than the simple ones [...] is rather preferred in legislative writing simply because the specialist community claims [...] that the simple ones tend to promote ambiguity and lack of clarity.

In (2) there are three such structures: *Nell'ipotesi di*, *in assenza di*, *con funzioni di*, while in (1) we find a P+N+P structure, *by virtue of*, which is one of the most frequent in this code. We also find another construction, *of the arbitration agreement* <u>*or*</u> *of a decision of the President of the Division*, which belongs to the second type of relevant structures:

- homogenous nominal groups connected with the conjunctions *and/or*. These allow exhaustive specifications and accurate lists of cases and situations but, at the same time, they make sentences generally long and intricate. They are defined by Bhatia (1993: 108) as

> [...] a sequence of two or more words or phrases belonging to the same grammatical category having some semantic relationship and joined by some syntactic device such as 'and' or 'or'. [...] This is an extremely effective linguistic device to make the legal document precise as well as all-inclusive.

---

1 "In case of arbitration with more than two parties involved, *in the absence of specific provisions in the arbitration clause on the number of arbitrators* <u>*or*</u> *the method of appointment* <u>*or*</u> *in the absence of an agreement on the* appointment *of a sole arbitrator among the parties on the same side,* the President of the Chamber shall appoint a Panel of three arbitrators, one of whom acting as President of the panel."

In (2) we find a binomial expression, *circa il numero o le modalità di nomina degli arbitri,* embedded in a longer and complex binomial linked by 'ovvero', a stronger synonym for 'o' (or): "[...] *in assenza di previsioni specifiche nella clausola arbitrale circa il numero o le modalità di nomina degli arbitri ovvero in assenza di accordo sulla nomina di uno stesso arbitro tra le parti aventi posizioni coincidenti* [...]".

- *nominalizations*, that is nominal forms very often used to replace the verbal ones, so that the text may apply as universally as possible, and be as detailed as possible; as Belotti (2002: 125) points out:

> In legal language nominalization is considered an effective device which can be used in order to de-emphasize or obscure the performer of the action and make provisions apply as broadly as possible [...]. Another reason for nominalization in legal texts is that draftsmen, by using nominal elements, can insert as many details as are required in a single sentence, thus making it all-inclusive [...].

In example (1) we find one of the most frequent nominalizations in the text: *upon receipt of* while in (2) the nominalization is *aventi posizioni coincidenti.*

These are the elements chosen for our analysis of the arbitration rules of ICAS and CCAS. Regarding such elements, sports arbitration rules do not seem to diverge from the trends of generic juridical discourse as in both codes we find a conspicuous presence of complex prepositional phrases, binomial/multinomial expressions and nominalizations. The following tables show the number of constructions identified in each text, and compare them to the number of sentences and words in the texts, with percentages.

	P+N+P	*B & M*	*NOM*	*Sentences*	*Words*
ICAS	125	187	76	266	7880
CONI	124	154	75	186	6318

Table 1. Number of constructions, sentences and words in each code.

	P+N+P	*B & M*	*NOM*
ICAS	46,9%	70,3%	28,6%
CONI	66,7%	82,8%	40,3%

Table 2. Percentage for each kind of construction compared to the number of sentences in each code.

	P+N+P	*B & M*	*NOM*
ICAS	1,58%	2,37%	0,97%
CONI	1,96%	2,44%	1,19%

Table 3. Percentage for each kind of construction compared to the number of words in each code.

The percentage tables refer respectively to the number of P+N+Ps, binomials and multinomials, and nominalizations compared to the number of total sentences, and the same number compared to the number of words in each text. Table 2 more clearly shows the relevance of these numbers. Indeed what stands out is the massive presence, in both texts, of binomial and multinomial expressions, almost 83 per cent in CCAS and 70 per cent in ICAS, and of the complex prepositional phrases, nearly 50 per cent in ICAS and almost 67 per cent in CCAS. This means that, as an average, in both codes about every two sentences there are up to two binomial or multinomial expressions and one PNP construction.

The tables also show that the Italian text contains a higher number of the constructions analysed, an average of 12 to 20 per cent more than in ICAS for each category. This may be due both to a different, more scrupulous attitude of the Italian legislators in order to be more precise and less ambiguous, and to the inherent grammatical and syntactic structure of the Italian language. A third and more socio-political reason could be the willing attempt of international legislators to write a text in English less complex than usual law codes, in order to make it accessible and clear to non-mother tongue speakers, as they probably constitute the larger part of the addressees of an international set of rules.

Averages of course hide the fact that in a large number of sentences, usually but not necessarily the longer ones, we find several

PNPs, binomials or multinomial expressions and nominalizations, while few, usually but not necessarily shorter ones, may contain just one of such constructions, if any. Moreover, in several cases, these constructions co-occur or else are embedded one within the other, i.e. a PNP and a nominalization, or in any other combination of the three as in the following example from CCAS:

(3) La Camera svolge le proprie funzioni *in composizione monocratica o collegiale secondo le disposizioni del presente Regolamento*, applicando le norme di diritto e le norme e gli usi dell'ordinamento sportivo nazionale e internazionale. (Art.1.4) [my italics and underlining][2]

Each of the expressions in italics makes up two different types, namely:

- a binomial construction and a nominalization (*in composizione monocratica o collegiale*)
- a PNP and a nominalization (*secondo le disposizioni del presente Regolamento*)

In addition, the underlined words make up two more binomial constructions so that, in not so long a sentence as (3), there are two nominalizations, one complex prepositional phrase and three binomial constructions. Example (4) is an even shorter sentence from ICAS:

(4) *Upon formation of* the Panel, the Court Office shall fix, subject to later changes, the amount and the method of payment of the advance of costs. (R64.2) [my italics and underlining]

Here we have an instance of nominalization sharing words with a PNP structure (*Upon formation of*), plus a further nominalization (*subject to later changes*) and a binomial expression (*the amount and the method of payment*). Such constructions, typical of juridical discourse, thus seem to be overwhelmingly present also in the sports arbitration codes analysed.

---

2 "The Chamber exercises its functions *through a sole arbitrator or a panel of arbitrators in conformity with the provisions of this Code*, according to the applicable regulations and rules of national and international sports law".

3. Placing the constructions in their co-text and context

Examples (3) and (4) show the importance of analysing the constructions in the actual sentence where they belong. Mere lists and statistics, though necessary for reference, do not really give an accurate enough idea of how the text works and of the significance of such expressions in the actual text. The importance of context for any linguistic study has been stressed by Firth (1935: 37), who states that "the complete meaning of a word is always contextual, and no study of meaning apart from a complete context can be taken seriously". Stubbs (1993: 8) takes up this concept by pointing out that "language should be studied in actual, attested, authentic instances of use, not as intuitive, invented, isolated sentences". In a more recent work (2002: 100), he makes the point clearer and more articulate introducing a more specific perspective:

> It makes little sense to describe the meaning of individual words in isolation, since words are co-selected with other words, and meanings are distributed across lager units. [...] Words and context are inseparable. If, for analytic convenience, we start from an individual word, then we can make predictions about the textual environment in which it is likely to occur. Equally, if we know something about the environment, then we can make predictions about the words which are likely to occur there [...].

Thus, while identifying the relevant constructions in the texts, we also studied their environment, the 'co-selections' that they trigger, their co-text, be it the few words immediately preceding and following them, or longer collocations such as whole sentences or parts of them. When several occurrences were found of the same construction, the co-text that seemed particularly interesting was chosen, either for its similarities with most of the other occurrences or for its connections with a similar co-text of a corresponding construction in the other code. In some cases, this choice was also influenced by technical reasons which will be discussed later.

A larger context was also needed because, as Evangelisti Allori (2004: 223-240) has pointed out, the distribution of information, and consequently the prominence and weight given to different aspects of the arbitration process vary in the two texts under examination, revealing different approaches due to the wider socio-political and cultural context. Thus, each of the constructions under analysis needed to be placed and studied in its actual position in the code, so that the whole context with its conceptual frame and distribution patterns could be taken into account. For this purpose, in the electronic glossary, a link was also provided between all the expressions and their positions in the text.

4. Correspondences and equivalences across languages

The general context is particularly relevant for our main aim, that is the comparison between the two codes to see which possible correspondences and equivalences can be found between constructions in each of them. As Malmkjaer (1993: 220) points out,

> There is obviously neither one fixed use nor one fixed meaning for each term in each language, and there is no one-to-one correspondence between the terms across the languages.

Therefore, what we were looking for was not a series of impossibly exact equivalences or even reciprocal translations, but interesting correspondences in both meaning and usage, with close attention to the wider context as well as to the co-text, while keeping in mind all discourse levels, lexical, morphological and syntactic (Tognini Bonelli 1996: 132). The kinds of features that can provide clues to possible correspondences between constructions in the two texts are the way the expressions collocate in the whole code, the role they have in their specific co-text, which words tend to gather nearby, which concepts they contribute to build or explain or tend to be part of. The complexity of such correspondences in meaning is highlighted by Halliday (1992: 16):

> If meaning is function in context, […], then equivalence of meaning is equivalence of function in context. What the translator is doing when translating or

> interpreting is taking decisions all the time about what is the relevant context within which this functional equivalence is being established [...].

Such functional equivalences were investigated in the two codes, and put side by side when found. In some cases they showed to be clear, close correspondences, since the words used and the co-texts and contexts in which they were found were very much alike, sometimes even expressed with the same structure, as in the following example:

(5) Upon their appointment, the members of the ICAS sign a declaration undertaking to exercise their function in a personal capacity, with total *objectivity AND independence*, in conformity with this Code. (S5) [my italics]

[...] ciascun arbitro deve produrre una dichiarazione attestante l'esistenza delle condizioni per lo svolgimento dell'incarico con imparzialità E indipendenza rispetto alle parti (Art.14.2) [my underlining][3]

At other times functional equivalences are expressed with different structures:

(6) *Upon expiration of* the time-limit set in Articles R41.2 and R41.3, the President of the Division shall decide on the participation of the third party, taking into account, in particular, the prima facie existence of an arbitration agreement as referred to in Article R39 above. (R41.4) [my italics]

Scaduto detto termine senza che la parte intimata abbia adempiuto è data notizia con le modalità previste dall'art.24 comma 3 lettera h) (Art.28.1) [my underlining][4]

Both cases are interesting to understand the reasons behind them, i.e. to determine whether the different language systems lead to such choices, or whether such choices were also or solely due to different legal discourse conventions. Just as interesting are the cases in which no correspondence could be found, as this could say much about the different prominence and weight given to certain kinds of information

---

3 "[...] each arbitrator shall produce a declaration attesting the existence of the conditions to exercise their functions with objectivity and independence with respect to the parties."

4 "If, after such time-limit expired, the summoned party didn't comply, it shall be notified in accordance with the provisions of article 24 paragraph 3 letter h)."

in the two codes, and therefore, there was a need for clear and unequivocal statements over different aspects of the process. In some cases correspondences cannot be found because the two codes set down different provisions; therefore, even if a particular aspect of the arbitration process is given equal prominence in both cases, specific details may be dissimilar. In such a case, no correspondent expressions can be identified. This is the case with the following nominalization in the ICAS text:

(7) The award shall be made by a majority decision, or, *in the absence of a majority*, by the President alone. (R46) [my italics]

The CCAS code does not allow an award to be made without a majority decision,[5] therefore a corresponding expression for 'in the absence of a majority' is not found in this text.

The different wider cultural and legal contexts which the two texts belong to can also prove quite relevant. Although both codes refer to the Civil Law system, ICAS chooses to abide by the Swiss law, in case no different choice is made by the parties, while CCAS is obviously connected to Italian law. Therefore, we find repeated expressions in the Italian text which do not have correspondences in the other one.

(8) *Oneri di legge da corrispondere ai componenti della Camera che hanno reso il parere: - se soggettivamente dovuti, agli onorari e alle spese vanno aggiunti gli importi relativi alla Cassa di previdenza e assistenza professionale e all'IVA. (I.4)* [my underlining][6]

The binomial expression in italics occurs three times in CCAS, thus emerging as a relevant feature. But it clearly applies to the Italian wel-

5 The specific part of the article concerning the award in the CCAS reads: "Sia il dispositivo sia il lodo completo di motivi devono essere in ogni caso sottoscritti dall'arbitro unico o da almeno la maggioranza del collegio arbitrale." (Art.20.4) ("Both the purview and the award together with the reasons therefor shall be in any case signed by the sole arbitrator or by at least the majority of the arbitration panel.")

6 "Fees owed to the members of the Chamber who rendered the opinion: – if subjectively owed, the amount related to the social security and assistance fund for professionals and to VAT shall be added to the fees and costs."

fare system and would have little sense in an international context. Similarly, the lack of correspondence could also be due to the different type of organization an international body needs in comparison with a national one. A few different binomial/multinomial expressions are used in ICAS without any possible correspondences in CCAS:

(9) the Court Office shall determine the final amount of the cost of arbitration, which shall include the CAS Court Office fee, the costs and fees of the arbitrators computed in accordance with the CAS fee scale, the contribution towards the costs and expenses of the CAS, and the costs of *witnesses, experts and interpreters*. (R64.4) [my italics]

(10) In the event of such a choice, the Panel may order that the parties bear all or part of the *translation and interpreting* costs. (R29) [my italics]

(11) R65.3 The costs of *the parties, witnesses, experts and interpreters* shall be advanced by the parties. [my italics]

Interpreters and translators are rarely if ever needed in disputes within a national context, while the ICAS text has to specify details about this matter a number of times. While examples (10) and (11) are the only ones featuring those constructions, the multinomial expression in example (9) is used again twice. It is interesting to note that examples (8)-(11) belong to parts of the texts where practical matters such as costs and expenses are stated. The different wider contexts seem to influence rules and decisions on such matters more than those on other aspects.

5. Technical implementation

The analysis of the two texts was completely carried out on their electronic versions, downloaded from the websites of the issuing bodies. The first step of the analysis consisted in identifying the constructions that would become the main objects of our study. The codes form a not too large corpus, therefore there was no need for extremely powerful and complicated tools. The *WordSmith Tools* software was mostly used in the beginning phase. The constructions we were looking for[7] are made of at least three words, but they basically focus on prepositions and conjunctions. So these were given as key words, and among the resulting clusters, the ones that actually made up the kind of constructions we were looking for were selected. Tables containing such constructions and their occurrences were then created. A double check with the *Search function* of the text editor was needed to make sure that occurrences were correctly counted, especially for complex prepositional phrases and for the multinomials, thus possibly tricking the software to double-counting each of them. Nominalizations were, instead, looked for in a manual way, since sorting through hypothetical collocates of *–ing* ending words or other possible clues to nominal forms would take just as long and would probably produce incomplete, unsatisfactory results. Once all the constructions were identified and counted, their co-texts and contexts were examined in order to select the most representative and interesting one in case of identical occurrences. These, too, were inserted in the tables.

The second step was the actual comparison of the constructions and contexts collected for the two codes, to find possible correspondences. Some correspondences were easy to identify, others were less obvious and were decided later on, when the general picture was much clearer. Finally, there were cases in which correspondences had to be looked for outside the tables of the analysed constructions, with a manual, more careful examination of the texts, their organization and structure, to find out whether and in what ways any parts of them matched with the contexts of the constructions which were still lacking an equivalent in each code. This was a slower, time-consuming part of the work than the previous one, especially as far as nominalizations were concerned.

At this point it was evident that the tables thus obtained were not practical and efficient enough to allow a proper evaluation of the results and further analysis of them. Proper interaction and the possibility to move quickly and efficiently from the list of constructions to their co-texts and correspondences and on to their wider contexts (and back) were needed, and HTML pages seemed the best tool for it. An

---

7 P+N+P and binomial & multinomial expressions; nominalizations had to be searched for differently.

HTML version of the tables and of their connections was designed, with the aim of producing a proper electronic glossary of the correspondences under examination. The glossary on CD-ROM opens up with a full screen *Home Page*, featuring links to its three main sections, P+N+P, binomial and multinomial expressions, nominalizations, and to both of the codes in their entirety. Figure 1 is a black and white screen shot of the Glossary Home Page:

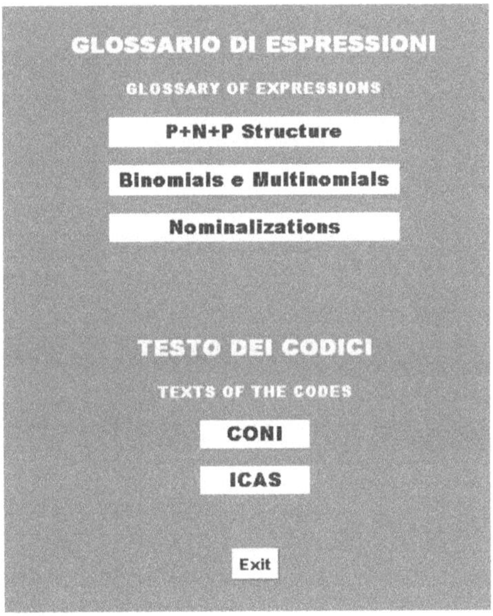

Figure 1. Home page of the CD-ROM.

Each section presents four links to as many pages: two of them point to the tables containing the simple lists of constructions (from CCAS and ICAS respectively), and two to the tables containing the constructions in their co-text and the corresponding constructions from the other text, when one was found. This, too, is presented with its co-text, i.e. one page is for the correspondences ICAS-CCAS, the other for those CCAS-ICAS. All the constructions in the tables have links to the part of the code where they are found and which is their actual context; in each code all constructions are linked to their position in the tables of correspondences.[8] It is possible to move from the lists of the constructions to their context in the code, from the tables of the correspondences to either of the codes and relative context, and from each code to the tables of correspondences. Figure 2 shows the organizational structure of the electronic Glossary, with the various links between pages. Here only the P+N+P Structure section is given as an example:

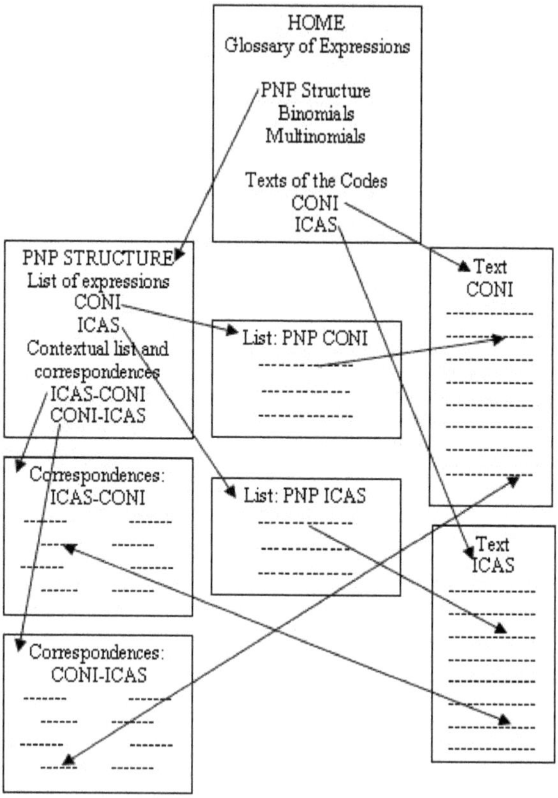

Figure 2. Links between pages in the electronic glossary.

8 As already mentioned, not all of the actual occurrences were linked: for each expression only the occurrence with the most representative and interesting co-text and context was chosen.

The most complex element to implement was the double link necessary in the codes when the same words are shared by two different constructions, i.e. P+N+P and nominalization. The final solution chosen for such cases is a very small pop-up menu, which appears next to the construction when the mouse passes over the link, and which shows the two possible choices, so that we can decide which table of correspondences we want to see, i.e. the P+N+P or the nominalization one. Because such pop-up menus tend to slow down the opening up and functioning of the pages, they were only employed when it was strictly necessary. This means that, when there were two possible occurrences of a construction, both relevant in a similar way but one also constituting a different structure, the one not sharing words with other types of constructions was chosen as co-text of the expression in the table. Finally, in all pages a BACK button can be found as well as a HOME button that links to the first page, which in turn has a CLOSE button, thus making the navigation easier and user-friendly.

6. A bridge across languages and field studies

The final product is an efficient, easy-to-use tool that gives a clear, immediate idea of the co-texts and contexts of all the constructions, as well as of their positions and distribution in the codes. At the same time, it provides a quick comparison between co-texts and contexts of the corresponding expressions in the two codes. Because it relates with different fields of studies on various levels, ranging from juridical discourse proper to translation to linguistics in the strict sense, this glossary will prove quite useful to a variety of users. In its mere glossary function, any translator working on legal texts of sports arbitration will find it helpful, because it allows them to study actual constructions in their original context along with their correspondences, and thus gives them "attested, authentic instances of use" (Stubbs 1993: 8).

More accurately than most dictionaries can do, it can help Italian jurists or law students, with not enough confidence and knowledge of the English language, to better understand the ICAS code or other similar codes, both because it provides an Italian equivalent of some core constructions and because it shows their collocation in the original context. This contributes to a deeper understanding of the texts and encourages comparative law studies, bridging the distance across juridical discourses in different languages. The same can be said, for English-speaking jurists who need to study the Italian code. By identifying "(degrees of) equivalences of concepts" this glossary may actually help to form a knowledge base of legal terms and expressions to "establish […] precision of terms and avoid ambiguity" as pointed out by Tessuto in this volume.

Finally, in its more specific features, and according to its original purpose, the glossary constitutes a useful instrument for all linguistics scholars who are interested in the comparison and the analysis of the strategies employed by the issuing bodies in such legal texts of sports arbitration, to try and understand whether these choices were made either because of inherent differences between the Italian and the English languages, or because of conscious different approaches and views in the legal matter, possibly due to different backgrounds or other similar socio-political reasons, or more probably because of a combination of these two reasons.

In many respects, though, the glossary and the whole project is still a work in progress and, as such, it is gradually developing and gathering more depth. In a more analytic direction, a distinction will be made between similar and different linguistic strategies employed by the two codes within the identified conceptual correspondences. This will be taken one step further by including some of the correspondences that were at first rejected because of the excessive divergence between them. In a more general direction, a more detailed analysis will be carried out about the significance and possible predominance of some types of constructions compared to the other types within each code. To this purpose, the possible connection between such significance and the position of the expressions in the general structure of each text will also be further investigated.

Finally, the analysis could be extended to arbitration codes other than sports-related arbitration, such as the UNCITRAL for instance, to inspect the similarities and differences of constructions and strategies between a code for international trade and the two codes for arbitration in sports. One of the issues worth investigating might be whether the two international codes in English, though dealing with different fields of social practice and activity, exhibit more similar strategies than the two codes of sports arbitration appearing in different languages.

References

Belotti, Ulisse 2002. The Language of Italian Arbitration Rules in English: Some Measurable Aspects. *Linguistica e Filologia* 15, 113-139.

Bhatia, Vijay K. 1993. *Analysing Genre. Language Use in Professional Settings*. London: Longman.

Comitato Olimpico Nazionale Italiano 2000. Il Regolamento della Camera di Conciliazione e Arbitrato per lo Sport. At <http://www.coni.it/fileadmin/arbitrato/GN24gen06.pdf>. [The CONI code that can be viewed in the official website at the moment of print was modified on January 24 2006. The version we have worked on is the previous one, dated 2000].

Evangelisti Allori, Paola 2004. International vs National Regulations: Rules and Practices in Two Codes for Arbitration in Sport. In Candlin, Christopher N. / Gotti, Maurizio (eds) *Intercultural Aspects of Specialized Communication*. Bern: Peter Lang, 223-240.

Firth, John R. 1935. The Technique of Semantics. *Transactions of the Philological Society*, 36-72.

Halliday, Michael A.K. 1992. Language Theory and Translation Practice. *Rivista internazionale di tecnica della traduzione* 0 (pilot issue), 15-25.

International Council of Arbitration for Sport 1994. Statutes of the Bodies Working for the Settlement of Sports-related Disputes. At <http://www.tas-cas.org/en/pdf/CodeEngnov2004.PDF>. [The ICAS code that can be viewed in the official website at the moment of print was modified and entered into force on January 1 2004. The version we have been working on is the previous one, dated 1994].

Malmkjaer, Kirsten 1993. Who Can Make Nice a Better Word Than Pretty? Collocation, Translation And Psycholinguistics. In Baker, Mona *et al.* (eds) *Text and Technology*. Amsterdam: Benjamins, 213-232.

Scott, Mike 2006. *WordSmith Tools 4.0*. Oxford: Oxford University Press.

Stubbs, Michael 1993. British Tradition in Text Analysis. In Baker, Mona *et al.* (eds) *Text and Technology*. Amsterdam: Benjamins, 1-33.

Stubbs, Michael 2002. *Words and Phrases. Corpus Studies of Lexical Semantics*. Oxford: Blackwell.

Tognini Bonelli, Elena 1996. *Corpus Linguistics at Work*. Amsterdam: Benjamins.

TARJA SALMI-TOLONEN

Negotiated Meaning and International Commercial Law

1. Introduction

This chapter examines some key concepts of transactional law in an international setting. In situations where professionals meet, such as project planning and contracting, issues are centred on communication and are essentially discursive. Participants negotiating business transactions come from various fields of expertise – and rarely from the same legal culture. Specialised knowledge is constructed and constituted in language, and differences in knowledge are differences in language. Therefore, it is also important to study language in connection with international commerce, and not only the multilingual aspect, but language use in general.

I will address the issues of language basically from the point of view of contracting, especially business to business contracting, and contract law. The chapter develops as follows: at the outset I shall outline the background of this work which I believe reflects new developments, both in present-day corporate contracting and lawyering practices; I will then discuss three different types of problems in international commerce that arise from concepts crucial to international contracting. *Non-conformity*, *avoidance*, and *impossibility of performance* can cause difficulties in contracting especially across borders. Differing interpretations and meanings of these terms may lead to litigation or arbitration. Finally, I will try to find remedies for problem situations and discuss the role language plays in the process, closing with some implications and conclusions. My principal starting point is that meanings are negotiated and that it is only by recognising this that contracting can be successful for all parties. I suggest that only by being aware of the differences in language use can problems be avoided and understanding reached. In my view, shared meanings are negotiated meanings.

2. The framework

The overall framework and point of view of this contribution lies in *proactive law*. This framework, which finds its origins in *preventive law*, is developed and promoted by a group of researchers and practising contract lawyers in Finland.[1] The basic idea in proactive law, apart from preventing problems arising, is to help people and businesses succeed. The thinking of the proactive law movement represents a shift from the traditional *ex post,* court-centred, backward-looking approach to a future-oriented *ex ante,* real-life approach. In other words, rather than treating contracts solely as means to avoid disputes, conflicts and litigation, practitioners of proactive law view them as means for planning ahead and for advancing cooperation and possibilities for all parties involved.

Legal linguistics is particularly meaningful in this approach because of the special relationship language and law have and because of the primacy of language. Law would not exist without language and speech acts precede any transactions governed by law. I will therefore explore ways in which linguistic explanation and legal linguistic knowledge can be of help to contracting parties.

Preventive law is a movement begun by Professor Louis Brown in the United States in the 1950s (Brown 1950, 1955). It has been pointed out that lawyers have engaged in preventive law ever since there have been lawyers and clients. Lawyers' duty is to assist their clients in arranging their affairs so as to reduce the risk of future legal problems. However, it has also been pointed out that until Louis Brown began his work in the United States there was no collection of

---

1 Preventive law was first brought to Finland by Helena Haapio LL.M., M.Q., an international contract counsel with Lexpert Ltd. A conference in Stockholm in June 2005 marked the extension of the proactive law movement to other Nordic countries.

principles known as 'planning' which would be applicable to almost any area of lawyering. The early stages in the development of preventive law were spent identifying these principles. In more recent years the approach has spread to an increasing variety of settings (Dauer 2003). The Finnish, or today the Nordic school or movement, applies the central insights of this work particularly in contracting and contract management.

3. The background

This paper examines some central concepts of transactional law in an international context. I use the expression 'transactional law' in the sense of "focusing primarily on the parties or their professionals in the formation, negotiation, documentation, or consummation of a business deal" (Klee 2003: 5). I will first outline the change and development which has taken place in contracting.

Although commercial contracts are negotiated and made at all levels in companies, they are often seen very narrowly only as legal instruments left for lawyers, signed and in optimal cases locked in the safe and never seen again. Expertise in contracting can be found at several different levels in companies: the management, project-management, purchasing or selling departments or production-management and the legal department. Cooperation between all these levels may not always be close-knit enough and in consequence profits may turn into losses. Such unwanted turns can to some extent be avoided by increasing knowledge of the factors that have impact in the negotiation process. In my view, this involves accepting that meanings are not necessarily defined in advance. Moreover, the parties should not presume equal understanding on the basis of a rule-governed system but accept that meanings and understandings are negotiated in the framework of an open dialogic universe (cf. Weigand/Dascal 2001: vii).

The aim of law and contracts is to provide rules for cooperation, to define rights and responsibilities according to which it may be determined who is right or wrong. The purpose of law is to search for ideals and present this ideal world in the form of provisions, rules and regulations. Bhatia (2004: 51) illustrates the ideal world of law in a clear manner. On the one hand, there is the ideal world of law and, on the other, the real world with facts, precedents, and legal reasoning. As was pointed out above, the proactive approach is a real-world approach. In contracting, the parties operate in the real world and the understanding of the writers is captured in a contract and then 'frozen'. The proactive approach favours dialogue and planning interactively, pondering and creating new knowledge by the contracting parties in cooperation, which is essential to its method. Rules and regulations form a framework whose purpose is to provide security. Basically, the aim is to find a balance between the static framework of legislation on the one hand and the flowing creativity of business strategies in the real world on the other.

In cross-border transactions, it is easy to assume that familiar words mean what we are accustomed to. What is believed to be self-evident and to go without saying may cause major misunderstandings leading to claims and disputes, even litigation. Despite the fact that the need for uniform coding in international commerce has long been recognised, problems have not completely disappeared. The legal profession may claim that the cause of problems are the non-lawyers who do not know the concepts but on the other hand it is also the lawyers who do not know the terminology and concepts of other legal orders. Since the language of contracting in international trade is English in the majority of cases, common law lawyers assign legal terms common law meanings whereas civil law lawyers tend to give them a more neutral or international meaning and of course in some cases treat them as translations equivalent to the terms in their own national code. These ubiquitous problems have nevertheless not stopped international trade from increasing. The present globalisation seems irreversible. One should therefore suggest remedies for overcoming or at least diminishing these problems. I believe that raising language awareness and increasing linguistic knowledge is a solution.

In section 4, I will discuss basically three types of problems: (1) context: national law vs. uniform international sales law, exemplifying same concept / different terminology and problems in distinguishing a special context concept from the general language meaning of the associated term; (2) context: two international codes, exemplifying same concept / different terminology; (3) context: national, international and uniform codes, exemplifying same concept / different interpretations and implications. The concepts I will discuss are concepts used in the international sale of goods. They are legal concepts found in national legislation and international conventions: the Finnish Sale of Goods Act and the Convention on Contracts for the International Sale of Goods 1980 (hereinafter CISG), the Model Law on International Commercial Arbitration 1985 (UNCITRAL), Principles of International Commercial Contracts 1994 (UNIDROIT), Commission on International Commercial Practice, Model Contract Clauses Relating to Force Majeure and Hardship 1978 (ICC), Principles of European Contract Law 1999 (EU Principles). These instruments provide the material for the study.

4. Concepts, terms, and interpretation

It is generally thought that legal language is basically about special vocabulary and terminology. True enough, special vocabulary is important, even crucial, but linguists have also shown that special vocabulary forms only a very small percentage of any law-related text. In order to prove the point to law students preparing for the Willem C. Vis Moot Court Competition in Vienna,[2] a collection of the winning memoranda[3] totalling 159,762 words, was analysed using WordSmith

2 This Moot is a commercial arbitration moot court. The goal of the Willem C. Vis Arbitral Moot is to foster the study of international commercial law and arbitration for resolution of international business disputes through its application to a concrete problem of a client and to train law leaders of tomorrow in methods of alternative dispute resolution.

3 Claimants' memoranda

University	*No of words*	*No of types*
Bonn	116,567	1,752
Cologne	125,048	1,924
Cologne	6,349	870
Copenhagen	16,252	1,781

Tools to see how frequently the essential legal terms occurred in the texts. The fifteen most frequent content words can be seen in Table 1 below. The left-hand column indicates the order of the word in the frequency list and the right-hand side the number of occurrences. The first really important words from the point of view of contracting are number 87, *breach*, with 191 occurrences, and number 92, *damages*, with 169 occurrences. Only 2,877 words occur more than twice and, as we know, the most frequent ones are form words, with, as nearly always the definite article at the top of the list.

In fact, only one of these words can lead to misunderstanding, namely 'goods', which is not well defined for instance in the CISG although it is fairly clear that 'goods' must consist of tangible corporeal things (more in Honnold 1991: 101). No other word on the list is likely to cause problems to professionals or experts from any field, be it law, engineering, or economics, most commonly involved in commercial contracting. The terms I am going to look at more closely and whose understanding and correct interpretation is important in international commercial contracting are not that frequent, although the 'non-conformity of goods' and 'avoidance' or 'termination' are very often the causes of conflict and most challenging for arbitrators. Of the words I am going to discuss below, *non-conformity* occurs in the data 24 times, *avoidance* 63, and *termination* twice.[4]

Basel	35,898	2,246
Heidelberg	18,060	1,834
Maastricht	22,301	2,002
Queensland	20,012	2,002
Freiburg	4,416	815
Overall	*159,762*	*5,759*

See <http://www.cisg.law.pace.edu> for the texts,

4 This is only natural since the moot is mostly about the CISG and *avoidance* is a CISG term.

	Word	*f*
16	contract	889
18	arbitration	840
19	respondent	836
22	CISG	766
27	claimant	703
39	law	407
41	goods	384
42	article	366
43	clause	361
45	parties	342
51	agreement	315
56	price	298
57	order	297
59	payment	288
60	convention	273
	Total	7365

Table 1. The most frequent words in the winning claimants' memoranda.

Well-known to all linguists but perhaps less so to individuals who negotiate and make contracts in companies, be they lawyers or other professionals, is the following line of argument (e.g. Moore/Carling 1982 11-12):

- Language cannot be separated from its users and communicative situations.
- Words are not containers whose contents are transferred from one interlocutor to another (from speakers to listeners or from writers to readers) unchanged.
- Meaning is a consequence of words and phrases rather than their inherent quality.
- The interpreters of a message do not get information from an expression as such but use the expression in order to have access to information which they already possess.
- Interpretation and meaning are always to some extent subjective.

I will next discuss the contracting situation in light of these arguments. First of all then the communicative event is contracting. Figure 1 illustrates a rather simplified situation, although one complex enough. It does not, out of necessity, contain the rather complex contract chains typical of present day contracting.[5]

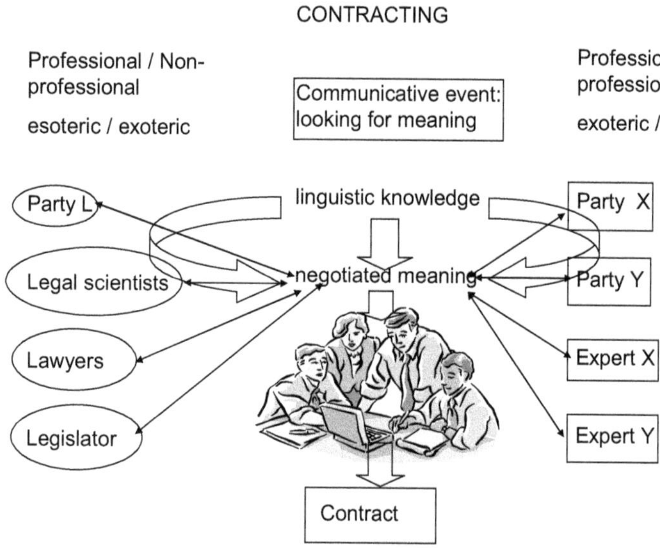

Figure 1. The audience and participants of the negotiation process.

On the left-hand side are several groups of legal professionals: Party L refers to the legal departments of the companies who are parties to the contract; legal scientists and researchers who are interested in contract law and, at least in the civil law countries, academics and researchers at the universities, who have traditionally had some influence on legislation; lawyers, i.e. the legal profession who are interested and/or engaged in contracting; the legislator, who governs the contracting process by legislation and amends legislation based on the feedback it gets from the real-world transactions. These participants are not necessarily physically present in the negotiations.

The contracting situation and also the written texts involved are always dialogic in a very explicit sense, not only in the Bakhtinian

5 I am referring here to companies outsourcing business processes, collaborating in complex partnership networks and new lifecycle and service models.

implicit sense. The texts are in dialogue with several other texts and their participants. According to the more traditional *ex post* approach, participants and audiences can be described in terms suggested by Fleck (1981) as exoteric (outsiders), a group constituted by the parties to the contract who are not legal professionals and who are represented by the esoteric group (insiders) who are legal professionals (cf. Salmi-Tolonen 2005: 67) In the real life approach the division has to be done differently. It is the parties involved in each contracting situation – whether legal professionals or other experts – who are the insiders. The outsiders again are all the others. If a conflict should arise and the dispute be brought before a court or an arbitral tribunal, the roles would change: then the arbitrators and the members of the court or tribunal would be insiders and the parties to the contract outsiders. Furthermore, as in all communication where law provides the framework, there is the legislator, abstract and impersonal, a party that never necessarily actually receives the message but is nevertheless one of the recipients.[6]

The function of the discourse varies depending on the audience rather than the discourse itself. To those directly involved, whether esoteric or exoteric, the contract provides a means for success, the guidelines, or a map, for further action and a tool for risk management; it is both informational and directive. However, to those who are not directly involved, the contract can be expository and informative and only secondarily, in case they should on some future occasion be acting in a different role, directive.

Kerbrat-Orecchioni (1980: 24) has pointed out that in her system, where presence/non-presence and speaking/non-speaking are the variables, most texts are addressed to a non-present and non-speaking audience. The audience of a contract[7] might fall into all four of these categories. We might call the parties of a contract the primary audience, consisting of the negotiators and the executors of the contract. On the other hand, there is the secondary audience whom the discourse involves, namely the legislator and legal professionals in

6 See also Trosborg's (1997) discussion of participants and contracts.

7 A contract should here be understood as a temporal entity, discourse, and a process rather than as a spatial entity, a collection of terms on paper duly signed and delivered.

case of conflict and eventually legal scientists. The legislator is addressed explicitly since the whole process is to a large extent governed by national or international legislation as well as case law. Then there is an audience that could be called onlookers: legal scientists, lawyers, the general public, and politicians who for various reasons are interested in the process and who form the audience Kerbrat-Orecchioni considers typical for written texts (see also Amossy 2000: 34 ff.).

In Figure 1, on the right-hand side, are the parties to the contract: Party X and Party Y. Expert X and Expert Y, who represent companies, have different types of expertise depending on the line of business the companies are engaged in. The aim is to reach a contract in a negotiation process; the parties are looking for a shared meaning which is to be written in the contract. The method for finding a shared meaning is negotiation. Although the parties are all qualified and business-savvy people they are in all probability experts and professionals in different areas and they need to construct the shared meaning between themselves. The arrows in Figure 1 show that expert knowledge and information are exchanged interactively between the parties as well as the audience. The contents of the contract are negotiated and the meanings should be shared. Only negotiated meanings are shared meanings and it is necessary for all participants to achieve this linguistic knowledge so that they know where meanings differ although expressions are the same. Most disputes arise from the parties not knowing what it is they have agreed upon.

Below I shall discuss concepts which represent the three categories outlined in section 3: 1) a concept that exists in both domestic law – Finnish law in this case – and international code but which has been found problematic at least partly because the expression and term chosen can be synonymous with a general language expression; 2) a concept that exists in two different international codes but is represented by a different term; and 3) a concept that is represented by the same term in different codes but is interpreted differently, with differing real-life consequences.

4.1. Non-conformity

Non-conformity is a term used in the CISG. Section II, Conformity of the Goods and Third Party Claims, Article 35 reads:

> 1) The seller must deliver goods which are of the quantity, quality and description required by the contract and which are contained or packaged in the manner required by the contract.
> 2) Except where the parties have agreed otherwise, the goods do not conform with the contracts unless they:
>   a) are fit for the purposes for which goods of the same description would ordinarily be used;
>   b) are fit for any particular purpose expressly or impliedly made known to the seller at the time of the conclusion of the contract, except where circumstances show that the buyer did not rely, or that it was unreasonable for him to rely, on the seller's skill and judgement;
>   c) possess the qualities of goods which the seller has held out to the buyer as a sample or model;
>   d) are contained or packaged in the manner usual for such goods, or where there is no such manner adequate to preserve and protect the goods.
> 3) The seller is not liable under subparagraphs a) to d) of the preceding paragraph for any lack of conformity of the goods if at the time of the conclusion of the contract the buyer knew or could not have been unaware of such lack of conformity.

Figure 2 depicts the contracting process as it proceeds from the intention of the parties to real-world consequences such as a building being constructed or a packing machine delivered at the seller's premises. Perfect contracts are both *complete* and *efficient*.[8] This means that nothing that is not taken into account can happen, and that there is no term in the contract which can be rewritten to one party's advantage except at another's expense. Perfect and complete contracts are possible in an ideal world. In the real world, the understanding of the parties to a contract may differ without their knowing it until problems arise.

---

8 On complete and explicit legislative communication see Bowers (1983: 3).

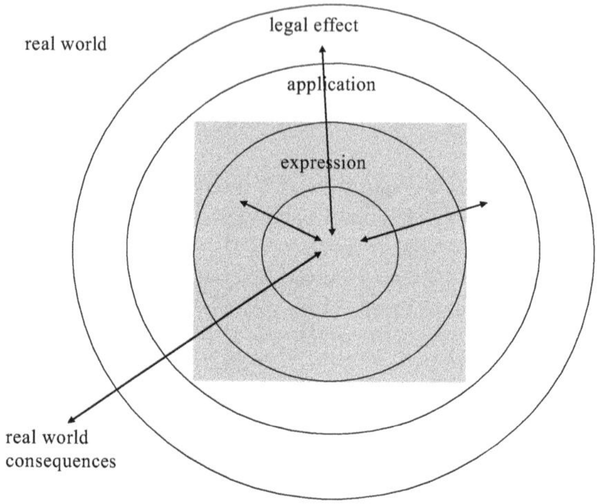

Figure 2. From intention to real world consequences in contracting.

Looking for the meaning of *conformity*, we can see at the outset that its meaning can be nothing but subjective. Its definition contains agreement and congruity or what is expected or required. In other words, the conformity of goods means that the goods meet the contractual specifications and non-conforming goods do not meet the specifications of the contract but deviate from what has been agreed on. At first sight, this seems straightforward enough, as the makers of the convention intended.

When interpreting international conventions such as the CISG, one should always take into consideration that they are the result of international unification efforts that, unlike domestic statutes, have not been drafted, at least not consciously, with any particular legal system or language in mind.[9] Laws often use concepts that are local inventions and lack equivalence in other legal systems (Honnold 1991: 207). Figure 3 illustrates the typical characteristics and compo-

9 One should note here that like any other writing, legal writing is culturally conditioned, and writers' notions about what convincing legal writing is like are inescapably rooted in each individual's experiences of learning his or her professional skills. In law, perhaps more than in any other professional field, conventions and traditions play a dominating role.

nents of the concept of non-conformity. As we can see, the occurrence depends on the provision in question or on the standard terms employed. YSE 98 refers to the standard terms generally used in Finland in construction contracts. The Finnish Sale of Goods Act provides in section 17, subsection 2:

> (2) Except where the parties have agreed otherwise, the goods must:
> (1) be fit for the purpose for which similar goods are ordinarily used;
> (2) be fit for any particular purpose for which the goods were intended if the seller knew or must have known of this purpose at the time of the conclusion of the contract and it was reasonable for the buyer to rely on the seller's skill and judgement;
> […]
> (3) If the goods do not conform with the provisions of paragraph (1) or (2), they are defective.

This is an unofficial translation in the sense that only the Finnish and Swedish language versions of statutes in Finland carry the force of law. The adjective 'defective' is confusing. However, even the Finnish noun *virhe*, used in the original authentic version, causes similar confusion. The provision does state the condition "if the goods do not conform" which is essential here but it is the adjective 'defective' that is confusing. The ordinary language meaning would lead anyone who does not know the legal language meaning to think that the goods are somehow imperfect, damaged or broken deviating from faultless goods. In legal terms, on the other hand, the imperfection refers to the goods in relation to the contract; i.e., the goods deviate from the contract.

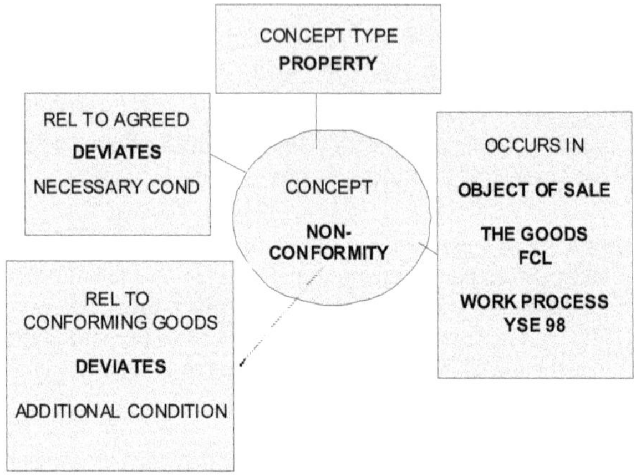

Figure 3. Characteristics of non-conformity as concept and concept type.

In Figure 3, we can see that where the non-conformity, or defect, occurs depends on the statute or the standard terms used in contracting. For instance, in the set of standard terms used in construction non-conformity can occur in the work process, whereas the Finnish Sale of Goods Act provides that conformity or non-conformity concerns the object of sale, the goods. In Figure 3, the features typical of the concept of non-conformity or defect are printed in bold. The concept relates to property and non-conformity may occur in the object of sale, the goods or, where the YSE98 terms are applied, the work process. The necessary and sufficient condition for non-conformity to exist is the deviation. An additional condition is that it deviates from flawless goods and if this is fulfilled the meaning is very close to the general language meaning of the word 'defective'. Next, I will discuss a concept that is recognised as a concept in contracting by international codification but under a different term.

4.2. Avoidance and/or termination

Avoidance is, one might say, a CISG term although the concept it represents is known in other uniform codes and EU Principles but represented in language by *termination*. The CISG and the UNIDROIT and EU Principles are internationally drafted instruments which combine elements from both civil law and common law systems. Where the parties come from countries that have ratified or acceded to the CISG, in most cases the CISG is the governing law. Article 72 of CISG declares that:

> In the case of a contract for delivery of goods by instalments, if the failure of one party to perform any of his obligations in respect of any instalment constitutes a fundamental breach of contract with respect to that instalment, the other party may declare the contract *avoided* with respect to that instalment [...]. (Italics added)

The UNIDROIT Principles do not use the word 'avoidance' but 'termination' when referring to such a situation. It might be argued that the different terminology of 'avoidance' or 'termination' may be of little significance since the real world consequence is the same. In either case the parties do not intend to fulfil their contractual obligations. However, the varying terminology may cause confusion among the contracting parties. It has been pointed out that in some cases the uniform codes and conventions complement each other, which means that it is necessary to know all related codes (Southerington 1999, 2000). A case in point is the relationship of the CISG and UNIDROIT principles. It has been argued that CISG Article 76:

> (1) If the contract is avoided and there is a current price for the goods, the party claiming damages may, if he has not made a purchase or resale under article 75, recover the difference between the price fixed by the contract and the current price at the time of avoidance as well as any further damages recoverable under article 74. If, however, the party claiming damages has avoided the contract after taking over the goods, the current price at the time of such taking over shall be applied instead of the current price at the time of avoidance.
> (2) For the purposes of the preceding paragraph, the current price is the price prevailing at the place where delivery of the goods should have been made or, if there is no current price at that place, the price at such other place as serves as a reasonable substitute, making due allowance for differences in the cost of transporting the goods.

as well as the counterpart UNIDROIT Principle Article 3.18:

> [Damages:] Irrespective of whether or not the contract has been avoided, the party who knew or ought to have known of the ground for avoidance is liable for damages so as to put the other party in the same position in which it would have been if it had not concluded the contract.

is merely an addition to CISG Article 74:

> Damages for breach of contract by one party consist of a sum equal to the loss, including loss of profit, suffered by the other party as a consequence of the breach. Such damages may not exceed the loss which the party in breach foresaw or ought to have foreseen at the time of the conclusion of the contract, in the light of the facts and matters of which he then knew or ought to have known, as a possible consequence of the breach of contract.

The purpose is to fully compensate the innocent party for a loss suffered due to a breach of contract. The provision attempts to clarify situations where despite avoidance of the contract a party seeks to demand damages if it has purchased goods from another source. The terminological confusion arises from the use of two different terms in international uniform coding which basically have the same content. This makes it necessary to have knowledge of all these complementing codes.

4.3. Impossibility of performance

Impossibility of performance as a concept provides a release from performance. This is a wide topic and will therefore only be touched upon briefly in this chapter. It is however important from the point of view of contracting, planning ahead and language. Basically there are three interpretations for impossibility of performance (Vihma 1956: 41-51). The first of these is a common sense, natural or logical interpretation referring to a situation where performance is not possible by any means at the time and in the manner agreed. A case in point is when in the sale of specific goods the goods are accidentally destroyed. The law may also allow for interpretations where performance is impossible in practice, called 'practical impossibility', in cases where the goods are not destroyed but for instance stolen. A third case of impossibility of performance, which Vihma calls 'juridical impossibility', occurs when performance would be illegal. Neither Finnish law nor the CISG refers to impossibility of performance as such but incorporate the idea in terms of more general principles (Hellner 1993: 61-64). It has also been noted that *force majeure* type of concepts have taken its place in the sale of goods. In English law impossibility is, however, an important concept and therefore important in the international sale of goods (Treitel 1994: 3).

Figure 4, adopted from Southerington (1999: 60) and modified here into flowchart format, provides a clear view of the interpretations and outcomes different codes provide. Here the instruments are the UNIDROIT and the EU Principles, which differ from the Finnish Sale of Goods Act, the CISG, and common law principles. They are based on a slightly different conception of contract in that exemptions are granted on a more lenient basis than these other instruments allow (Southerington 1999: 60). At the top of Figure 4, we find the very first requirement in relation to the contract, namely changed circumstances. The second node shows three types of impossibility, the next one their cause and then the effect. The final line indicates the outcome and the concept as understood in the UNIDROIT and the EU Principles. Both of these sets of rules were completed in the 1990s and presumably reflect the recent developments in contract law, hence the more flexible views. In brief, without knowledge of the origin and development of legal instruments and their relation to each other, one should not interpret a term in the context of contracting. One should at least have enough knowledge to see an alarm flashing whenever there is room for interpretation and then discuss the competing potential meanings with the other parties. One should plan ahead, where appropriate, and anticipate alternate ways of dealing with unexpected but nevertheless foreseeable situations.

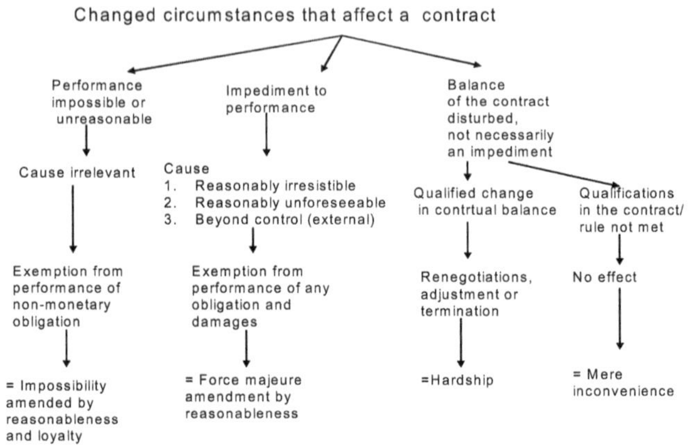

Figure 4. Exemptions under the UNIDROIT and the EU Principles.

5. Implications and conclusions

I have discussed above three types of conceptual and terminological problems occurring in international commercial contracting. In the framework of proactive law, the implications are that negotiation is to be understood not only as a specific dialogue type in commercial transactions but as a methodological concept for describing and explaining interaction and what we do when we use language (cf. Weigand/Dascal 2001: vii). This requires the acceptance that meanings are not defined in advance and that presupposing equal understanding, especially in international commercial contracting, can turn out to be costly. In law, there is a rising interest in what has come to be called language risk (Jayme 2001: 28-30). Who carries the risk if the parties to a contract assign different meanings to the same clause in a contract? The clause does not always have to be ambiguous, given that meanings are to some extent subjective. We might ask whether problems can be seen as caused by the discrepancies between law as an academic discipline and law in practice and between knowledge of the role of language in legal education and in international trade. Bhatia (2004: 212-213 and elsewhere) calls for collaboration between researchers and experts in different professions for creating a common discourse which would make sense to us and to members of the discourse culture we work with. In order to achieve this, we need expert knowledge, we need legal knowledge and, on top of these we need linguistic knowledge in order to achieve this. To sum up I will briefly explain how linguistic knowledge and legal knowledge are related.

5.1 Linguistic knowledge and legal knowledge

Contracting in either a monolingual or multilingual environment is, to my mind, an interplay of multiple sources of knowledge – in particular linguistic knowledge and legal knowledge. Next I attempt to characterise linguistic knowledge and legal knowledge as I see them. In a narrow sense, we can say that legal knowledge is knowledge of propositions of law. In a broad sense, as it is understood here, it is the knowledge of legal culture in its broadest sense, including legal systems, a legal order, legal institutions, history and practices and practitioners (see also Salmi-Tolonen 2004). Legal Knowledge is:

- language-dependent
- communal / interactional
- institutional.

Firstly, legal knowledge is language-dependent because law is constituted in language and could not exist without it (see Searle 1995: 60-66). Secondly, legal knowledge is communal or interactional in the sense that linguistic knowledge is:

- language-related / textual / descriptive / encyclopaedic
- communal / interactional
- functional.

When we put these two together, we can see that according to this line of thinking, legal linguistic knowledge is:

- communal
- interactional
- institutional and functional.

These two types of knowledge are manifested in legal discourse. Legal discourse is socially constructed and negotiated. Bhatia observes that "at the very heart of most frameworks for the analysis of discourse, especially as genre, is the belief that there is no universal form of discourse for structuring knowledge. There can only be 'a consensus of an agreement' (Bruffee 1986: 777 in Bhatia 2004: 185). The consensus of an agreement is the objective of negotiation understood as a methodological concept, as I have used it here.

5.2. Conclusions

The argument that language cannot be separated from its users and communicative situations is a commonly accepted argument. Meanings are subjective. If meanings are not negotiated, not even a linguist can say exactly what is meant. Linguistic methods can help point out patterns of language use that give clues to intended meanings (cf. Shuy 2002). The implications are that we need to:

- raise the level of language awareness
- increase linguistic knowledge
- be aware that meanings are subjective and that shared meanings can only be found by negotiating.

Unfortunately, direct knowledge transmission from one person to another is impossible. Despite research findings to the contrary, people still believe in direct transmission of knowledge. Studies on learning emphasise active construction of knowledge instead of direct transmission (e.g. Kirchner 2002). Ideas, messages, and knowledge are always interpreted by the receivers. Their knowledge-base in general, previous knowledge and experiences, as well as expectations, affect the way they interpret messages. Therefore, instead of monologue and self-evident meanings we need dialogue and negotiation.

References

Adam, Jean-Michel / Bonhomme, Marc 1997. *L'argumentation publicitaire; Rhetoric de l'eloge et de la persuasion*. FAC, Paris: Editions Nathan.

Amossy, Ruth 2000. *L'argumentation dans le discours: Discours politique, littérature d'idées, fiction*. FAC, Paris: Editions Nathan.

Bhatia, Vijay K. 2004. *Worlds of Written Discourse. A Genre-based View*. London: Continuum.

Bowers, Frederick 1989. *Linguistic Aspects of Legislative Expression*. Vancouver: University of British Columbia Press.

Brown, Louis M. 1950. *Manual of Preventive Law*. New York: Prentice Hall.

Brown, Louis M. 1955. *How to Negotiate a Successful Contract*. Prentice Hall: Englewood Cliffs.

Dauer, Ed 2003. Preventive Law, Past, Present and Future. A paper read at *Future Law, Lawyering and Language*, May 12-13, 2003, Helsinki organised by the University of Lapland and the Academy of Finland.

Engberg, Jan 2004. Statutory Texts as Instances of Language(s): Consequences and Limitations on Interpretation. *Symposium Creating and Interpreting Law in a Multilingual Environment. Brooklyn Journal of International Law*. Volume 29, 2004, Number 3, 1135-1166.

Fleck, Ludwik 1981. *The Genesis and Development of a Scientific Fact*. Chicago: University of Chicago Press.

Hellner, Jan 1993. *Speciell Avtalsrätt II. Kontraktsrätt*. 2. häftet. Allmänna ämnen. Second ed. Stockholm: Juristförlaget

Hoey, Michael 2005. *Lexical Priming. A new theory of words and language*. London: Routledge.

Honnold, John 1991. *Uniform Law for International Sales*. Philadelphia: Deventer.

Jayme, E. 1999. Langue et droit. Rapport général. Jayme, E. (ed.) *Langue et droit. Xve Congrès international de droit comparé*. Bruxelles: Bruylant, 11-34.

Kerbrat-Orecchioni, Catherine 1980. *L'Énonciation de la subjectivité dans le langage.* Paris: A. Colin.

Kirchner, Paul 2002. Cognitive load theory: implications of cognitive load theory on the design of learning. *Learning and Instruction* 12/2002, 1-10.

Klee, Kenneth N. 2003. Teaching Transactional Law. *Law Review*, University of California, Los Angeles School of Law, Research Paper Series, 1-16.

Moore, Terence / Carling Christine 1982. *Understanding language: towards a Post-Chomskyan linguistics.* London: Macmillan Palgrave.

Pilke, Nina 2000. *Dynamiska fackbegrepp. Att strukturera vetande om handlingar och händelser inom teknik, medicin och juridik.* Acta Wasaensia No. 81. Vaasa.

Poikela, Teija 2003. Conformity of Goods in the 1980 United Nations Convention of Contracts for the International Sale of Goods. *Nordic Journal of Commercial Law,* 2003/1, 1-68.

Salmi-Tolonen, Tarja 2004. Legal Linguistic Knowledge and Creating and Interpreting Law in Multilingual Environments. *Symposium Creating and Interpreting Law in a Multilingual Environment. Brooklyn Journal of International Law.* Volume 29, 2004, Number 3, 1167-1191.

Salmi-Tolonen, Tarja 2005a. Persuasion in judicial argumentation: The Opinions of the Advocates General at the European Court of Justice. In Halmari, Helena / Virtanen, Tuija (eds) *Persuasion Across Genres.* Pragmatics and Beyond. New Series 130. Amsterdam: John Benjamins, 59-101.

Salmi-Tolonen, Tarja 2005b. Kielen merkityksestä sopimustoiminnassa. [The Meaning of Language in Contracting] Haapio, H., Lintumaa, S., Järvinen, M., af Hällström, E. Taivalmaa, P., Lehto, J., Nystén-Haarala, S., Pohjonen, S., Salmi-Tolonen, T., Koivu, S., Leskinen, J. (eds) Yritysten *sopimus- ja vastuuketjut. Sopimusten hallinta käytännössä.* [Contract and Responsibility Chains in Business. Managing Contracts in Practice] Helsinki: Tietosanoma Oy, 285-296.

Salmi-Tolonen, Tarja 2005c. Terminologiaa ja sen taustaa: Kielen merkityksestä sopimustoiminnassa. [On Terminological Background. The Meaning of Language in Contracting]. In Haapio,

H., Sipilä, R., Kousa, M., Palmu, B., Koskelainen, K., Nystén-Haarala, P., Lehto, J., Pohjonen, S., Salmi-Tolonen, T., Koivu, S., Leskinen, J. (eds) *Sopimusten ja häiriötilanteiden hallinta rakennusprojekteissa.* [Managing Contracts and Disturbance Situations in Construction Projects] Helsinki: Tietosanoma Oy, 266-279.

Searle, John 1995. *The Construction of Social Reality.* Harmondsworth: Penguin Books.

Shuy, Roger W. 2002. To Testify or Not to Testify? In Cotterill, Janet (ed.) *Language and the Legal Process.* Basingstoke: Palgrave Macmillan, 3-18.

Southerington, Tom 2000. *Impossibility of Performance and Other Excuses in International Trade* (1999) (unpublished LL.M. thesis, University of Turku, Faculty of Law). *See also Exemptions from Contractual Obligations in International Commercial Law, in Kansainvälisestä kaupasta* [On International Trade] Antti Aine & Anne Kumpula (eds), 2000. 281-303.

Treitel, G. H. 1994. *Frustration and force majeure.* London: Sweet & Maxwell.

Trosborg, Anna 1997. "Contracts and social action" In Gunnarsson, Britt-Louise / Linell P. / Nordberg B. (eds), *The Construction of Professional Discourse.* London: Longman. 54-75.

Vihma, Väinö 1956. *Suorituksen mahdottomuus varallisuusoikeudellisessa sopimussuhteessa.* [Impossibility of performance in contracts in view of the law of property.] Vammala: Suomalaisen lakimiesliiton julkaisuja [Publications of the Finnish Lawyers' Association].

Weigand, Edda / Dascal, Marcelo (eds) 2001. *Negotiation and Power in Dialogic Interaction.* Amsterdam: John Benjamins Publishing Company.

MARTIN SOLLY

Uberrimae fidei: Language Choice and Cultural Undertones in the Insurance of International Trade

1. Introduction

It is hundred years since the drafting of the United Kingdom Marine Insurance Act 1906 (henceforth MIA 1906). This statute codified the law and language of marine insurance and is still the main legal and linguistic point of reference for marine insurance in the United Kingdom. It has also strongly influenced the law and language of marine insurance in other English-speaking common law jurisdiction countries. London became the marine insurance capital of the world in the nineteenth and twentieth centuries and is still an important centre for international marine insurance and dispute resolution. This is because the English law of marine insurance is relatively certain and well-developed, because the English court system is seen to be reliable and impartial and because the use of standard forms[1] is favoured in international trade (ALRC 2000: 13).

Because of the way the law of insurance has developed in the United Kingdom, it contains legal concepts and has underlying cultural characteristics which are embodied in the language of MIA 1906. This chapter will examine the language of some of these legal concepts and how it has influenced the language choice used in some of the marine insurance statutes and proposed statutes of other English-speaking countries, thus in countries which with the passage of time are becom-

1 These days buyers and sellers will almost certainly adopt a recognised and established form of contract, typically those contained in Incoterms 1990, where the incidents are well known and whose successful use and efficiency have been proven by the passage of time. These generally allocate the insurance of the goods being carried overseas to the buyer or the seller depending on the nature of the goods and the form of contract adopted (Day/Griffin 1993).

ing increasingly removed from the legal, cultural and linguistic boundaries of the United Kingdom.

2. Culture-bound legal concepts

Although this chapter deals with legal concepts, its main focus will be to examine the role of language in the construction of these concepts. Legal concepts are embodied in the language in which they are formulated and any change to the language can alter the concepts. The legal concepts dealt with here have been chosen as sharing certain characteristics: they are legal concepts specifically linked to the language of marine insurance; they are legal concepts presented in language which can be considered 'culture-bound'. Thus we deal with the 'avoidance of gaming or wagering contracts' section in the legal concept of insurable interest, with the principle of *uberrimae fidei* (utmost good faith) and the legal concept of 'non-disclosure', and with the 'implied warranty of seaworthiness'. Because of the cultural context of the time, it was essential for the legislators to identify these concepts in the existing usage and to include them in MIA 1906. It is suggested here that the language used in these clauses of MIA 1906 reflects the cultural context in which the United Kingdom traditions of marine insurance grew up and were formulated.

This chapter will look at the treatment of these legal concepts in the statutory legislation of a number of other English-speaking common law jurisdiction countries. The history of these countries over the last hundred years obviously reflects their political, cultural and legislative 'growing apart' from the United Kingdom. And there are of course strong geographical and temporal factors. From a language point of view, this 'growing apart' is well documented: linguists now talk of a range of Englishes, each with its distinctive history and characteristics (see, for example, McArthur 1998). Moreover, the very nature of the common law system with its judge-made decisions means that there will be different case law in the different national jurisdictions; there will therefore be divergence from English law which in particular cases will produce different outcomes. And we further note that as regards Australia, the areas of insurable interest, non-disclosure and breach of warranty – the legal concepts we focus on here – have all been reformed significantly in non-marine insurance, and their retention in the Australian Marine Insurance Act 1909 is the subject of some criticism (Hetherington 2000).

3. Materials

Much of the law of international marine insurance is based on MIA 1906; this is particularly true of the English-speaking countries and of the standard contract forms used in international trade. In this chapter we will look at some of the other Marine Insurance Acts (in draft or statutory form), in order to observe the language choice used to deal with the legal concepts discussed here. Some countries, such as Australia and New Zealand passed their Marine Insurance Acts closely based on the United Kingdom statute soon after MIA 1906, respectively in 1909 and 1908. Indeed the Australian Act is in all relevant respects the same as MIA 1906 (Hetherington 2000). However there have been minor amendments to the United Kingdom statute that have not always been followed elsewhere (ALRC 2000: 2).

Traditionally those national common law legal systems without their own Marine Insurance Acts generally referred to MIA 1906. This was the case in the United States until 1955 when the Supreme Court ruled in Wilburn Boat Company v Fireman's Fund (348 US 310) that it is for the states to regulate marine insurance: "Prior to William Boat, it had been the practice for US courts to look to British law for meaning and definition in the field of marine insurance" (Volk 1998). Since then, the laws governing marine insurance in the United States "have been in a muddle" (Volk 1998) and no federal body on the subject has been developed. Similarly both Canada and South Africa also relied on the legal traditions contained in MIA 1906; however there has been considerable pressure on the national legislatures to pass their own acts. Thus Canada passed its own Marine Insurance Act in 1993 and a draft proposal has been drawn up for a South African Marine Insurance Act.

Amendments have also been proposed to the Australian Marine Insurance Act.

The documents that we have chosen to deal with here and to compare with MIA 1906 all come from common law systems and are the Australian Marine Insurance Act of 1909 (as we have seen, almost identical to MIA 1906, but especially interesting because of the proposed amendments), the Canadian Marine Insurance Act of 1993 and the 1997 draft version of the South African Marine Insurance Act. These will be respectively referred to as MIA 1909, MIA 1993 and MIA 1997. Reference will also be made to the reforms which are being suggested for the Australian Act. The analysis here is of course primarily linguistic: for the accuracy and precision of its legal observations, the chapter relies on two law textbooks: *Law of Marine Insurance* (Hodges 1996) and *The Law of International Trade* (Day and Griffin 1993).

4. Analysis

The language choices found in the sections of the various marine insurance acts examined here conform to the many of the well-known characteristics of the specialised language of the law (Crystal/Davy 1969; Tiersma 1999; Gotti 2005). Thus the sections contain highly specific terms (whose meaning is then defined), sometimes including archaic vocabulary and Latin and Old French terms, repetition, binomial and multinomial expressions, certain modal verbs, qualifying conditional expressions, evaluative adjectives and adverbs, depersonalisation, a somewhat particular punctuation and layout and so on. They also contain that careful balance between precision/certainty and flexibility/vagueness that characterises so much of the language choice in successful legislative provisions (for a discussion of this in relation to MIA 1906 see Solly 2005). We give two comments here which illustrate the balance in relation to drafting statutes. The first as regards certainty:

> This is probably one of the most debatable points about English drafting. Although it is desirable that a provision should normally only have one clear meaning it is an ideal that is often difficult to achieve [...]. (Holland/Webb 2003: 187)

The second as regards flexible language:

> It allows a legislature to use a general term without having to articulate in advance exactly what is included in it, [...] permits the law to adapt to differing circumstances and communities within a jurisdiction. And it enables the law to deal with novel situations that are certain to arise in the future, as well as changing norms and standards. (Tiersma 1999: 80)

We will first look at the language relating to the three culture-bound legal concepts introduced in Section 2 here, comparing the choices favoured by the four different texts. We will then examine two further legal/linguistic interfaces linked to the flexibility issue to see if there are substantial differences in the way they are treated in the different texts, namely the concept of 'reasonableness' and the use of some conditional expressions which are considered to underpin the lasting success of MIA 1906.

4.1. Insurable interest and 'gaming or wagering'

The aim of the insurance policy is to place the assured in the position in which he or she would have had no damage to the subject matter of the policy occurred. Thus the assured must have some kind of legally recognised 'insurable interest' in the subject matter of the policy, so that he or she can be indemnified for its loss or damage. The essence of an insurable interest in marine insurance is that property in which the assured has some legal or equitable interest is at risk from marine perils. If the assured has no such interest in the subject matter, and no reasonable expectation of acquiring one, any insurance he or she effects on the subject matter will, under MIA 1906, be void as a gaming or wagering contract (Day and Griffin 1993: 119).

It is suggested here that this legal concept and its wording reflect the history of marine insurance in the United Kingdom. It would seem that there were strong links between the origin of marine insurance in

England and the habit of gambling on the outcome of battles, sieges and trading ventures in the late seventeenth and early eighteenth centuries.[2] This draws our attention to a possible confusion between gambling and insurance in the early days of the language of insurance. Some of the 'underwriters' at Lloyds made contracts which were merely wagers on public or private events. Without the rule of insurable interest, a person could insure a vessel with the hope that it would sink and collect the insurance. Thus, as we have pointed out above, under MIA 1906 (4.1) "Every contract of marine insurance by way of gaming or wagering is void". This precision aims to avoid a possible confusion in the language of insurance that today might be considered superfluous. This section in MIA 1906 reflects legal principles set out clearly in other United Kingdom statutes specifically related to gaming or wagering, both before and after the enactment of the statute. By the Gaming Act 1845 all contracts by way of gaming and wagering are void (Bone 2001: 181). More specifically relevant to marine insurance, by the Marine Insurance (Gambling Policies) Act 1909 it is an offence to effect a contract by way of gambling on loss of maritime perils (Bone 2001: 276). So it might be legitimate to question whether this legal principle really needs to be reiterated in the more recent versions of MIA looked at here, MIA 1993 and 1997 (see Table 1).

Every contract of marine insurance by way of gaming or wagering is void. (MIA 1906. 4.1)	Every contract by way of gaming or wagering is void. (MIA 1993. 18.1)
Every contract of marine insurance by way of gaming or wagering is void. (MIA 1909. 10.1)	Every contract by way of gaming or wagering is void. (MIA 1997. 4.1 draft)

Table 1. Avoidance of wagering or gaming contracts.

2 Jonathan Swift referred to the business of betting on the War of the Spanish Succession (1701-1714), reporting in 1711 in *The Conduct of the Allies* that the 'insurers' at the Royal Exchange kept a book of the great towns in the Low Countries complete with the odds on whether they might be chosen for attack and for how long they might withstand a siege. Swift was of course writing against the war and the government of the time in the pamphlet; nevertheless, it is evidence of what seems to have been a widespread practice at the time (Childs 2003: 52).

Nevertheless, as we can see in Table 1, the wording is practically the same in all four versions, although the two more recent MIAs specify 'every contract' and not 'every contract of marine insurance', thereby eliminating what might be considered redundant repetition. We also note that neither of these more recent versions sees the need to change the language of the somewhat archaic 'gaming or wagering' formula. Nor does either of them choose the more current word 'gambling' rather than 'gaming', a choice taken by Hodges in her comprehensive study of the Law of Marine Insurance, where the index refers to 'gambling and wagering' contracts (1996: 636), but the text to the 'gaming and wagering' sections of MIA 1906 (1996: 2). 'Wagering or gaming' is moreover an example of that much discussed word-doubling so favoured by English legal language, where the alliterative power of the phrase is considered to be at least as responsible for its continuing use as its legal value (Tiersma 1999: 14-15). The fact that the section is drafted in all four different versions with the all-inclusive determiner 'every' and the conjunction 'or' suggests these are considered felicitous choices which need no changing. 'Gaming or wagering'[3] has come to be used as a technical term which at first might have offered a choice, but which has become 'codified' by its use in the statute, and thus instantly recognisable to the discourse community to whom it is addressed. Statutes are formally addressed by the legislators to the public at large, but in reality are primarily for lawyers and judges (Bhatia 1994: 137).

4.2. 'Uberrimae fidei' and the duty of disclosure

The very foundation of a United Kingdom contract of marine insurance rests on the principle of *uberrimae fidei* and the duty of disclosure stems from the principle of utmost good faith (Hodges 1996: 83-84). The insurance policy is a contract of *uberrimae fidei* which means that the assured must act with 'the utmost good faith' towards the insurer and in particular, must disclose to the insurer all material facts relevant

---

3 Hodges uses both 'gaming and wagering' and 'gaming or wagering' on the same page (1996: 2), perhaps a lesser degree of precision is required of the writer of the textbook than of the drafter of a statute.

to the application for insurance. The onus of disclosure is therefore on the assured, whose failure to disclose or misrepresentation of a material circumstance could render the contract void. This is different from the obligation not to misrepresent material facts and is linked to the origins of English marine insurance. This legal concept of disclosure in insurance has led to considerable debate in the insurance and legal community in common law jurisdictions outside the United Kingdom (see, for example, ALRC 2000). The concept of disclosure is of course linked to that of non-disclosure and thus to that of silence, which has been the subject of much scrutiny across various disciplines.[4]

In the expression *uberrimae fidei*, the Latin *uberrimae*, the superlative of the adjective *uber/uberis* is usually translated by the English 'utmost', hence 'utmost good faith'. It is translated this way in MIA 1906 and 1909 and in the current edition of Osborn's Law Dictionary (Bone 2001: 389): although in a previous edition it was translated as 'of the fullest confidence' (Bird 1983: 332). The inclusion of the maximising adjective 'utmost' before the adjective 'good' suggests that a high degree of good faith is required to satisfy Section 17 (Hodges 1996: 83), thus much more than a minimum requirement of an absence of bad faith. This provides the courts with the possibility of identifying different degrees of good faith, here requiring the highest possible degree. The use of language to convey this legal principle seems to change in the more recent MIAs. Indeed if we look at Table 2 we notice that MIA 1993, the Canadian statute, makes no use of the Latin *uberrimae fidei*; MIA 1997, however, still uses Latin but lowers the degree of good faith requested from the 'utmost good faith' to 'good faith' – *bonae fidei*.

4 In a discussion of felicity conditions in performative utterances, Austin pointed out "that there are many non-verbal procedures by which we perform exactly the same acts as we perform by [...] verbal means". However, these require a convention to be invoked and "the circumstances in which we purport to invoke this procedure must be appropriate for its invocation. If this is not observed, then the act that we purport to perform would not come off – it will be, one might say, a misfire" (1979 [1961]: 237-238). Silence is also a tool for lawyers in their control and management of courtroom discourse (Conley/O'Barr 1998). From an intercultural stance, Beamer/Varner observe that high-context and low-context cultures differ in their interpretation of silence: "While Westerners typically view silence as gaps in conversation, the Japanese believe silence is part of conversation." (2001: 184)

INSURANCE IS *UBERRIMAE FIDEI* A contract of marine insurance is a contract based upon the utmost good faith, and, if the utmost good faith be not observed by either party, the contract may be avoided by the other party. (MIA 1906. 17)	UTMOST GOOD FAITH A contract is based on the utmost good faith and, if the utmost good faith is not observed by either party, the contract may be avoided by the other party. (MIA 1993. 20)
INSURANCE IS *UBERRIMAE FIDEI* A contract of marine insurance is a contract based upon the utmost good faith, and, if the utmost good faith be not observed by either party, the contract may be avoided by the other party. (MIA 1909. 23)	INSURANCE IS *BONAE FIDEI* A contract of insurance is a contract based upon good faith, and, if the requisite degree of good faith be not observed by either party, the contract may be avoided by the other party. (MIA 1997 draft 17.1)

Table 2. *Uberrimae fidei* – utmost good faith.

The words 'by either party' in MIA 1906 Section 17 emphasise the reciprocity of the duty of utmost good faith and make clear that it is required of both parties and is thus a mutual obligation We note the choice of the determiner 'either' rather than 'both' or 'all' or 'any': 'either' indicates a choice between two options, but here refers to the parties to the marine insurance policy and thus operates inclusively and is all-embracing. The legal effect of a breach of utmost good faith is contained in the words 'the contract may be avoided by the other party'. Here the operative word is the modal 'may' (Hodges 1996: 85). The modal grants the right to avoid the contract, but 'may' has also been chosen because it does not contain the obligation to take this course of action. In other words it refers to a possible option and not to a necessary obligation

The words 'void', 'avoid' and 'avoidance' have meanings in legal English which are quite different from those in general English. This is especially so as regards 'avoid' and 'avoidance', where the general English definitions convey the sense of 'refrain from', 'evade', rather than the legal English 'nullify' or 'quash' (OED). In the same dictionary 'void' in general English is given as 'empty, vacant' and in legal English as 'invalid, not binding' (OED). Osborn's law dictionary defines 'to avoid' as 'to make void' and 'void' as 'of no legal effect, a nullity' (Bone 2001). In the context of this statute the word has strong legal force. Thus breach of utmost good faith could return both parties to a pre-contract situation. Moreover, because this is the only remedy mentioned in s 17, if one of the parties chooses this option, this is the only remedy available (Hodges 1996: 85). When we come to the section on disclosure, the first subsection is exactly the same in the United Kingdom, Australian and draft South African statutes. Here we report it in its entirety

> Subject to the provisions of this section, the assured must disclose to the insurer, before the contract is concluded, every material circumstance which is known to the assured, and the assured is deemed to know every circumstance which, in the ordinary course of business, ought to be known by him. If the assured fails to make such disclosure, the insurer may avoid the contract. (MIA 1906. 18.1; MIA 1909. 24.1; MIA 1997. 18.1)

There are however certain differences in the Canadian statute, MIA 1993, especially as regards the order in which the various legal provisions are presented. Comparing the language of MIA 1993 with that of the other versions, we can see that the drafters of the Canadian statute have taken considerable pains to improve the section.[5] Section 21 starts in quite a similar way to the other statutes, with most of the changes into language which can be considered more accessible and up to date. Thus the first sentence is truncated (rendering it shorter and more user-friendly) and the rest of the legal provision, presented as a single section in the other MIAs, comes in later subsections of Section 21 as we see below:

> Subject to this section, an insured must disclose to the insurer, before the contract is concluded, every material circumstance that is known to the insured. (MIA 1993 21. 1)
> [...] an insured is deemed to know every circumstance that, in the ordinary course of business, ought to be known by the insured; (MIA 19993 21. 6.a).
> If an insured or an agent of an insured fails to make a disclosure as required by this section, the insurer may avoid the contract. (MIA 1993 21.7)

5 Many of the language choices in MIA 1993 reflect the intention of the Canadian legislators to preserve "the substance of the provisions of the British Act while modifying the form in which they are expressed to meet the current drafting standards" (Parliament of Canada *Commons Debates* 23 March 1993, 1025, reported in ALRC 2000: 3).

In the first subsection 'the provisions' has been cut, 'the assured' has become the wider less specific 'an insured', and 'which' is replaced by 'that'; the last sentence expands 'the assured' to include 'an insured or an agent of an insured', while 'a disclosure' is specifically 'as required by this section'.

4.3. Implied warranty of seaworthiness

The third legal concept dealt with here is the concept of 'seaworthiness', which is included in the section on warranties. It does not manifest such clearly culture-bound characteristics as the other two. However, we suggest that it reflects the legal usage and cultural context on which MIA 1906 was based. Despite its Anglo-Saxon ring the term 'seaworthiness' dates from the nineteenth century and is defined as "to be in a fit condition to undergo a voyage and to encounter strong weather" (OED). Moreover, the legal concept of the implied statutory warranty of seaworthiness (in the section on warranties) is one of those considered to be in need of reform by the Australian Law Reform Commission (ALRC 2000). An implied warranty is a term of a contract regarded by law as so obviously fundamental to the contract that it applies without having to make any express provision for it: "So indispensable is the term that it is tacitly understood that it is to be read into the policy though it does not appear on the face of it" (Hodges 1996: 123). The definitions of 'the warranty of seaworthiness' provided by the MIAs examined here can be seen in the Table 3.

WARRANTY OF SEAWORTHINESS In a voyage policy there is an implied warranty that at the commencement of the voyage the ship shall be seaworthy for the purpose of the particular adventure insured. (MIA 1906 39.1)	WARRANTY OF SEAWORTHINESS There is an implied warranty in every voyage policy that, at the commencement of the voyage, the ship will be seaworthy for the purpose of the particular marine adventure insured. (1993 37.1)
WARRANTY OF SEAWORTHINESS In a voyage policy there is an implied warranty that at the commencement of the voyage the ship shall be seaworthy for the purpose of the particular adventure insured. (MIA 1909 45.1)	WARRANTY OF FITNESS OF CRAFT In a voyage contract there is an implied warranty that at the commencement of the voyage the craft shall be reasonably fit to encounter the ordinary risks of the particular adventure insured. (MIA 1997 39.1)

Table 3. Warranty of seaworthiness of ship / fitness of craft.

Here the subsections of the 1906 and 1909 Acts are exactly the same; there are however some changes in the Canadian and South African provisions. In actual fact the South African Act makes no specific reference to 'seaworthiness', but we have included its Section 39.1 as it is the same number as that of MIA 1906 even though it is headed 'Warranty of fitness of craft' and refers to the same legal issue. We notice the use of the very specific time marker 'at the commencement of the voyage' in all four versions, thus the implied warranty of seaworthiness is applicable at a particular time and place, indeed it applies only when the ship sets sail from that particular place (Hodges 1996: 127). The Canadian provision specifies 'every voyage policy' and substitutes 'will' for 'shall'. This use of the modal 'will' rather than the stronger directive 'shall' is a clear choice by the drafters of the Canadian Act. Indeed, a comparison of the incidence of modals 'shall' and 'will' in the statutes, reveals that the former is the preferred choice in MIA 1906 and MIA 1997 (three occurrences of 'will' in both statutes, as against 39 and 32 respectively for 'shall'). In MIA 1993 there are 14 occurrences of 'will' and eight of 'shall'.[6]

The South African definition seems somewhat different from a language point of view, but in actual fact it includes language to be found in the next subsection of the other statutes defining 'seaworthy' presented below in Table 4. In the three subsections we notice the similarity of the language and the careful but limited changes made in the Canadian provision: 'when' becomes 'if' and the adventure is specifically a 'marine adventure'.

A ship is deemed to be seaworthy when she is reasonably fit in all respects to encounter the ordinary perils of the seas of the adventure insured. (MIA 1906 39.4)
A ship is deemed to be seaworthy when she is reasonably fit in all respects to encounter the ordinary perils of the seas of the adventure insured. (MIA 1909 45.4)
A ship is deemed to be seaworthy if it is reasonably fit in all respects to encounter the ordinary perils of the seas of the marine adventure insured. (MIA 1993 37.5)

Table 4. Definition of 'seaworthy'.

6 MIA 1909 has not been included in these frequency counts, given its similarity to MIA 1906.

The South African draft legislation does not contain this definition, but as we have seen above, neither does it make any reference to 'seaworthy' and thus no definition is required. Nevertheless the language is similar to that of its Section 39.1, as we see above (in Table 3). In the South African draft statute, as we have seen, the warranty is termed 'Warranty of fitness of craft'. From a language point of view, 'fitness of craft' might be considered more user-friendly to the non-lawyer than 'seaworthiness'. And we notice that the word 'ship' has been exchanged for the more inclusive 'craft' and that the criteria used to measure the fitness are different: 'seaworthy for the purpose of' has become 'reasonably fit to encounter the ordinary perils of'. This is similar to the definition of 'seaworthy' given in the other texts (Table 4), but is without the more inclusive 'in all respects'. For Hodges (1996: 125), the two words in the statutory definition which require elaboration are 'reasonably' and 'ordinary' and both words are maintained in all four of the texts discussed here. She emphasises that the standard of fitness is not one of perfection, but only of 'reasonableness':

> To be seaworthy, a ship is not expected to be able to weather every conceivable storm or withstand every imaginable peril of the sea. All that is required of her is that she be reasonably suitable for the particular voyage. (Hodges 1996: 125)

As regards the 'ordinary perils of the seas' this means that the ship need only be capable of withstanding the normal vicissitudes of the voyage. However, "even severe weather, hurricanes, cyclones and strong gales could be considered as 'ordinary' perils of the seas if they are conditions expected of a particular region" (Hodges 1996: 126). Thus 'seaworthiness' is a relative and flexible term. It varies according to the nature of the voyage contemplated: a ship may be seaworthy for one voyage and not for another. There is no fixed or absolute standard of seaworthiness: the wording of MIA 1906 (39.1) itself makes this clear: it states that the ship shall be seaworthy for the "purpose of the particular adventure insured" (Hodges 1996: 127).

4.4. Reasonableness

The flexible concept of reasonableness is one of the cornerstones of the common law system and the law of marine insurance is no exception. We examine it here because standards of reasonableness may change over time (Tiersma 1999: 79) and outside cultural and territorial bounds. The texts discussed in this paper constantly refer to the concepts of 'reasonable' and 'reasonably' (MIA 1906, 23 and 8 times; MIA 1993, 20 and 8; MIA 1997, 16 and 13). Thus there is little change as to the frequency of its use, suggesting the continuing importance of the concept despite the passage of a considerable period of time between the Acts. We note however that there is no specific section in MIA 1997 providing a precise definition as regards 'reasonable time, reasonable premium, or reasonable diligence' and, as we can see in Table 5, MIA 1993 limits it to 'the purposes of this Act'.

Where by this Act any reference is made to reasonable time, reasonable premium, or reasonable diligence, the question what is reasonable is a question of fact. (MIA 1906 88)
Where by this Act any reference is made to reasonable time, reasonable premium, or reasonable diligence, the question what is reasonable is a question of fact. (MIA 1909 94)
Any question as to what constitutes a reasonable time, a reasonable premium or reasonable diligence for the purposes of this Act is a question of fact. (MIA 1993 91)

Table 5. Reasonable time, etc., a question of fact.

4.5. Flexible qualifying conditions

It is generally accepted wisdom that the language of the law dislikes language change if it is not absolutely necessary. Indeed one definition of successful legislation is legislation which is drafted in such a way that it stands the test of time. From this point of view MIA 1906 is regarded as a highly successful statute, as we see in this comment by Luxford (1995, reported in ALRC 2000: 9): "The significant achievement of the MIA is that its provisions have managed by and large to be applicable to the evolution in the marine insurance market over the last 90 years." As regards language choice, Hetherington (2000) notes that there are "obsolete terms and concepts in the Marine Insurance Act". He was of course referring to the Australian Act MIA 1909, however the Australian Law Reform Commission report highlights one of the linguistic devices used in the Act as one of the main reasons for its success: the flexibility contained in qualifying conditional expressions such as 'unless the policy otherwise provides', 'subject to any express provision in the policy', 'unless the contrary be expressed' and 'unless otherwise agreed', which enable the parties to "add to, fill out or explain the terms of the policy" (ALRC 2000: 8). It is thus, for example, common for some warranties otherwise implied by the MIA to be waived or modified in contracts of marine insurance (ALRC 2000: 9).

Looking at the frequency of the use of these qualifying conditional expressions in the various texts, we observe that 'unless the policy otherwise provides', which occurs 14 times in MIA 1906, only occurs twice in MIA 1993 and once in MIA 1997. This perhaps suggests that the legislators have found the Act 'overflexible' in this regard. We find a similar decline in the use of the expression 'subject to any express provision in the policy' (10 occurrences in MIA 1906, only 3 in MIA 1993 and none in MIA 1997). We do not find the same frequency of use variation in the other two expressions: 'unless the contrary be expressed' (used once in MIA 1906, not used in MIA 1993 and only used once in MIA 1997) and 'unless otherwise agreed' (3 occurrences in all three texts).

5. Conclusion

MIA 1906 still dominates the law of marine insurance in the English-speaking world and in international trade for various reasons: legal, practical and commercial, and, as we have seen, it is widely recognised as a highly successful statute. Here we have concentrated on the role of language, and suggest that the continuing success of MIA 1906 is a testament to its creators' drafting skills, even in those controversial areas where culture-bound legal concepts might have been expected to become obsolete. Indeed MIA 1906 has in many ways codified the language of marine insurance in other English-speaking countries, so that even where change might be desirable and has indeed been seriously proposed (MIA 1997, ALRC 2000), there is also fear that implementing change might lead to commercial disadvantage, precisely because of the language change.[7] MIA 1993 is an example of a successfully modified statute, especially as regards the culture-bound legal concepts discussed here and the form in which they are expressed, but the Australian and South African drafters of proposed reforms seem to focus their attention more on the language of MIA 1906 than that of MIA 1993; this provides further evidence of the language skills of its principal drafter, Sir Mackenzie Chalmers, even after the first centenary of the statute's enactment.

References

Austin, John L. 1979 [1961]. Performative utterances. In *Philosophical Papers*. Oxford: Oxford University Press, 233-252.

Australian Law Reform Commission (ALRC) 2000. *Discussion Paper 63: Review of the Marine Insurance Act 1909*. <http://www.austlii.edu.au/au/other/alrc/publications/dp/63/ch3.html>.

Bhatia, Vijay 1994. Cognitive Structuring in Legislative Provisions. In John Gibbons (ed.) *Language and the law*. London: Longman, 136-155.

Beamer, Linda / Varner, Iris 2001. *Intercultural Communication in the Global Workplace*. Boston: McGraw-Hill.

Bird, Roger (ed.) [7]1983. *Osborn's Concise Law Dictionary*. London: Sweet and Maxwell.

Bone, Sheila (ed.) [9]2001. *Osborn's Concise Law Dictionary*. London: Sweet and Maxwell.

Childs, John 2003. Fortune of War. *History Today* 53/10, 51-55.

---

7 Much of the resistance to change in Australia is through fear that any changes to the Act "might result in a competitive disadvantage for the Australian insurance industries in view of the close association between the Australian Act and the United Kingdom legislation, the dominance of the London marine insurance market and the *industry practice of using standard wordings*" (Hetherington 2000, our emphasis).

Conley, John / O'Barr, William 1998. *Just Words: Law, Language, and Power.* Chicago: University of Chicago Press.

Crystal, David / Davy, Derek 1969. *Investigating English Style.* London: Longman.

Day, D. Michael / Griffin, Bernadette [2]1993. *The Law of International Trade.* London: Butterworths.

Gotti, Maurizio 2005. *Investigating Specialized Discourse.* Bern: Peter Lang.

Hetherington, Stuart 2000. Reform Meets Resistance in Australia. *The Marine Advocate* 11. <http://www.marineadvocate.com/i11_insu.htm>.

Hodges, Susan 1996. *Law of Marine Insurance.* London: Cavendish.

Holland, James / Webb, Julian 2003. *Learning Legal Rules.* Oxford: Oxford University Press.

Luxford Derek 1995. The Marine Insurance Act: Chronologically Challenged Legislation? Paper presented at the Maritime Law Association of Australia and New Zealand Annual Conference, Wellington NZ, 5-8 November.

Marine Insurance Act 1906. UK (6 Edw 7 c 41). <www.uctshiplaw.com/mia1906.htm>.

Marine Insurance Act 1909. Australia. <http://www.austlii.edu.au/au/legis/cth/consol_act/mia1909170/s11.html>.

Marine Insurance Act 1993. Canada (1993, c. 22). <http://laws.justice.gc.ca/en/M-0.6/text.html>.

Marine Insurance Act 1997. Draft Proposal for South Africa – Redraft March 1997. <www.uctshiplaw.com.marins.htm>.

Mc Arthur, Tom 1998. *The English Languages.* Cambridge: Cambridge University Press.

Solly, Martin 2005. Vagueness in the Discourse of Insurance: the case of the Marine Insurance Act 1906. In Bhatia, Vijay / Engberg, Jan / Gotti, Maurizio / Heller, Dorothee (eds) *Vagueness in Normative Texts.* Bern: Peter Lang, 313-334.

Tiersma, Peter 1999. *Legal Language.* Chicago: The University of Chicago Press.

Volk, Kenneth 1998. A Muddle in Marine Insurance. *The Marine Advocate* 4. <http://www.marineadvocate.com/i4_insu.htm>.

Part 2 :
European Legal and Institutional Language

GIGLIOLA SACERDOTI MARIANI

Linguistic 'Checks and Balances' in the Draft EU Constitution

1. The Union establishes the Constitution, the Constitution establishes the Union

In July 2003, Valery Giscard d'Estaing, Chairman of the European Convention handed the 'Draft Treaty Establishing a Constitution for Europe' to the Italian Presidency of the European Council, in the hope that it would be signed in May 2004, ahead of the European elections that were scheduled in June. In the concluding part of his official declaration, Giscard d'Estaing optimistically stated:

> Le projet de la Convention est un succès parce qu'il fixe les équilibres nécessaires entre les peuples, entre les Etats, nouveaux et anciens, entre les institutions, entre rêve et réalité. Ce projet est une réussite parce que c'est un projet fini, complet jusque dans les détails, sans options. Il répond à l'intérêt général. C'est dans cet esprit que le Président de la Convention, conjointement avec les deux Vice-Présidents, a appelé la Présidence italienne – et personnellement le Président du Conseil européen Silvio Berlusconi – à garder ce texte intact. Le remettre en cause, même partiellement, le menerait à l'échec. Le Président de la Convention a confiance en la Présidence italienne; elle sera à la hauteur de cette responsabilité, et l'Union européenne pourra, le 9 mai 2004, signer sa Constitution de Rome.

We may wonder why the Constitution (or should we say the 'Treaty'?)[1] was not signed in May 2004 and I believe that we may find

---

1 This is not a verbal quibble or a semantic argument; it is a issue for which politicians and jurists have not given a precise answer. On June 17, 2004 – while I was presenting this paper in the course of the international conference entitled 'The Formulation of Legal Concepts across Systems and Cultures', that was held in Rome – the EU leaders were meeting in Brussels to reach the

a partial answer to this question if we analyze the rendering of some concepts in different languages.

I have tackled and compared three versions (English, French and Italian) of this legislative text, that brings something new into existence, that is an interesting example of performative discourse, and I must say that I was overwhelmed and intrigued by it, because its performativity, although set in a formal and ritualized framework, is quite complex. It is a very special instance of constitutional discourse in the sense that it draws on a far wider intertext of different legal documents, in terms of juridical notions and technical lexis. And I do not think it would be stretching a point too far, to maintain that the language of this charter, representing the final stage of a debate that lasted for many years and developed through a number of different revisions and amendments, reveals traces of consensus-building and of compromises. Moreover, the collective speaker encoding the text seems to suffer from 'split personality'; it is not easy to understand who is the speaker and who is the addressee, who is the donor and who is the donee or recipient! For sure there are too many organs around: the European Parliament, the Council of the European Union, the European Commission, the European Court of Justice, the Court of Auditors. Suffice it to say, here, that one gets the impression of facing a split personality or, if you wish, a text that speaks to itself, just by skimming the long preamble or by reading the first clause of the first Article:

---

final agreement on the Draft. That day, on the front page of the *International Herald Tribune*, under the title 'Europe of 25 sharpens its charter-writing pencils', I read the following lines: "As late as Monday ministers were still unsure what the document should be called. Officials present at a meeting of foreign ministers in Luxembourg said there was a debate over whether leaders were preparing a 'Constitution' or a 'Treaty'. Ireland's foreign minister, Brian Cowen, settled the point with typical EU compromise by saying it was a 'Constitutional Treaty'."
Similar uncertainty surrounds the question of whether the European document establishes a federation or a confederation. Scholars maintain that if we focus on the elements of democratic control that the document proposes, it seems more confederal and less federal. If we focus on the power that it gives to the central government, it looks more federal.

> Reflecting the will of the citizens and States of Europe to build a common future, this Constitution establishes the European Union, on which the Member States confer competences to attain objectives they have in common. The Union shall coordinate the policies by which the Member States aim to achieve these objectives, and shall exercise in the Community way the competences they confer on it.
>
> Inspirée par la volonté des citoyens et des États d'Europe de bâtir leur avenir commun, cette Constitution établit l'Union européenne, à laquelle les États membres confèrent des compétences pour atteindre leurs objectifs communs. L'Union coordonne les politiques des États membres visant à atteindre ces objectifs et exerce sur le mode communautaire les compétences qu'ils lui transfèrent.
>
> Ispirata dalla volontà dei cittadini e degli Stati d'Europa di costruire un futuro comune, la presente Costituzione istituisce l'Unione europea, alla quale gli Stati membri conferiscono competenze per conseguire obiettivi comuni. L'Unione coordina le politiche degli Stati membri dirette al conseguimento di tali obiettivi ed esercita sul modello comunitario le competenze che essi le trasferiscono.

As we can realize, the Constitution is the main participant of this paragraph: it seems to be more controlled and thoughtful in English, but more passionate in French and in Italian, since it is so 'inspired' as to create the Union; and, a few seconds later, the Union – the newborn baby, a female in French and Italian – is invested with responsibility, and seems ready for her performance, as indicated by the institutional processes that follow in the same clause.

2. A new vocabulary for Eurospeak

Compared to many existing constitutions – think of the first written Constitution in the world, the US one, which is all contained within four handwritten pages, seven articles and about 4,400 words – the EU charter is very long… perhaps too long: a verbal avalanche of over 60,000 English words put together by a Convention of 108 members in a little less than a year and a half.

Out of the 24 versions – being equally authentic – that are to be found in the official website of the European Convention, I downloaded the complete English, French and Italian texts. In the same official website I also examined the glossary for each language, which is preceded by an introduction worth quoting; it unveils the attitude of the English drafter who speaks of a 'European venture', thus implying a risky, dangerous undertaking – a concern that is not revealed by the French and Italian versions:

> The European venture has been going on for 50 years. Special terms have come to denote the concepts, rules, processes and institutions that emerge from it. […] These words from the "European vocabulary" frequently appear in the Convention's working papers, so it is useful to know what they mean. Also, some of the definitions listed here provide an understanding of how the Union now functions and what are its core principles.

> L'Europe se construit depuis 50 ans. Les règles, les processus et les institutions issus de cette construction ont donné naissance à un vocabulaire particulier. […] Ces mots du "vocabulaire européen" reviennent fréquemment dans les documents de travail de la Convention, connaître leurs sens est donc utile. De plus, les quelques définitions proposées ici permettent de comprendre le fonctionnement actuel de l'Union et ses grands principes.

> L'Europa si sta costruendo da 50 anni. Per designare i concetti, le regole, i processi e le istituzioni nati da questa costruzione, è nato un vocabolario specifico. […] Questi termini del "vocabolario europeo" tornano frequentemente nei documenti di lavoro della Convenzione, pertanto è utile conoscerne il significato. Inoltre, le definizioni qui proposte consentono di comprendere il funzionamento attuale dell'Unione e i suoi principi

In the list of keywords (amounting to many pages for each language) we find terms, acronyms, expressions – now frequently heard in debates, conferences and round tables promoted by academics and think-tanks – accompanied by useful definitions and explanations. From them we learn the meanings of 'the three pillars of the European Union',[2] of 'CFSP', of 'variable geometry Europe', of 'Europe *à la carte*', of 'opting in' and 'opting out', of 'hard core', of 'multi-speed Europe', of '*acquis*'.

---

2 The explanation of this phrase is introduced by a metalinguistic note: "In Community parlance people often refer to the three pillars of the EU Treaty to designate the three categories into which are divided the various areas where the Union is active to varying degrees and in different ways".

The French term '*acquis*' is used in most of the versions of Article 43 (fourth clause)[3] – from Irish Gaelic to Rumanian to Dutch – because no satisfactory translation seems to have been agreed upon, considering what the lexeme implies, comprises or represents! We can call it a neologism, a loan word, a term of European legalese, but for sure it is a symbol of intercultural, interlinguistic mediation, that needs extensive definitions and explanations, as the ones we find in the web:

> The Community *acquis* or Community patrimony is the body of common rights and obligations which bind all the Member States together within the European Union. It is constantly evolving and comprises:
> the content, principles and political objectives of the treaties;
> Community legislation and the case law of the Court of Justice;
> the declarations and resolutions adopted by the Union;
> measures relating to the common foreign and security policy;
> measures relating to justice and home affairs;
> international agreements concluded by the Community and those concluded by the Member States between themselves in the field of the Union's activities.
> When further countries join the European Union, full compliance with the Community *acquis* is one of the requisites for accession.
>
> L'acquis communautaire correspond au socle commun de droits et d'obligations qui lie l'ensemble des Etats membres au sein de l'Union européenne. Il est en évolution constante et comprend:
> la teneur, les principes et les objectifs politiques des traités;
> la législation communautaire et la jurisprudence de la Cour de justice;
> les déclarations et les résolutions adoptées dans le cadre de l'Union;
> les actes relevant de la politique étrangère et de sécurité commune;
> les actes convenus dans le cadre de la justice et des affaires intérieures;
> les accords internationaux conclus par la Communauté et ceux conclus par les Etats membres entre eux dans les domaines d'action de l'Union.

---

3 In the three versions, that clause recites as follows:
"Acts adopted in the framework of enhanced cooperation shall bind only participating States. They shall not be regarded as an *acquis* which has to be accepted by candidates for accession to the Union.

"Les actes adoptés dans le cadre d'une coopération renforcée ne lient que les États participants. Ils ne sont pas considérés comme un acquis devant être accepté par les candidats à l'adhésion à l'Union.

Gli atti adottati nel quadro di una cooperazione rafforzata vincolano solo gli Stati partecipanti. Non sono considerati un *acquis* che deve essere accettato dai candidati all'adesione all'Unione".

> Lorsque de nouveaux Etats adhèrent à l'Union européenne, une des conditions fixées à leur adhésion est qu'ils se conforment intégralement à l'acquis communautaire.

> L'*acquis* comunitario corrisponde alla piattaforma comune di diritti ed obblighi che vincolano l'insieme degli Stati membri nel contesto dell'Unione europea. Esso è in costante evoluzione ed è costituito:
> dai principi, dagli obiettivi politici e dal dispositivo dei trattati;
> dalla legislazione comunitaria e dalla giurisprudenza della Corte di giustizia;
> dalle dichiarazioni e dalle risoluzioni adottate nell'ambito dell'Unione;
> dagli atti che rientrano nella politica estera e di sicurezza comune;
> dagli atti che rientrano nel contesto della giustizia e degli affari interni;
> dagli accordi internazionali conclusi dalla Comunità e da quelli conclusi dagli Stati membri tra essi nei settori di competenza dell'Unione.
> Allorché nuovi paesi aderiscono all'Unione europea, una delle condizioni per la loro adesione è che si conformino integralmente all'*acquis* comunitario.

3. Translating the Charter

Going back to the versions of the Charter, which we can read on the web, I realized that they are all formatted in the same way; I mean to say that for each language we can find a file of 265 orderly and neat pages, printed according to the same style sheet. As a sample, I have chosen a page that, because of its contents, allows us to pay homage to one of our editors, Paola Evangelisti Allori, and her University. Page 147 of any version, under the heading 'Section 4 – Education, Vocational Training, Youth and Sport', presents Article 182 that reads as follows:

> 1. The Union shall contribute to the development of quality education by encouraging cooperation between Member States and, if necessary, by supporting and complementing their action. It shall fully respect the responsibility of the Member States for the content of teaching and the organisation of education systems and their cultural and linguistic diversity.
> The Union shall contribute to the promotion of European sporting issues, given the social and educational function of sport.

2. The Union action shall be aimed at:
(a) developing the European dimension in education, particularly through the teaching and dissemination of the languages of the Member States;
(b) encouraging mobility of students and teachers, inter alia by encouraging the academic recognition of diplomas and periods of study; [...]
(g) developing the European dimension in sport, by promoting fairness in competitions and cooperation between sporting bodies and by protecting the physical and moral integrity of sportsmen and sportswomen, especially young sportsmen and sportswomen.

1. L'Union contribue au développement d'une éducation de qualité en encourageant la coopération entre États membres et, si nécessaire, en appuyant et en complétant leur action. Elle respecte pleinement la responsabilité des États membres pour le contenu de l'enseignement et l'organisation du système éducatif ainsi que leur diversité culturelle et linguistique.
L'Union contribue à la promotion des enjeux européens du sport, eu égard à sa fonction sociale et éducative.
2. L'action de l'Union vise:
a) à développer la dimension européenne dans l'éducation, notamment par l'apprentissage et la diffusion des langues des États membres;
b) à favoriser la mobilité des étudiants et des enseignants, y compris en encourageant la reconnaissance académique des diplômes et des périodes d'études; [...]
g) à développer la dimension européenne du sport, en promouvant l'équité dans les compétitions et la coopération entre les organismes sportifs ainsi qu'en protégeant l'intégrité physique et morale des sportifs, notamment des jeunes sportifs.

1. L'Unione contribuisce allo sviluppo di un'istruzione di qualità incentivando la cooperazione tra Stati membri e, se necessario, sostenendone ed integrandone l'azione. Rispetta pienamente la responsabilità degli Stati membri per quanto riguarda il contenuto dell'insegnamento e l'organizzazione del sistema di istruzione e le diversità culturali e linguistiche.
L'Unione contribuisce alla promozione delle sfide europee dello sport, data la sua funzione sociale e istruttiva.
2. L'azione dell'Unione è intesa:
a) a sviluppare la dimensione europea dell'istruzione, segnatamente con l'apprendimento e la diffusione delle lingue degli Stati membri;
b) a favorire la mobilità degli studenti e degli insegnanti, promuovendo tra l'altro il riconoscimento accademico dei diplomi e dei periodi di studio; [...]
g) a sviluppare la dimensione europea dello sport promuovendo l'imparzialità nelle competizioni e la cooperazione tra gli organismi sportivi e proteggendo l'integrità fisica e morale degli sportivi, in particolare dei giovani sportivi.

This Article – even if it concerns all of us, dealing as it does with teaching, languages and sports – presents a range of issues, tasks, objectives, activities jumbled or muddled together that do not have anything to do with the legal system or with legal concepts. And while we wonder why the Constitution should deal with those issues (since we already have our Erasmus/Socrates programmes, and all sorts of international agreements), we find an immediate answer in the fact that the EU constitutional framers were willing to establish not only a body of laws, but also a social code of common practices and guidelines.

But there is more to say on this Article: its first clause offers an example of how the translation of very common words can be poor, inaccurate, imprecise, or even deceptive: the English 'sporting issues' are not the same as the French 'enjeux du sport', and the Italian 'sfide dello sport' are not the same as 'sporting issues'.[4]

---

4 Most astonishing is also the English translation of Article 23 ("Formations of the Council of Ministers"), clause 2, that reads as follows:
"1. The Legislative and General Affairs Council shall ensure consistency in the work of the Council of Ministers. [...]
2. The Foreign Affairs Council shall, on the basis of strategic guidelines laid down by the European Council, flesh out the Union's external policies, and ensure that its actions are consistent. It shall be chaired by the Union Minister for Foreign Affairs.

1. Le Conseil législatif et des affaires générales assure la cohérence des travaux du Conseil des ministres. [...]
2. Le Conseil des affaires étrangères élabore les politiques extérieures de l'Union selon les lignes stratégiques définies par le Conseil européen, et assure la cohérence de son action. Il est présidé par le ministre des Affaires étrangères de l'Union

1. Il Consiglio legislativo e degli affari generali assicura la coerenza dei lavori del Consiglio dei ministri. [...]
2. Il Consiglio "Affari esteri" elabora le politiche esterne dell'Unione secondo le linee strategiche definite dal Consiglio europeo e assicura la coerenza della sua azione. È presieduto dal ministro degli affari esteri dell'Unione".

While the French and Italian drafters use such a common and 'neutral' verb as "élabore"/"elabora", the English one chooses "flesh out" – a very peculiar term, in this legal discourse, considering its etymological meaning: "to stimulate the hunting instinct of hounds or falcons by giving them small quantities of raw flesh".

On the other hand, we appreciate the English version of the second clause (under letter g.), that is 'politically correct', in the sense that it includes sportswomen together with sportsmen!

Another 'translation' of the Charter that is 'politically' and 'scientifically' correct is the SMS version I found in the web,[5] that scholars of languages and linguistics should not ignore!

Dedicated to President Giscard d'Estaing, that version presents a very pertinent epigraph by Umberto Eco. It is destined to "younger generations", in order to make them familiar with the European Institutions, but I believe all of us can understand the words of the front page and of Article 11 (clause 2), with the help of the official French version:

Pro G 2
TRE-T 1STITUAN 1 KONSTITU6ON
POOR L'€P

Projet de
TRAITE INSTITUANT
UNE CONSTITUTION POUR L'EUROPE

Traduction établie par
WILLIAM ABITBOL
à l'intention des jeunes générations

A valeri Js1/4Dst1
A Valéry Giscard d'Estaing

La langue de l'Europe c'est la traduction.
Umberto Eco

Art 11: Katégori 2 konPtans
2. lorsk la konstitu6on @ribu a lunion 1 konPtans partaG avek lé zéta manbr dan 1 domN Dterminé, lunion & lé zéta manbr on le poovwar 2 léJferé & dadopT D zakt juri10kmnt obligatwar dan ce domN. lé zéta manbr exRs leur konPtans dan la mezur oo lunion napa exRC la6N oo a D6D 2 CC 2 l'exRC.
Art 11: Catégories de compétences
2. Lorsque la Constitution attribue à l'Union une compétence partagée avec les États membres dans un domaine déterminé, l'Union et les États membres ont le pouvoir de légiférer et d'adopter des actes juridiquement obligatoires

5 <http://www.france-referendum.org>.

dans ce domaine. Les États membres exercent leur compétence dans la mesure où l'Union n'a pas exercé la sienne ou a décidé de cesser de l'exercer

Needless to say, this 'translation' – because of its novelty – is accompanied by an elementary vocabulary (of which I quote only a few entries), where 'jeunesse' is given the same relevance as 'institutions européennes':

Vocabulaire européen élémentaire	voKbulR €P1 LmantR
Assemblée élue	a100blé LU
Citoyen	6tway1
Citoyenneté européenne	6twayNT €PN
Clause de flexibilité	kloz 2 flexibiliT
Commission européenne	komi6on €PN
Compétence	konPtans
Consensus	kon100sus
Coopération	koPra6on
Cour des Comptes	kour D kont
Culture	Qltur
Décision	d6zion
Destin commun	dSTin kom1
Disposition	10pozi6on
Domaines de compétence partagée	domN 2 konPtans partaG
Droits de l'Homme	drwa 2 lom
Election	Lek6on
Eligibilité	LiJBeeLeeT
Europe	€p
Européen	€P1
Jeunesse	jEnS
Institutions européennes	1stitu6on z€PN
Lignes directrices	liñ 10rectris
Libre circulation des personnes	libr 6rQlation D prson
Loi-cadre	looa-KDr
Nationalité	na6onaliT
Non-discrimination	non-10crimina6on
Principe	pr1 6p
Personnalité juridique	pRsonaliT juri10k
Pétition	Pti6on
Respect	rSP
Subsidiarité (principe de)	sub6 10ariT (pr1 6p 2)
Système Européen de Banques Centrales (SEBC)	6Tm €P1 2 bank 100tral (et se baisser)

4. From Alexander Hamilton to Tony Blair

Let us resume the main issue of this paper. As one can understand from my title, I was inspired by the famous definition that is commonly given of the American frame of government – 'a system of checks and balances'. The original expression (where 'balances' correctly come before 'checks'!) – used by Alexander Hamilton in *The Federalist* 9, dated 1787 – acquires more sense when it is cited within its co-text and is linked with a fragment of *The Federalist* 51, attributed to James Madison:

> The efficacy of various principles is now well understood, which were either not known at all, or imperfectly known to the ancients. The regular distribution of power into distinct departments – the introduction of legislative balances and checks – the institution of courts composed of judges holding their offices during good behavior – the representation of the people in the legislature by deputies of their own election [...]. (Cooke 1961: 51)
> It may be a reflection on human nature, that such devices should be necessary to control the abuses of government. But what is government itself, but the greatest of all reflections on human nature? If men were angels, no government would be necessary. If angels were to govern men, neither external nor internal controls on government would be necessary. In framing a government which is to be administered by men over men, the great difficulty lies in this: you must first enable the government to control the governed; and in the next place oblige it to control itself. (Cooke 1961: 349)

Madison's reflection on human nature – though written in 1788 – is still topical: since men are not angels, not even in Europe, not even 217 years later, checks/balances/controls are surely needed within the European borders.

Even Valery Giscard d'Estaing was inspired by American constitutional history. When he was first 'minted' as Chairman of the European Convention, he suggested he might be "Europe's Benjamin Franklin, a senior figure lending his authority to the process".[6] But when the Draft was published, he compared himself to Thomas Jefferson, by saying: "I tried to play a little bit the role that Jefferson played in Philadelphia, which was to instil leading ideas into the system. [...]

---

6 <http://www.nationalreview.com/comment/comment-murray062303.asp>.

Jefferson was a man who wrote and produced elements that consolidated the Constitution". Giscard d'Estaing ignored the fact that Jefferson was not present at the Philadelphia Convention, because he was serving his country as minister in Paris![7]

As far as I am concerned, another source of inspiration was Tony Blair's double comment, or ambivalent mood. Some time ago, making a comparison between the existing European Treaties and the proposed Constitution, he said that the latter was a "tidying-up exercise" and did not represent any significant change. However, on April 20, 2004, in the House of Commons, in the course of his "statement on the forthcoming negotiation over the new European Treaty", Blair affirmed: "I want to make clear that in this negotiation Britain will co-operate fully in helping Europe work better, but work better as Europe of sovereign nation states. There are certain areas of policy where *maintenance of control of our affairs is essential.*"[8] First, he listed those areas and then he ridiculed some comments of the Eurosceptics as alarmist exaggeration. He had to demolish their fears that the Constitution, superimposed on the British unwritten set of conventions, would inaugurate an organic process of centralization, leading to the atrophy of the nation state and the hypertrophy of the superstate.

He tried to put an end to a series of legends that had propagated about the Charter, such as "the hardy perennial that the Germans would take over our nuclear weapons and no doubt the shape of our bananas too!" "All of it, nonsense" – he added – "myth designed to distance people's understanding of what the European Constitution is about".[9]

7 Apart from the French President's historical blunder, I believe that Thomas Jefferson would be distressed to have his name associated with the draft document: that 'champion' of limited government would be appalled at the paternalistic, centralizing ideas that the EU Constitution seems to embody!

8 <http://www.guardian.co.uk/uk_news/story/0,1197044,00.html> My emphasis.

9 <http://www.telegraph.co.uk/opinion/main.jhtml?xml=/opinion/2004/03/30/>.

5. In the name of transparency

As a matter of fact, there are parts of the document that are not easy to understand, or to interpret, although in its preface we can read that the Convention

> proposes measures to increase the democracy, transparency and efficiency of the European Union, by developing the contribution of national Parliaments to the legitimacy of the European design, by simplifying the decision-making processes, and by making the functioning of the European Institutions more transparent and comprehensible.
>
> propose des mesures pour accroître la démocratie, la transparence et l'efficacité de l'Union européenne, en développant la contribution des parlements nationaux à la légitimité du projet européen, en simplifiant les processus décisionnels, en rendant le fonctionnement des Institutions européennes plus transparent et plus lisible.
>
> propone misure volte ad accrescere la democrazia, la trasparenza e l'efficienza dell'Unione europea, accrescendo il contributo dei parlamenti nazionali alla legittimazione del progetto europeo, semplificando il processo decisionale, rendendo il funzionamento delle istituzioni europee più trasparente e leggibile.

Does the proposed Constitution really simplify "the decision-making process", does it really make "the functioning of the European Institutions transparent and comprehensible"? I wonder! I doubt it!

In the quoted paragraph, transparency is promised in the first and in the fifth lines,[10] and the adjective 'transparent' is used several times in the Draft; it is a kind of a mantra, but an empty magic formula, because the language, that should help in making the text (that

10 Curiously enough, the word 'transparency' appears in the official glossary, as if it were a neologism or a special lexeme of Eurospeak. This is the English version: "The term 'transparency' is frequently used in the language of the institutions to mean openness in the working of the Community institutions. It is linked to a variety of demands for broader public access to information and EU documents and more easily readable instruments (simplification of the Treaties, consolidation and better drafting of legislation). Complaints regarding a lack of transparency tend to reflect a feeling that the European institutions are remote and that decision-making procedures are difficult for the ordinary European citizen to understand."

is 'the functioning') transparent and comprehensible, fails to do so in several parts of the document.

What is transparent and crystal clear, in the Draft, is… the vagueness of the language of some clauses, which seem to be the result of political compromises, the result of a tough, diplomatic negotiation of meaning. As a matter of fact, the interpretation of several parts of the Charter is not entirely a matter of processing linguistic information, but, more importantly, it relies on taking account of a host of ideological, cultural, institutional and contingent factors underpinning some lexical/syntactical choices and non-choices.

Let us ponder upon some lexical choices/non-choices of those 108 members of the Convention whose contribution to the text is based on different personal/historical/linguistic/legal backgrounds.

I believe that the Convention used the word 'Constitution' as evidence of a growing awareness in Europe of the need of a real federal Europe, although the terms 'federation' and 'federal' never show up in the text or, better, the F-words (!), which appeared in a previous version of the draft, were deleted from this one,[11] because some countries objected to the use of those terms, as carrying negative connotations, as representing the threat which the EU poses to Member States' sovereignty. And also the word 'sovereignty' is carefully avoided in the text. But Article 6 defines Europe, for the first time, as a legal entity in its own right, capable of exercising sovereign power directly, rather than through the Member States. And the basis for that sovereignty is set out by Article 45, where, as far as some clauses are concerned, the speaker, more than a lawgiver, looks like a benefactor, expressing solidarity and identity with the addressee, trying to demonstrate that the European institutions are not as remote as the ordinary European citizen might believe:

> 2. Citizens are directly represented at Union level in the European Parliament. Member States are represented in the European Council and in the Council of Ministers by their governments, themselves accountable to national parliaments, elected by their citizens.
> 3. Every citizen shall have the right to participate in the democratic life of the Union. Decisions shall be taken as openly as possible and as closely as possi-

11 The statement that the EU would exercise power "on a federal basis" was replaced with the words "in the Community way".

ble to the citizen.
4. Political parties at European level contribute to forming European political awareness and to expressing the will of Union citizens.

2. Les citoyennes et les citoyens sont directement représentés au niveau de l'Union au Parlement européen. Les États membres sont représentés au Conseil européen et au Conseil des ministres par leurs gouvernements, qui sont eux-mêmes responsables devant les parlements nationaux, élus par leurs citoyens.
3. Toute citoyenne ou tout citoyen a le droit de participer à la vie démocratique de l'Union. Les décisions sont prises aussi ouvertement et aussi près des citoyens que possible.
4. Les partis politiques de niveau européen contribuent à la formation de la conscience politique européenne et à l'expression de la volonté des citoyennes et des citoyens de l'Union.

2. I cittadini sono direttamente rappresentati a livello dell'Unione nel Parlamento europeo. Gli Stati membri sono rappresentati nel Consiglio europeo e nel Consiglio dei ministri dai rispettivi governi, che sono essi stessi responsabili dinanzi ai parlamenti nazionali, eletti dai loro cittadini.
3. Ogni cittadino ha il diritto di partecipare alla vita democratica dell'Unione. Le decisioni sono prese nella maniera più aperta e più vicina possibile al cittadino.
4. I partiti politici di livello europeo contribuiscono a formare una coscienza politica europea e ad esprimere la volontà dei cittadini dell'Unione.

According to this Article, Member States – represented in the equivalent of a senate – are complementary to the direct representation of the people in the European Parliament, but are not the primary source of legitimacy. And Article 25 makes clear that it is the European Parliament the body which the Commission, as the executive arm, is responsible to; and it is the Parliament that is entrusted the ultimate democratic power of forcing the executive to resign. Finally, Article 10 sets out clearly that the Constitution and laws adopted by the European institutions shall have supremacy over the laws of the Member States.

6. Linguistic 'checks and balances'

But there is more to say on the issue: No. 10 is one of the Articles included under the heading 'Title III: Union Competences', and, if we analyse Articles 9-13 in a row, we understand that the fundamental issue at stake, here, is what we would call the 'horizontal separation of powers'. However, the word 'power' in the English version, appears only once (Art. 11, c. 2), when the Union and the Member States have nothing to worry about, because they are 'bound' together in adopting 'binding acts', as we shall see further on.

From Article 9 to Article 13 and all through the Constitution, in the English version (according to my frequency list), there is very little 'power' and there are very few 'powers'! 'Competence' is the term adopted and – I would say – diplomatically adapted or negotiated. As a matter of fact, even if one of the definitions of 'competence' in the Collins' English dictionary of 1979 is "the state of being legally competent or qualified", the term in English does not have the same implication of the Italian *competenze*, which is perfect in this context and co-text.[12] In this Charter, 'competence' seems to be European jargon or legalese for legislative power, or, if you wish, a lexeme of 'English Eurospeak'. Here, I believe, we have a relevant instance of intercultural and interlinguistic mediation, an example of a drafter selecting a lexeme because of its graphical/visual/etymological uni-formity with

12 With a short autobiographical (although scholarly!) digression, I shall try to cast light on these concepts. When I published my books and essays on the US Constitution and the *Federalist* (Sacerdoti Mariani 1985, 1997), I had to tackle the translation of the term 'power/s', several times. For each co-text, I had to adopt a different solution in Italian. The term, that appears in Art. 1, Sect. I, in the clause "All legislative powers herein granted shall be vested in a Congress", became, in my translation, "tutte *le competenze* legislative qui previste saranno conferite a un Congresso", but for Art. 1, Sect. VIII, where the Constitution recites: "The Congress shall have power to lay and collect taxes, […] to borrow money, […] to regulate commerce, […]", the solution I adopted was the following: "Il Congresso avrà le seguenti *attribuzioni:* imporre e riscuotere tasse, […] contrarre prestiti, […] disciplinare il commercio […]". On the other hand, Art. 2, Sect. I, which begins with "The executive power shall be vested in a President […]" was rendered into Italian as "*Il potere esecutivo* sarà conferito a un Presidente […]".

French and Italian, but at the expense of semantic precision. Perhaps 'competence' sounds less powerful than power, less dangerous, less threatening, and gives the impression that the danger would be the same in the three languages and that the United Kingdom, France and Italy might be equally affected or infected by the same power. As if, with a linguistic compromise, the three countries might reduce the anxiety about the famous demarcation dispute; as if, in a way, a linguistic device might 'check and balance' the allocation of powers between Union and States, since the predominant concern is that these articles provide scant protection for state rights, scant safeguard against an ever increasing shift of power from the states to the Union. This linguistic compromise is revealed by the following tables of concordances drawn up by processing the three versions of Articles 9–13:

```
Concordance for "competence*"
Text: Art9-13.doc

nfers on the Union exclusive competence in a specific area, only
ution confers on the Union a competence shared with the Member S
 States shall exercise their competence to the extent that the U
ded to cease exercising, its competence. 3. The Union shall have
ce. 3. The Union shall have competence to promote and coordinate
ates. 4. The Union shall have competence to define and implement
ut thereby superseding their competence in these areas.6. The sc
e Union shall have exclusive competence to establish the competi
e Union shall have exclusive competence for the conclusion of an
 it to exercise its internal competence, or affects an internal
etence1. The Union shall share competence with the Member States
Constitution confers on it a competence which does not relate to
Articles 12 and 16.2. Shared competence applies in the following
however, the exercise of that competence may not result in Membe
t III. Article 12: Exclusive competence 1. The Union shall have
 Article 13: Areas of shared competence 1. The Union shall share
ciples1. The limits of Union competences are governed by the pri
 conferral. The use of Union competences is governed by the prin
set out in the Constitution. Competences not conferred upon the
s for exercising the Union's competences shall be determined by
*********** TITLE III: UNION COMPETENCES Article 9: Fundamental
t within the limits of the competences conferred upon it by the
s Institutions in exercising competences conferred on it, shall
ot fall within its exclusive competence the Union shall act only
```

Concordance for "compétence*"
Text: 9-13FR.doc

```
ectifs qu'elle établit.Toute compétence non attribuée à l'Union
ution attribue à l'Union une compétence exclusive dans un domain
ution attribue à l'Union une compétence partagée avec les états
 états membres exercent leur compétence dans la mesure o l'Union
cer.3. L'Union dispose d'une compétence en vue de promouvoir et
res.4. L'Union dispose d'une compétence pour la définition et la
s pour autant remplacer leur compétence dans ces domaines. 6. L'
ves 1. L'Union dispose d'une compétence exclusive pour établir
he. 2. L'Union dispose d'une compétence exclusive pour la conclu
r lui permettre d'exercer sa compétence interne, ou qu'elle affe
.Article 13: Les domaines de compétence partagée 1. L'Union disp
gée 1. L'Union dispose d'une compétence partagée avec les états
onstitution lui attribue une compétence qui ne reléve pas des do
sans que l'exercice de cette compétence puisse avoir pour effet
 sans quel'exercice de cette compétence puisse avoir pour effet
es qui ne relèvent pas de sa compétence exclusive, l'Union inter
que e de l'espace, l'Union a compétence pour mener des actions,
*************TITRE III: LES COMPÉTENCES DE L'UNION Article 9:
on régit la délimitation des compétences de l'Union . Les princi
 regissent l'exercice de ces compétences .2. En vertu du princip
on agit dans les limites des compétences que les états membres l
les modalités d'exercice des compétences de l'Union sont détermi
a Partie III.Article 12: Les compétences exclusives 1. L'Union d
ux articles 12 et 16. 2. Les compétences partagées entre l'Union
```

Concordance for "compet*"
Text: EUIT913.doc

```
nze esclusive 1. L'Unione ha competenza esclusiva per definire l
 questa stabiliti. Qualsiasi competenza non attribuita all'Union
 settori che non sono di sua competenza esclusiva, l'Unione inte
e attribuisce all'Unione una competenza esclusiva in un determin
e attribuisce all'Unione una competenza concorrente con quella d
ti membri esercitano la loro competenza nella misura in cui l'U
i esercitarla.3. L'Unione ha competenza per promuovere le polit
coordinamento. 4. L'Unione ha competenza per la definizione e l'
la Costituzione, l'Unione ha competenza per svolgere azioni inte
ttavia sostituirsi alla loro competenza in tali settori.6. La po
 della pesca. 2. L'Unione ha competenza esclusiva per la conclus
one. Articolo 13: Settori di competenza concorrente 1. L'Unione
concorrente 1. L'Unione ha una competenza concorrente con quella
senza che l'esercizio di tale competenza possa avere per effetto
iuto umanitario, l'Unione ha competenza per avviare azioni e con
senza che l'esercizio di tale competenza possa avere per effetto
*****************TITOLO III: COMPETENZE DELL'UNIONE Articolo 9:
li 1. La delimitazione delle competenze dell'Unione si fonda sul
ribuzione. L'esercizio delle competenze dell'Unione si fonda sui
ione agisce nei limiti delle competenze che le sono conferite da
e modalità d'esercizio delle competenze dell'Unione sono determi
```

Next to these lists, we should quote the entire clause two of Article 11, where, as stated above, the term 'power' appears in the English version (corresponding here to the French *pouvoir* and the Italian *facoltà*):

> *Article 11: Categories of competence*
> 2. When the Constitution confers on the Union a competence shared with the Member States in a specific area, the Union and the Member States shall have the power to legislate and adopt legally binding acts in that area. The Member States shall exercise their competence to the extent that the Union has not exercised, or has decided to cease exercising, its competence.
>
> 2. Lorsque la Constitution attribue à l'Union une compétence partagée avec les États membres dans un domaine déterminé, l'Union et les États membres ont le pouvoir de légiférer et d'adopter des actes juridiquement obligatoires dans ce domaine. Les États membres exercent leur compétence dans la mesure où l'Union n'a pas exercé la sienne ou a décidé de cesser de l'exercer.
>
> 2. Quando la Costituzione attribuisce all'Unione una competenza concorrente con quella degli Stati membri in un determinato settore, l'Unione e gli Stati membri hanno la facoltà di legiferare e adottare atti giuridicamente obbligatori in tale settore. Gli Stati membri esercitano la loro competenza nella misura in cui l'Unione non ha esercitato la propria o ha deciso di cessare di esercitarla.

Although the entire list of policy areas to be included within the sphere of 'shared competence' is given later, in Article 13, the rules are established in this clause. Here, we have the impression that 'shared competence' is a misnomer, because we do not know how extensive is the 'extent' (referred to in the fourth line), in the sense that the paragraph does not specify under which procedures and acts the Union will decide not to exercise its power and does not give motivations for that prospective choice. Will it be because of a whimsy idea on the side of the Union? Moreover the Member States can only legislate in those areas the EU decides to give back to them – but how long should they wait for that decision? Does the EU need a special reason or season for it? 'Shared' and the corresponding Italian and French terms (*partagée* and *concorrente*) do communicate the idea of a balanced power, but the French and Italian 'measures' seem to make the scales turn in the Union's favour! It is the Union that has the final check!

Clauses three and four of Article 9 are also worth citing as examples of another kind of 'linguistic checks and balances' of this Charter:

> *Article 9: Fundamental principles*
> 3. Under the principle of subsidiarity, in areas which do not fall within its exclusive competence the Union shall act only if and insofar as the objectives of the intended action cannot be sufficiently achieved by the Member States, either at central level or at regional and local level, but can rather, by reason of the scale or effects of the proposed action, be better achieved at Union level.
> 4. Under the principle of proportionality, the content and form of Union action shall not exceed what is necessary to achieve the objectives of the Constitution.
>
> 3. En vertu du principe de subsidiarité, dans les domaines qui ne relèvent pas de sa compétence exclusive, l'Union intervient seulement et dans la mesure où les objectifs de l'action envisagée ne peuvent pas être atteints de manière suffisante par les États membres tant au niveau central qu'au niveau régional et local mais peuvent l'être mieux, en raison des dimensions ou des effets de l'action envisagée, au niveau de l'Union.
> 4. En vertu du principe de proportionnalité, le contenu et la forme de l'action de l'Union n'excèdent pas ce qui est nécessaire pour atteindre les objectifs de la Constitution.
>
> 3. In virtù del principio di sussidiarietà, nei settori che non sono di sua competenza esclusiva, l'Unione interviene soltanto se e nella misura in cui gli obiettivi dell'azione prevista non possono essere sufficientemente raggiunti dagli Stati membri, sia a livello centrale sia a livello regionale e locale, ma possono, a motivo della portata o degli effetti dell'azione in questione, essere meglio raggiunti a livello di Unione.
> 4. In virtù del principio di proporzionalità, il contenuto e la forma dell'azione dell'Unione non vanno al di là di quanto necessario per il raggiungimento degli obiettivi della Costituzione.

We may be surprised to find, in this document, eulogistic adjectives taking the comparative form, as 'better' here, that is referred to the European Union – which thus is implicitly defined superior to the Member States, whose action, on the contrary, is supposedly 'insufficient'. Evaluation markers of this kind would belong quite properly to a preamble, rather than to the body of the legislation itself.[13] But, in spite of their vagueness (how better is better? how sufficient is suffi-

13 I am thinking of the US Constitution preamble and of its "more perfect Union".

cient? how necessary is necessary?), they are common in the draft and can be seen as fulfilling some kind of indirect persuasive function that everything is under control and well balanced on the side of the Union. This is only an instance of how the document deviates from traditional patterns characterizing legal discourse. In this text we have a high frequency of lexical choices that tend to connote the absolute political/social legitimacy of the institutions, powers and organizational principles that the document is creating, and the unquestionable good relationship being established by the Constitution itself between the central power and the constituent units and the Member States among themselves.

The short selection of eulogistic terms given below – in the list – includes adjectives and adverbs of the corpus that were retrieved in order to identify the repeated word clusters they form. And one should not be surprised to find out that they occur within traditional patterns that characterize legal discourse, such as tautological expressions. They help emphasize the mutually beneficial ties – the 'checks and balances' – between different levels of governance in the Union:

```
Concordance for "*ly"
Text: EUcosten.doc

nce.2. Member States shall actively and unreservedly support the
 expenditure develops in an orderly manner and within the own re
upervises, determines or appreciably influences imports or expor
isions and, united ever more closely, to forge a common destiny,
s openly as possible and as closely as possible to the citizen.4
 ensuring that it acts consistently, efficiently and on a colleg
 Member States.2. The Union equally respects the status of philo
 Such data must be processed fairly for specified purposes and o
affairs handled impartially, fairly and within a reasonable time
 Decisions shall be taken as openly as possible and as closely a
 shall conduct their work as openly as possible.2. The European
 establishment makes a particularly valuable contribution to the
lectoral mandate or are politically accountable to an elected as
posed as to reflects satisfactorily the demographic and geograph
opean Parliament shall be regularly consulted on the main aspect
ouncil of Ministers shall regularly verify that the grounds on w
tes shall be treated on a strictly equal footing as regards det
onths if such measures are strictly necessary. It shall act afte
tes shall actively and unreservedly support the Union's common f
```

This is only a partial list of some meaningful selected examples; most revealing are the terms clustering round the idea of 'completeness' and 'consistency', of 'contact', 'cooperation', 'coordination', which, in turn, are supposed to be 'close', 'constant', 'mutual', 'loyal', 'stronger', and that are being 'prompted', 'fostered', 'encouraged', 'stimulated', 'ensured': it is a lexical chain of a special relationship – at least on paper!

7. Concluding remarks

I wish to conclude with a comment on 'necessary' that appears in the last quotation (Article 9, clause 4), after showing a list of concordances which is the result of my retrieving the third part of the document (from page 157 to the end) in its English version:

```
Concordance for "*necessar*"
Text: EUcoste3.doc

ileges and immunities as are necessary for the performance of it
provided in time to allow, if necessary, for prior consultations
ssion shall take any measure necessary to facilitate the success
adopt the European decisions necessary for defining and implemen
of Ministers shall adopt the necessary European decisions. Such
e available to the Union, if necessary the duration, and the con
 of the action and adopt the necessary European decisions. As l
, Member States may make the necessary arrangements as a matter
 shall, whenever it deems it necessary, appoint, on the initiati
 of Member States having the necessary capability and the desire
ibute to identifying and, if necessary, implementing any useful
shall establish the measures necessary for the implementation of
r States shall contribute if necessary to the implementation of
shall establish the measures necessary for the implementation of
of Ministers shall adopt the necessary European decisions on a p
 Commission, shall adopt the necessary European regulations or d
ing of the agreement and, if necessary, its provisional applicat
hall be required to take the necessary measures to comply with t
 shall, if it considers this necessary, state which of the effec
shall be required to take the necessary measures to comply with
 decision on the question is necessary to enable it to give judg
shall be required to take the necessary measures to comply with
ases before it prescribe any necessary interim measures. Article
 be based on records and, if necessary, performed on the spot in
```

```
or, if these do not have the necessary powers, with the competen
or, if these do not have the necessary powers, the competent nat
 any document or information necessary to carry out its task. In
s have access to information necessary for the audit of Union ex
eedings and shall take all the necessary initiatives with a view
tive. It may, if it deems it necessary, take part in the Concili
edings and shall take all the necessary initiatives with a view
 decision shall lay down the necessary measures relating to reso
 Commission shall submit any necessary information to the Europe
 Member State, to the extent necessary to enable them to be used
residents shall take all the necessary steps to promote consulta
work laws shall lay down the necessary measures in the fields of
ncerned. It shall note where necessary that any conditions of pa
transitional measures deemed necessary with regard to the applic
Affairs. It shall note where necessary that any conditions of pa
transitional measures deemed necessary with regard to the applic
 law or framework law where necessary for the performance of the
 Member States shall, where necessary, assist each other to this
e such steps as it considers necessary for the protection of the
le of Man only to the extent necessary to ensure the implementat
ber States, including, where necessary, the regional legislation
etings shall take place, when necessary, to discuss questions re
tion is of the view that the necessary arrangements for the esta
inisters shall establish the necessary measures for the election
e concerned has not taken the necessary measures to comply with
```

'Necessary', together with the adjective 'appropriate', is one of the most notable cases of the Draft linguistic indeterminacy.[14] It is one of those terms that Blanquit would have defined "un mot de gomme" and on which a famous judge, Marshall, in 1819, made a remarkable observation, which is still topical (q. in Sacerdoti Mariani 1985: 35):

> The word has not a fixed character peculiar to itself: It admits of all degrees of comparison; and it is often connected with other words, which increase or diminish the impression the mind receives of the urgency it imports: A thing may be necessary, very necessary, absolutely or indispensably necessary. To no mind would the same idea be conveyed by these several phrases. This word, then, like others is used in various senses; and in its construction, the subject, the context, the intention of the person using them, are all to be taken into view.

A close analysis of the concordances of 'necessary', and 'appropriate' – either alphabetized to the left or to the right – reveals that wherever

---

14 That reminds us of the vagueness of the US Constitution, where, in the so-called 'implied powers clause' (Art. 1, Sect. VIII, c. 18), the ambiguous terms are "necessary and proper".

the two terms are used, in this constitution-making discourse, they are to be considered as an index of compromise between conflicting powers and as an act of remitting the determination of the meaning and reason of the text to another time and another body, a 'checked time', a 'balanced body'... when and where... – resuming Madison's expression – men might become angels!

References

Cooke, Jacob E. (ed.) 1961. *The Federalist*. Cleveland and New York: The World Publishing Company.

Sacerdoti Mariani, Gigliola 1985. Il 'verbo' della Costituzione. In Sacerdoti Mariani, Gigliola / Reposo, Antonio / Patrono, Mario (eds) *La Costituzione degli Stati Uniti d'America. Duecento anni di storia, lingua e diritto*. [*The USA Constitution. Two Hundred Years of History, Language and Law.*] Milano: Mondadori, 25-42.

Sacerdoti Mariani, Gigliola / Reposo, Antonio / Patrono, Mario ^{1}1991, ^{3}1995. *Guida alla Costituzione degli Stati Uniti d'America. Duecento anni di storia, lingua e diritto*. [*A Guide to the USA Constitution. Two Hundred Years of History, Language and Law.*] Milano: R.C.S. Libri.

Sacerdoti Mariani, Gigliola (ed.) 1997. *Il federalista*. Torino: Giappichelli.

<european-convention.eu.int/doc_register.asp?lang=EN&Content=DOC>
<register.consilium.eu.int/pdf/en/03/cv00/cv00850en03.pdf>
<european-convention.eu.int/doc_register.asp?lang=FR&Content=DOC>
<register.consilium.eu.int/pdf/fr/03/cv00/cv00850fr03.pdf>
<european-convention.eu.int/doc_register.asp?lang=IT&Content=DOC>
<register.consilium.eu.int/pdf/it/03/cv00/cv00850it03.pdf>
<european-convention.eu.int/glossary.asp?lang=EN&Content=>
<european-convention.eu.int/glossary.asp?lang=FR&Content=>

<european-convention.eu.int/glossary.asp?lang=IT&Content=>
<www.worldpress.org/Europe/1232.cfm>
<news.bbc.co.uk/1/hi/world/europe/3252628.stm>
<www.guardian.co.uk/uk_news/story/0,1197044,00.html>
<politics.guardian.co.uk/eu/story/0,1195999,00.html>
<www.guardian.co.uk/guardianpolitics/story/0,1195662,00.html>
<politics.guardian.co.uk/print/0,3858,4891342-107988,00.html>

MARINA DOSSENA

'The times they're a-changing': The Abolition of Feudal Tenure (Scotland) Act 2000 and Linguistic Strategies of Popularization

November 28th 2004 was the date of commencement of the Abolition of Feudal Tenure (Scotland) Act 2000. While this might seem a long overdue act in European (or, indeed, English) eyes, it is in fact going to have a remarkable impact even on ordinary citizens, in that it will not just suppress a label evocative of medieval times, but will also influence the mechanisms by means of which burdens can (or cannot) be imposed on property. The aim of this chapter is therefore to discuss the linguistic strategies by means of which the legal text is made more accessible to the general public – a process that in the end may prove far from neutral, as strategies have been observed to vary according to the encoder's stance in relation to the reform itself.

In particular, the chapter intends to concentrate on the use of definitions and examples as privileged *loci* of plain language encoding (Asprey 1997; van der Staak 1997), in order to assess the expression of stance by means of periphrasis. While special attention will be given to adverbials and adjectives (see Hunston/Thompson 2001), the role played by modality will not be overlooked (see Trosborg 1997; Gotti/Dossena 2001). Finally, it will be interesting to note that the expressions of critical assessment observed, albeit somewhat infrequently, in the popularization of scientific discourse (Gotti 2003: 304-305) are especially emphasized in those texts in which the aim of guiding the recipients' evaluation of the subject matter is more prominent. In such cases the use of 'personalized' examples and (often jocular, i.e. emotional) intertextual references provide the materials upon which the recipients' response is elicited, so that consensus is actually constructed around the encoder's statements through explicit reliance on shared cultural elements.

After an overview of the Act itself, my analysis will discuss four types of sources aimed at illustrating the text to the public: the Explanatory Notes issued by the Scottish Executive, the text issued by a non-profit charitable company in co-operation with a firm of solicitors and estate agents, and the texts issued by two law firms, one of which argues explicitly against the Act.[1] Given their relative heterogeneity, no attempt will be made here at quantitative investigations of data, but simply at a qualitative overview of their main rhetorical strategies in relation to their pragmatic aim, whether this is more informative or argumentative, and to what extent it is dependent on cultural specificity.

1. The Abolition of Feudal Tenure (Scotland) Act 2000 – Background notes

In recent years there have been numerous developments in the Scottish legal system, both in relation to international developments[2] (especially within the European Union) and, in particular, owing to the passage of the Scotland Act 1998, which (re-)established a Parliament[3] with a wide range of powers. These include legislative competence in relation to health, education, industry, local government, social work and housing, economic development and transport, criminal and civil law and home affairs, environment, agriculture, forestry and fishing, sport and the arts. In particular, Scottish Private Law is within the competence of the Parliament.

As regards land tenure, the 2000 Act had been preceded by other initiatives whose aim was to reform it. For instance, the Convey-

1 All the texts are available online – see References.

2 For instance, a case in point concerns arbitration. Owing to the specificity of the Scottish legal system, Scotland is not subject to the Arbitration Act 1996 which applies to the rest of the United Kingdom, but the UNCITRAL Model Law on International Commercial Arbitration does apply in Scotland by virtue of Section 66 and Schedule 7 of the Law Reform (Miscellaneous Provisions) (Scotland) Act 1990 (see Dossena 2003).

3 Scotland had had a Parliament till 1707, when the Act of Union was passed.

ancing and Feudal Reform (Sc) Act 1970 had modernised heritable securities[4] and created new ways of changing land conditions. The Land Tenure Reform (Sc) Act 1974 had allowed for the redemption of feu duty and the Land Registration (Sc) Act 1979 had provided for a new Land Register.[5] As for the abolition of the feudal system, the Scottish Law Commission had been studying the issue since 1991, and a Report was brought before Parliament in February 1999. The Abolition of Feudal Tenure (Scotland) Act 2000 was finally passed on 9th June 2000.

In practice, this means that the feudal system applied in Scotland until 28th November 2004, which was the appointed day for commencement under the Abolition of Feudal Tenure (S) Act 2000. Until that day all land in Scotland (except Udal[6] land in Orkney and Shetland and Allodial[7] Land owned by the Prince of Wales) was owned by the Crown, which had granted rights in land to tenants-in-chief, who in turn had created sub-tenants, and so on to those who enjoy actual possession of the land, that is those who have the *dominium utile* of it. The 2000 Act replaces the feudal system with a scheme of absolute ownership – even the Crown's paramount feudal superiority disappears. However, there will still be restrictions on how an owner can use land – for instance, the planning and building control systems remain, and this has already been seen to have important consequences on sheltered housing.[8] Burdens will also be maintained or enforced for conservation purposes: for instance, if the owner is a 'conservation body', such as the National Trust for Scotland, as its aims are (at least partially) in the public interest.

---

4 The Scots Law of Property distinguishes between heritage (e.g., land and buildings) and moveables (that is, objects that are physically moveable and moveable rights).

5 This is expected to supersede the Register of Sasines, which has been in use since 1617.

6 This refers to a form of freehold tenure.

7 This refers to the holding of land in absolute ownership: hence *the allodial system* is generally opposed to the *feudal system*.

8 According to the Title Conditions Bill (intended to supplement the 2000 Act: see <www.scottish.parliament.uk/parl_bus/legis.html>) in future a sheltered housing complex, or at least one in which all the flats have been sold, will be treated as a 'community' with all the burdens applicable to individual flats becoming, if they are not already, mutually enforceable.

2. Popularization and argumentation

As we have seen, the shift from a feudal system to one of absolute ownership is going to have important consequences for citizens, not least because it involves a significant cultural change in the attitude to the concept of 'property' itself. For this reason, although the text of the Act is accompanied by Explanatory Notes issued by the Executive, several law firms have published their own explanations on their websites. For this study I have selected a few that represent different attitudes to the new Act, one of which is very clearly in opposition to it and employs the highest number of popularization strategies, including intertextual references ranging from *Hamlet* to well-known films. It will thus be seen that making legal texts more 'user-friendly' can in fact be a way of guiding citizens' assessment, thus suggesting and promoting opinions, rather than facts. In order to proceed gradually, linguistic features will be discussed in their varying occurrences in the different texts.

2.1. Features of text organization and presentation

The texts taken into consideration here immediately strike us for their similarities or differences already at the level of text organization. While the Explanatory Notes (EN) present themselves as very similar, both typographically and in terms of text structure, to the text of the Act itself, the other texts immediately present themselves as 'user-friendly' either in their structure or in their opening statement. The site of a non-profit company (CAL),[9] for instance, defines its text as "A Practical Guide for Community Groups" and indicates a specific author, in addition to a reference to the law firm that has provided its assistance – a clear indicator of text reliability for the benefit of the reader:

---

9 It may be of interest to note that this is the only site that makes extensive use of colour, graphics and varying fonts. In this respect, it appears to be in line with what is argued by Eagleson (1997: 19-23), where he underlines that design and layout can contribute to textual intelligibility and clarity in a crucial way.

> Written by Andy Wightman
> With the assistance of MacLeod & MacCallum (Solicitors and Estate Agents)
> Inverness, April 2001 [CAL].

It then continues with a hypertextual table of contents; this also includes a link to a glossary and other useful links to sites like Her Majesty's Stationery Office, the Law Society of Scotland and the Scottish Law Commission. The sites of the law firms, instead, appear to approach the texts rather differently: one (M) presents a "Summary of the Act's main provisions" under the title

> Know How : Property Matters : Guide to the abolition of feudal tenure (Scotland) act 2000.

The other (G) presents its text with a title clearly reminiscent of tabloid journalism, with decreasing font size, a pun[10] within an elliptical question and an exclamatory answer, followed by a proverb that prepares the way for the expression of the encoder's negative stance towards the reform:

> Land Reform in Scotland;
> Irritated?
> – you should be!
> *"To change and to change for the better are two different things."* – German proverb.[11]

As we will see, this is also the text in which cultural elements are most forcefully employed for argumentative purposes. Interestingly, the only link provided at the end of the text is to the Act itself, though with the caveat that, as it is the full text, it is "for eager-beavers only" – an idiom that is meant to discourage the ordinary reader from ap-

10 This refers to the "Discharge of Rights of Irritancy", since with the reform the Superior can no longer 'irritate' the feu (meaning that he can no longer take legal action to bring the feu to an end).

11 On proverbs, fixed idioms and set phrases used argumentatively see Morley (2004). In this case, however, the proverb is not employed to introduce a counterargument, but to summarize the encoder's opinion and to present it as universally acceptable, thanks to the alleged 'universality' of the proverb as the epitome of received wisdom.

proaching the text.[12] In addition, this phrase is preceded by various other indications that the text is not exactly recommended reading, as far as this firm is concerned:[13]

> The Act is a *hefty* tome, so we will consider just one example here (*believe me, one is enough*).

> This all sounds a bit *heavy-going*, so instead have a look at the diagram.

As regards images, these only appear in the texts encoded by CAL and G as diagrams of the feudal system. While CAL presents this in a very linear way (Figure 1) and provides an example in a specific box with a further diagram, G presents just one diagram illustrative of an example in which almost jocular pseudonyms are employed (Figure 2). Leaving aside multimodal communication as a popularization strategy, since this would be beyond the scope of this chapter, my analysis is now going to concentrate on linguistic features signalling greater or lesser user-friendliness. In particular, we shall focus on elements signalling distance from the legal text and proximity to the recipient,[14] especially in the clarification of definitions and examples and in the use of modality, adjectives and adverbials to signal evaluation. At the same time, we shall discuss the use of intertextual references for the expression of stance.

---

12 In such cases the encoder appears to have an ambiguous attitude towards the potential empowerment of the recipient (see Bhatia, this volume): while the text purports to facilitate the recipient's understanding of the text, it consistently stresses the importance of turning to the law firm for assistance, thus highlighting the mediating role of a third party between the text and the recipient.

13 In all quotations italics show added emphasis.

14 Shuy (1998, esp. ch. 5) discusses various ways in which legal discourse can be made more or less 'lay-friendly', and therefore both more comprehensible and (ideally) more acceptable. In such cases the encoder expresses greater proximity to the recipient in order to facilitate understanding and avoid conflict – on such issues in more general terms see Gotti/Heller/Dossena (2002).

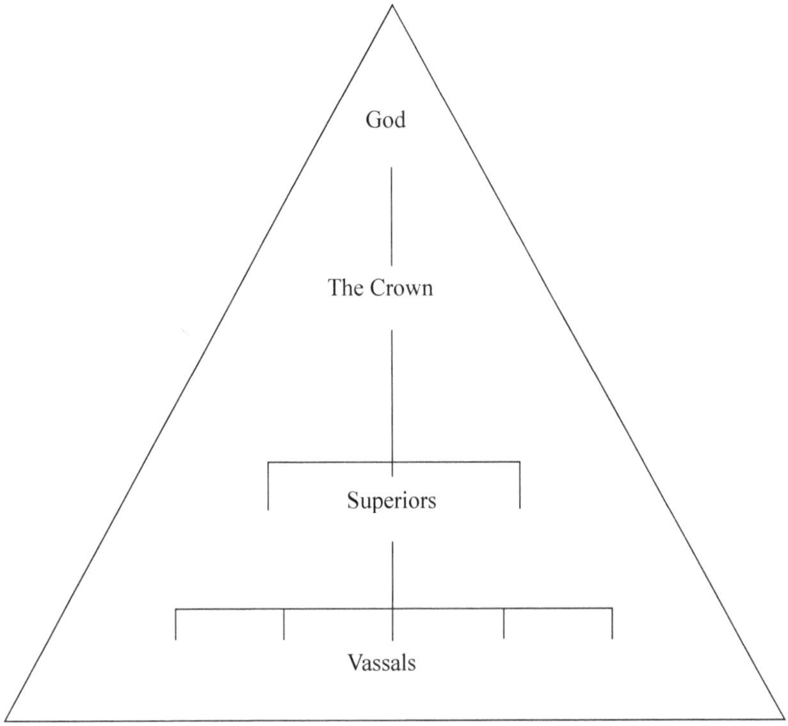

Figure 1. The Feudal Pyramid (CAL).

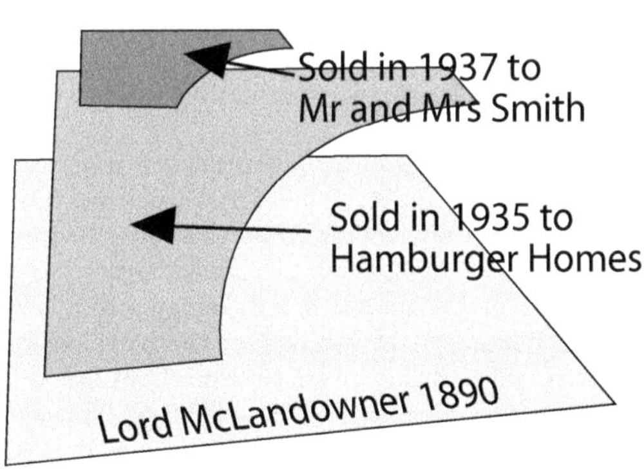

Figure 2. Illustration of the feudal system in G.

2.2. Encoding distance and proximity

Since the texts taken into consideration here are meant to 'popularize' the Act – that is, to make it accessible to the general public, but not to provide what lawyers could take to be an 'authentic interpretation' of the legal text itself, encoders are careful to signal that their summaries and explanations do not have any kind of binding force. This is made especially clear by EN:

> 1. These Explanatory Notes have been prepared by the Scottish Executive in order to assist the reader of the Act. *They do not form part of the Act and have not been endorsed by the Parliament.*
> 2. The Notes should be read in conjunction with the Act. *They are not, and are not meant to be, a comprehensive description of the Act.* So where a section or schedule, or a part of a section or schedule, does not seem to require any explanation or comment, none is given.

Disclaimers feature in the other texts as well; for instance, M states:

> Note: This paper contains *a summary* of the provisions of the Act only. While it is believed to be accurate, *no guarantee can be given*, and recipients should seek individual legal advice on their specific circumstances.

Similarly, CAL stresses the importance of obtaining professional advice prior to action (see fn. 12):

> This briefing is intended to provide *general* guidance on how the Abolition of Feudal Tenure etc. (Scotland) Act 2000 affects you as the owner of land or property.
> It is written as far as possible in a way that should make it easy to understand in general (as opposed to strictly legal) terms.
> It is *not intended as a definitive or comprehensive interpretation of the Act.* Rather it is intended to draw attention to the Act's *main* provisions and what action, if any, you might have to take or might wish to take as a consequence.
> As in all such matters, it is *intended as a guide only* and *should not be relied on as the basis of any legal action.* It is important that if, having read it, you think that there might be implications for you, you contact your solicitor for detailed advice. Given the nature of the Act, there are certain actions that you may be entitled to take but which have to be dealt with within a set timetable or you will lose such rights. It is thus even more important that you seek legal advice soon if you feel that the Act might affect you in any way.

The same appeal is repeated at the end of the text, when advice is given to the reader as to what should be done:

> Action to be taken
> All owners of superiority interests in land should now commence to review their property holdings so as to identify (1) burdens which they will wish to try to preserve, and the best means of doing so, and (2) compensatory payments for the extinction of feu duty, which they will wish to claim. The appropriate steps should then be taken. Should you require assistance with such matters, please contact the person with whom you normally deal at [M], of the firm's Scottish Parliamentary Group or of the Commercial Property department. [M]

> 16. Do I need to do anything?
> If you are a vassal you might care to check out what burdens exist in your title. The onus is on the superior however, to take any action to preserve them. If they do not then, on the appointed day, they are extinguished. If you wish them to go then it would be advisable not to draw attention to their existence in the hope that the superior will not take any action. If you feel that there is something worth preserving then it might be advisable to contact the superior to discuss a mutual agreement to preserve them. (See Section 19 of the Act)
> BEFORE DOING ANYTHING IT IS RECOMMENDED THAT YOU CONTACT YOUR SOLICITOR FOR ADVICE
>
> If you are a feudal superior, the onus is on you to take action to check:
> – what rights you have over land, which has been sold by you or by past owners of your land
> – to see whether there are any conditions which have been placed on property, which you would like to preserve
> – or whether there is any feuduty, which will be extinguished on the appointed day and for which you wish to be compensated.
>
> You will then need to determine whether you can, under the terms of the Act preserve such conditions. As a general rule if you do not take any action by the appointed day or within a specified period afterwards, you will lose any rights to take such action.
> BEFORE DOING ANYTHING IT IS RECOMMENDED THAT YOU CONTACT YOUR SOLICITOR FOR ADVICE

As seen above, CAL appears to be guiding users in more detailed ways, though this may involve repetition and therefore a certain degree of redundancy. G, instead, does recommend that their readers should seek legal advice, though stressing that further changes could occur and reassuring their readers that, at the time of writing, the firm is preparing more helpful documents:

> So what should interested parties – landlords, lenders, homeowners etc – do? Relax – it is not here yet
> [...] You will be concerned to know that the underlying law of real burdens will be amended and separate legislation will be enacted and brought into force, it is thought, on the same date – we can only hope that this may well help clarify some of the more 'vague' elements of the Act which seem to lend themselves to nothing but protracted litigation. The rumours that reach [G]as to the contents of that separate legislation do not suggest a likelihood of a good result. [...] In the next year we will be providing each group of people affected by these changes with a Survival Checklist.

In this respect, it may be interesting to observe that the encoder criticizes the Act on account of its supposed 'vagueness': while this reflects a layperson's general perception of legal discourse as 'vague', i.e. 'unclear', the specialist, and indeed the linguist, recognize that vagueness is in fact an intrinsic feature of legal texts (see Endicott 2000), which can actually be an asset if it allows for interpretative flexibility and culturally-dictated adaptations of internationally-accepted frameworks (see Bhatia *et al.* 2005). Here the encoder appears to dispossess itself of its *persona* as a law firm, in order to adopt the one that is presupposed to reflect the recipient. In practice, the encoder appears to abandon its cultural world, in order to enter the one attributed to the recipient, albeit somewhat stereo-typically.

2.2.1.The virtual dialogue with the recipient

Concerning the ways in which recipients are addressed, impersonal forms occur throughout the EN and M texts; as a result, these appear to be very similar, although the former is much longer than the latter. CAL, instead, establishes a kind of virtual dialogue with the reader.[15] This is made explicit in the table of contents, where out of seventeen questions one is in fact a comment allegedly made by the reader ("I thought feudalism had been abolished a long time ago!"), while three are questions allegedly posed by the reader:

> 7. So how does [the Act] affect me?
> 8. Who is my feudal superior and how do I contact them? [...]
> 16. Do I need to do anything?

---

15 This communicative strategy has in fact been observed also in earlier scientific discourse – see Dossena (2001a).

A virtual dialogue with the recipient is also mimicked by G, in whose text the encoder frequently appeals to the reader by means of elliptical questions, the use of direct forms of address and discourse markers like *well*:

> To know why the future has its problems we need to have a quick look at where Scottish Land law currently is and why they want to change it.. Sitting comfortably? Well, let me begin…
> We are back to the usual 'why change what isn't broken'?' query. Well, of course the system is not 'broken' in the objective sense of the word;

Within this framework it becomes important to see how examples and explanations are offered in the various texts, in order to see whether these are used informatively or, in fact, argumentatively, in order to construct consensus around a certain view of the Act. In EN definitions are – predictably – fairly neutral, although their stylistic proximity to legal discourse is – just as predictably – quite high:

> 7. The system of land tenure in Scotland is overwhelmingly feudal in nature. In theory, this means that the land is held under the Crown as ultimate feudal superior. Historically, the Crown would make a grant of land in return for military or other services and the grantees would in turn make sub-grants for other services and so on. Those making grants – the 'superiors'– retained a legal interest in the land ('dominium directum'), and so a hierarchical structure was created with each property having a number of owners, co-existing simultaneously. Only one of these, the 'vassal', has what in normal language would be regarded as ownership of the property ('dominium utile').
>
> 60. *Subsection (2)* abolishes the security (debitum fundi) which a superior previously had over the feudal property for unpaid feuduty and redemption money.

In the examples above we see that Latin phrases are employed in brackets after their practical definitions (either as translations into English or as periphrases). Latin, however, does not occur in similar ways in any of the other texts, although they all employ periphrases for definitions, most typically introduced by the phrase *in other words* or indeed *in simple terms*, in which use of the evaluative adjective is certainly not accidental:

> It will not be possible to create a feudal estate after the Appointed Day. In other words, land will not be transferable by way of a feu disposition. [M]

> As its title implies, the Act abolishes the feudal system of land tenure. In other words it brings an end to the system whereby title to land is held as part of a chain of hierarchical interests. The Act introduces a system of simple ownership of land. […]
> Feudal tenure has its roots in the 11th and 12th century when the Scottish Crown began to assert its authority over the country. It did this by granting feu charters over extensive estates which conferred rights and privileges (usually administrative and legal powers) to the nobility in return for obligations (usually financial and military) to the Crown. Over time this system evolved into the system of land tenure that we have today. In simple terms, feudal tenure is a system of land ownership where a person – the vassal – does not own land outright but holds it on terms set by another person – their feudal superior. The ultimate Superior (or Paramount Superior) is the Crown, which historically derives its authority from God. All land held under feudal tenure (at least in theory) originates from a Crown charter [CAL]

CAL actually stresses the opposition between 'general' and 'strictly legal' terms in its introduction:

> This briefing […] is written as far as possible in a way that should make it easy to understand *in general (as opposed to strictly legal) terms.*

On the other hand, EN frequently signals that concepts are expressed in 'non-feudal language' in the Act itself:[16]

> 15. [Part 2] restates, in non-feudal language, the established rules for the transfer of ownership of land in Scotland.

They also emphasize the fact that the Act has made the law more accessible by doing away with 'obsolete and unnecessary words':

> The Act provides for the repeal of 46 entire Acts, as well as over 300 sections and Schedules and many obsolete and unnecessary words in other Acts.

Reference to modernisation is taken up in the text issued by G, instead, for its own argumentative purposes:

---

16 On the attempt, on the part of the Scottish Parliament, to approximate 'plain English' see also Marrone (this volume).

> In moving that the Abolition Bill be passed, Jim Wallace, MP, said "I believe that the Bill... abolishes 800 years of feudal tenure in Scotland... (and) will modernise and greatly simplify Scottish land law".
> Simplification of Scottish land law? Em... I think not – if you can bear it, read on to see how only lawyers could make a bad law even worse.
> Let's replace the Superior Law with an inferior one

The paragraph opens with another pun ('Superior' meaning 'Feuar' in the feudal system), preceded by a touch of self-irony ("only lawyers could make a bad law even worse"): a clear case of *captatio benevolentiae* on the part of the encoder. Again, the choice of such adjectives as 'obsolete and unnecessary' in EN is not accidental – indeed, adjectives and adverbials have been shown to play a crucial role in the expression of stance even in 'normative' texts (see Mariani Sacerdoti, this volume), and these texts are no exception: CAL is explicitly defined as a 'practical' guide for community groups. On the other hand, G – the text that criticizes the Act most forcefully – begins with a reference to 'snappy populist' titles for which the legislator is claimed to have a taste – two adjectives the negative connotation of which is indisputable:

> Always keen on snappy populist titles, the Scottish Parliament passed The Abolition of Feudal Tenure etc (Scotland) Act 2000, part of which came into force on 9th June 2000. [G]

As regards adverbials, these are often observed to co-occur with modal verbs, especially when their value is epistemic:[17]

> *Clearly* there *will* be occasions when a superior is unable to come to an agreement with a vassal to preserve a burden. There may also be valid feudal burdens imposed to protect valued amenity interests which are not saveable as ordinary non-feudal burdens under section 18. [EN]
> Abolition of feudal tenure *will* apply equally in urban and rural areas, *perhaps* having greater practical impact in the former. [EN]
> Interests are created in favour of 'neighbouring' owners to enforce conditions – this *will* in due course become a 'loony neighbour charter' – *surely* this was not what was needed? [G]

17 On adverbial modality and its harmonic co-occurrence with modal auxiliaries in legal texts see also Dossena (2001b, 2001c).

As regards modal auxiliaries themselves, their use in argumentation can be illustrated by the following quotation, in which the encoder stresses the necessity to be informed ("you need to know about this"), predicts relevance for the reader ("it will affect you") and envisages hypothetical damage for the recipient ("'it may cost you a lot of money"):

> if you are a lender, landlord, tenant, or home-owner you need to know about this – it will affect you, it may cost you a lot of money. [G]

In this case, we observe a kind of 'reversed canon' in the text: the semantic strength of the auxiliaries decreases (from *need* to *will* to *may*) as their pragmatic strength increases (the possibility of 'cost' being outlined at the end of the sentence in order to obtain maximum attention from the reader). On the other hand, CAL proves much more cautious in indicating that the reform may affect the recipient: distal modal forms (especially *might*) occur much more frequently than in the other text:

> This briefing [...] is intended to draw attention to the Act's main provisions and what action, if any, you *might* have to take or *might* wish to take as a consequence. [...] It is important that if, having read it, you think that there *might* be implications for you, you contact your solicitor for detailed advice. Given the nature of the Act, there are certain actions that you *may* be entitled to take but which have to be dealt with within a set timetable or you will lose such rights. It is thus even more important that you seek legal advice soon if you feel that the Act *might* affect you in any way.

The sense of urgency conveyed to the reader is thus considerably decreased.

2.3. Culture-bound references

In legal texts encoded within a specific legal system it is no surprise to come across vocabulary pertaining to highly specific situations and only understood in that cultural context; as in the case of Udal and Allodial land mentioned above, we observe this phenomenon in a paragraph in which reference to glebe land (i.e., a portion of land assigned to a clergyman) is made. In the text below, which provides examples of feudal superiors in towns, as opposed to the situation in the country, we also find that the encoder mentions the New Town of Edinburgh as a totally transparent indicator of a certain place and a certain type of housing:

> In towns and cities it is common to find that one's feudal superior is the descendant of the individual or organisation, which originally owned and (frequently) developed the land. Thus in *Edinburgh* the original owners (now in the form of trusts) of the *New Town* are today the feudal superiors. Elsewhere it is common to find corporate bodies such as insurance companies owning portfolios of superiorities. This was done as part of their investment strategy in the days when the payment of feu duties still represented a significant source of income to feudal superiors. Other bodies such as the *Church of Scotland* have extensive superiority interests in property that has been developed on former *glebe land* (which involves large numbers of tenement flats and other buildings in the cities). [CAL]

While use of specific vocabulary and cultural references stresses their cultural relevance, it may also be indexical of their restriction if the reference is intertextual and can only be understood by recipients who share the very same cultural background. For instance, this is the case of the references to films and TV series that will be discussed below, in which information is blended with references to the world of entertainment, in order to obtain the recipients' consensus.

2.3.1. Edutainment?

G, the text that claims to be informative while actually guiding the recipient's view of the reform, has been found to convey meaning by means of references to plays, films and even TV series that the recipient is expected to recognize, in order to 'share the joke'.[18] As a matter of fact, all these jocular intertextual references aim at *captatio benevolentiae* by means of an appeal to emotions disguised under the deliberate manipulation of the exact reference either at the level of wording, or at the pragmatic level; in this way an external, apparently unrelated, comment is made to seem relevant in the context.

---

18 This is a strategy clearly aimed at pre-empting potential disagreement – if the two interlocutors share 'a joke', the encoder may assume that the recipient also shares his views and opinions in more general terms (see Shuy 1998: 98).

If we look at these instances in detail, we find three references to films, one to Shakespeare's *Hamlet*, and one to a TV series (*Star Trek*). As we can see in Table 1, of the three references to films, two include a quotation from the script; the source is given in all three, as it is in the case of *Hamlet*, while the reference to the TV series is left for the recipient to decode, in the assumption that it is a perfectly recognizable catch-phrase for anybody.

Text	*Source*
My mind is going! I can feel it! I can feel it! (*2001: A Space Odyssey*)	Film
Maybe not today, maybe not tomorrow, but soon… (*Casablanca*)	Film
The Good, the Bad and the Ugly? (*The Ugly, the Ridiculous and the Stupid?*)	Film
If it be not now, yet it will come – the readiness is all (Shakespeare; *Hamlet*)	Drama
It's a legal system, Jim,[19] but not as we know it?	TV

Table 1. Intertextual references in G.

References to time occur twice (*Casablanca* and *Hamlet*) and both are employed to stress that the reform is imminent, hence the recipient should prepare for it by gathering information. Finally, one film title is rephrased to convert it into a very negative assessment of the reform, followed by what might actually be interpreted as a self-deprecating remark:

> When this Act properly comes into effect, unfortunately the only winners are going to be the lawyers. [G]

Another pragmatic strategy of recipient involvement frequently employed in (G) is the use of colloquialisms, in order to make the text appear closer to the recipients' everyday usage: on occasion, however, this may even sound patronizing, as the recipient could appear to be portrayed as rather ignorant, if not a drunkard, and rather uninterested in legal subtleties anyway:

19 Reference is made here to Jim Wallace, MSP (not MP, as erroneously indicated in the text), current Deputy First Minister of Scotland. The original phrase ("It's a form of life, Jim, but not as we know it") refers to the protagonists being typically involved with surprising instances of extra-terrestrial life.

> While it would be inaccurate to say that this Act has dominated conversation *in the drinking-holes of Scotland,* it is (regrettably some would say) a matter of some importance to anyone who has interests in property in Scotland.
>
> Scots land law revolves around a system known as the feudal system. *Now this sounds like some form of medieval torture* and when learning it that seems not so very far from the truth. Scottish land law is medieval but what does the feudal system mean?
>
> Existing feudal restrictions may continue to survive if the provisions of the Act in this respect (*which I won't bore you with*) are met and the appropriate action in terms of the Act is taken by a Superior to ensure their continuance.

The idiomatic quality of this text is highlighted by its indirect reference to another proverb within the paragraph:

> as with most situations where we are *forewarned*, we are *forearmed* and we should be preparing ourselves for change

and also by its capacity to use both such colloquial lexical items as 'botched' and sophisticated 'parlance', 'feudal' in its French-sounding suffix and deftly contrasted with the 'plain-English' term to which both encoder and recipient ("you or I") would equate it. Maximum proximity between the two subjects of interaction is thus achieved when their identity is explicitly made to overlap:

> It is depressing that an opportunity to modernise our property system appears to have been *botched.*
>
> the system comprises a hierarchy of interests with someone called the 'Superior' at the top of the tree and the party known as the 'Feuar' (or in even more *ancient parlance*, the 'Vassal') having the significant interest in the land which *you or I* would equate to ownership..

The text concludes its argument with a Latin phrase, almost imitating stereotypical legal discourse; this, however, is promptly translated first into everyday English, and immediately after that in an idiom that takes the register back to an imitation of spoken informal interaction:

> There is a Latin phrase used in the law res ipse locitur which translates as 'things speak for themselves'. Enough said. [G]

Of course the other, less argumentative, text in CAL had not ignored controversy, but had put it far more mildly, employing hedging devices ('some controversy, some critics') and *argue* as the *verbum dicendi* introducing the perplexities:

> There was some controversy during the passage of the Act in the Scottish Parliament regarding the future of the Crown. Some critics argued that abolishing the Crown, as the ultimate owner of land would diminish the direct stake that society had in the ownership of land in Scotland. This would, they argued, promote the notion of a more absolute form of landownership, eliminate the public interest in the tenure system, and weaken the ability of Parliament to legislate on land in future.

It had also provided a summary of how the legislator had addressed the issue in a specific paragraph, while still signalling (in italics) that some points would need to be clarified further:

> Such concerns have been addressed to an extent by the preservation of the key Crown rights of prerogative including the interests of the Crown in ownerless property and the regalia majora (those rights in land must be forever retained by the Crown). *It remains unclear to what extent the public interest is still represented in the new land tenure arrangements.*

Once again, in this text information is conveyed as objectively as possible, avoiding argumentative overtones either in lexical choices or in syntactic organization.

3. Concluding remarks

Although a quantitative investigation of the texts discussed in this chapter was clearly beyond its remit, their very heterogeneity has allowed us to see that their informative aim is in fact achieved in different ways and, above all, with varying parallel attempts at argumentation. On the one hand, we have observed how the texts in EN and CAL actually try and make the legal text more accessible to ordinary citizens by means of paraphrases, examples and clear textual organization. M basically summarizes the reform, while highlighting the role that the law firm can have in assisting the citizens requiring legal advice – in practice, it advertises itself while giving an overall impression of informing the public. Finally, G offers a subjective view of the reform, which is illustrated to the public by means of linguistic strategies that leave no doubt as to the encoder's negative opinion of the text; at the same time, the encoder constantly seeks the recipients' support by means of winks and nods referring to their everyday world, especially the world of entertainment. References to films, drama, TV series, proverbs and idioms are supposed to evoke a familiar scenario for the recipients, who are thus led to concur with the views of an encoder who purports to be 'one of them'. In this case, the legal text is both explained and evaluated for the benefit of the reader. In the process, encoders approach a different culture from their own, although the image they may have of it still reflects their expectations and maybe also their prejudices.

References

Asprey, Michelle M. 1997. Marketing Legal Services in Plain Language. In Engberg/Trosborg (eds), 27-43.

Bhatia, Vijay / Engberg, Jan / Gotti, Maurizio / Heller, Dorothee (eds) 2005. *Vagueness in Normative Texts*. Bern: Peter Lang.

Dossena, Marina 2001a. *For the aduancement of the commoun weilth*: Hypotheses in Scots Scientific Discourse of the 16th-17th Centuries. A Preliminary Investigation. *Scottish Language* 20, 47-65.

Dossena, Marina 2001b. *Committed Wittingly Willinglie and of Purpose*: Exclusiveness and Intensification through Non-Verbal Modality in Early Modern English Legal Texts In Gotti/ Dossena (eds), 113-131.

Dossena, Marina 2001c. *The cruel slauchtyr that vas cruelly exsecutit*: Intensification and Adverbial Modality in the Helsinki Corpus of Older Scots – A Preliminary Overview. *Neuphilologische Mitteilungen* 102/3, 287-302.

Dossena, Marina 2003. Arbitration in Scotland: Local Specificity and International Homogeneity. In Bhatia, Vijay / Candlin, Christopher / Gotti, Maurizio (eds) *Legal Discourse in Multilingual and Multicultural Contexts: Arbitration Texts in Europe*. Bern: Peter Lang, 87-109.

Eagleson, Robert D. 1997. Lawyers and Linguists Working Together: Enlightening the Community and Upholding the Law. In Engberg/Trosborg (eds), 1-25.

Endicott, Timothy A.O. 2000. *Vagueness in Law*. Oxford: Oxford University Press.

Engberg, Jan / Trosborg, Anna (eds) 1997. *Linguists and Lawyers – Issues we Confront*. Tostedt: Attikon.

Gotti, Maurizio 2003. *Specialized Discourse. Linguistic Features and Changing Conventions*. Bern: Peter Lang.

Gotti, Maurizio / Dossena, Marina (eds) 2001. *Modality in Specialized Texts*. Bern: Peter Lang.

Gotti, Maurizio / Heller, Dorothee / Dossena, Marina (eds) 2002. *Conflict and Negotiation in Specialized Texts*. Bern: Peter Lang.

Hunston, Susan / Thompson, Geoff (eds) 2001. *Evaluation in Text. Authorial Stance and the Construction of Discourse*. Oxford: Oxford University Press.

Shuy, Roger W. 1998. *Bureaucratic Language – Government and Business*. Washington, D.C.: Georgetown University Press.

Staak, Jan van der 1997. Standard Structures: Basic Concepts Used as Frames to Explain Words in Legal Discourse. In Engberg/Trosborg (eds), 27-43.

Trosborg, Anna 1997. *Rhetorical Strategies in Legal Language. Discourse Analysis of Statutes and Contracts*. Tübingen: Narr.

Websites (accessed 04.06.04)

<www.scotland-egislation.hmso.gov.uk/legislation/scotland/acts2000/20000005. htm>.

<www.scotland-legislation.hmso.gov.uk/legislation/scotland/en2000/2000en05.htm> [EN].

<www.caledonia.org.uk/land/feudal2.htm> [CAL].

<www.mms.co.uk/html/article/knowhow-property-abolitionfeudal.htm> [M].

<www.golds.co.uk/articles/articles_prop_feudalreform.htm> [G].

GIUDITTA CALIENDO / MARCO VENUTI

EU Discourse on Enlargement: The Negotiation of Meaning*

1. Introduction

This chapter presents the different stages of the negotiation of meaning in the delicate diplomatic process of European enlargement. It focuses on the active role played by language, which is not only an instrument to describe European construction but also forms a part of the construction process itself. In particular, we analyze the position of Turkey and how its relations with the EU are reflected in and affected by the documents issued by the Commission and the European Council, in order to highlight significant differences in their respective attitudes towards that country.[1]

A political and historical analysis of the main events that led to the current situation is necessary to understand the wider context in which the European institutions acted. Such an understanding is required to evaluate the language used in the formulation of their documents, where conditionality becomes an instrument to negotiate between messages of obligation and concession. Our chapter therefore provides an overview of the main steps of EU enlargement with par-

---

* The authors discussed and conceived the article together. Namely, Giuditta Caliendo is responsible for Sections 2, 4, 6 and Subparagraph 5.1. Marco Venuti is responsible for Sections 1, 3 and Subparagraph 5.2. The work presented here is part of a national project on Intercultural Discourse in Domain-specific English.

1 At the time our analysis was carried out, Turkey had not yet opened accession negotiations with the EU. We therefore refer to events that took place and documents that were issued before the 2004 Brussels European Council, when an agreement was found on the possible opening of negotiations with Turkey on 3 October 2005.

ticular reference to EU-Turkey relations, and a description of the roles played by the Commission and the European Council in the different steps of the process. We then focus on the linguistic analysis of two types of EU texts, the Annual Reports of the Commission and the Conclusions of the European Council, in order to show how the interpretation of these documents depends on both the language analysis and the understanding of the wider historical and political context. Our study will show how, over the years, the EU attempted to maintain diplomatic and economic relations with Turkey without officially committing itself to opening accession negotiations.

2. EU enlargement

The history of European enlargement has always been linked to a set of conditions, which has evolved and increased over the years. The first requirement appeared very simple: in 1957, the Treaty of Rome stated that "any European State may apply to become a member of the Community" (Treaty of Rome 1957, Art. 237). Therefore, 'European identity' originally appeared as the only basic condition to apply for membership. It remained such until Britain, Ireland and Denmark joined the Community in 1973. The first change of approach occurred in the mid 70s, when the new candidates to EU accession, Greece, Portugal and Spain, were making a transition from authoritarian rule to democracy. As a result, in 1978 it was established that "respect for and maintenance of representative democracy and human rights in each Member State are essential elements of membership in the European Communities" (Declaration on Democracy, Copenhagen European Council 1978).

The end of the Cold War and the growing number of applicant States from Central and Eastern Europe induced the Community to set out more explicit requirements for membership. As a consequence, in 1993, the Copenhagen European Council set political and economic conditions, the so called 'Copenhagen criteria', stating that "Membership requires stability of institutions guaranteeing democracy, the rule of law, human rights and respect for and protection of minorities, a functioning market economy" (Copenhagen Council Conclusions 1993, Paragraph 7). Later on, as a response to the Turkish-Cypriot issue and to Cyprus's application for EU membership, a new political condition was set at the 1994 Essen European Council: good neighbourliness, i.e. the obligation to solve any border dispute before accession (Smith 2003: 130-133).

This historical overview shows that, as years went by, candidate countries have been subject to more and tougher membership conditions and that Membership conditionality has affirmed itself as an instrument in the hands of the EU to influence domestic and foreign policies of applicant countries.

2.1. A European strategy for Turkey

Turkey has always represented a sensitive issue in the EU political sphere and the attitude towards this country has changed over the years according to new political scenarios. As early as 1963, Turkey signed an Association Agreement with the European Community (also called the 'Ankara Agreement') for the establishment of a customs union[2]. This event confirmed Europe's positive attitude towards Turkey at the time. This country seemed encouraged to join the EU, being offered a trade agreement that might eventually lead to full membership. Such a positive attitude was dictated by the fact that, although Turkey was not economically influential, it represented a strategic ally in Europe as the Southern pillar of NATO. As shown in Table 1, Turkey applied for membership in 1987, well before all the other States that joined the EU on 1 May 2004. In spite of that Turkey remains the only country listed in that table still to open negotiations with the EU.

---

2 "As soon as the operation of this Agreement has advanced far enough to justify envisaging full acceptance by Turkey of the obligations arising out of the Treaty establishing the Community, the Contracting Parties shall examine the possibility of the accession of Turkey to the Community." (Agreement establishing an Association between the European Economic Community and Turkey, Art. 28).

Country	Application	Accession negotiation	Membership
Turkey	1987	?	?
Cyprus	1990	1998	2004
Malta	1990	2000	2004
Hungary, Poland	1994	1998	2004
Romania, Bulgaria,	1995	2000	2007
Slovakia, Latvia, Lithuania	1995	2000	2004
Estonia	1995	1998	2004
Czech Republic, Slovenia	1996	1998	2004

Table 1. Dates of the Enlargement process.

This long time-gap and a general weak support for Turkey's accession after the Ankara Agreement was due to the fact that, after the end of the Cold War, Turkey's strategic importance in terms of security had gradually decreased, while the EU felt a growing pressure for admission from the former Communist countries. Furthermore, the Turkish-Greek dispute over Cyprus was becoming a major concern. As a result, in 1997, ten years after its first application, Turkey was still considered by Europe simply as a country 'eligible' for accession:

> The Council confirms Turkey's *eligibility* for accession to the European Union. Turkey will be judged on the basis of the same criteria as the other applicant States. (Luxembourg Council Conclusions 1997, Paragraph 31, italics added, as in all the other quotations)

The Luxembourg Council represented the saturation point, also because its Conclusions granted Cyprus the opening of negotiations while no mention at all was made of Turkey. This generated an extremely bitter reaction from Turkey, as reported by the Commission in the following year:

> Turkey reacted negatively to the results of the European Council, considering that it had received discriminatory treatment compared with the other applicant countries. Ankara stated that [...] it was suspending political dialogue with the Union and therefore no longer wished to discuss with it issues such as relations between Greece and Turkey, Cyprus or human rights. (The Commission Annual Report on Turkey 1998: 5)

As a consequence, the EU acknowledged the need to make some concessions in order to keep diplomatic ties alive. In the 1999 Helsinki

European Council, Turkey was finally recognized the status of 'candidate' country:

> Turkey is qualified as a *candidate State* destined to join the Union on the basis of the same criteria as applied to other candidate States. (Helsinki Council Conclusions 1999, Paragraph 12)

However, the acknowledgement of candidate status does not necessarily trigger an immediate start of accession negotiations. This is proven by the fact that, although Turkish status changed in form, the actual situation remained the same since in the whole text "there is no commitment to actually opening accession negotiations and accession itself today still appears somewhat enigmatic" (Maresceau/Lannon 2001: 14). In doing so, the European Council has achieved its aim to establish as close relations with Turkey as possible without granting it actual membership.

3. Data and methodology

In order to analyze the different stages of the EU-Turkey relation through the use of language, two types of EU documents were taken into consideration: the Conclusions of the European Council and the Annual Reports of the Commission. European Councils are summits of the Heads of State and Governments and their Conclusions set the political guidelines to be adopted by the Union. The five Council Conclusions selected for this study have been particularly concerned with the issue of Enlargement: Copenhagen 1993, Essen 1994, Luxembourg 1997, Helsinki 1999, Copenhagen 2002. As far as the Commission is concerned, it represents the mediator in the enlargement process in that it acts as a key point of contact between the EU and non-member States. The Commission paves the way for enlargement by making investigations on candidate states. Through the Annual Reports, it briefs the European Council on the progress made by each candidate and on what remains to be done in order to open negotiations. Although the role of the Commission in the enlargement process is essentially supportive and positive, the high authority is always represented by the European Council that officially decides to launch the Accession process:

> The European Council has considered the current situation in each of the eleven applicant States on the basis of the Commission's opinions [...]. In the light of its discussions, it has decided to launch an accession process comprising the ten Central and East European applicant States and Cyprus. (Luxembourg Council Conclusions 1997, Paragraph 10)

Our corpus contains the Annual Reports on Turkey published from 1998 until 2003, before the start of accession negotiations. For research purposes we also used *WordSmith Tools* (Scott 1998), which helped us to carry out concordance-based analyses of the texts. However, the different scope and size[3] of the two texts prevented a parallel analysis: while the Annual Reports are entirely devoted to Turkey, the selected Council Conclusions concern the European enlargement in general, in which Turkey only represents a limited section. As a result, our analysis will not be focused on the same linguistic features across the two text types. In order to draw some conclusions on the attitude of the Commission and of the European Council with regard to Turkish accession, we therefore decided to concentrate our attention on those text features that best characterized the different roles played by the two EU institutions.

The interaction between the analysis of language structure and the wider historical and institutional context is necessary if we need to make sense of complex events related to the delicate diplomatic field of international relations. The knowledge of relevant historical events, particularly the dispute over Cyprus, and an understanding of the different objectives of the institutional participants involved are instrumental to the analysis of the texts under scrutiny. Our approach is essentially that of an analysis of 'discourse as social practice' which:

> [...] takes the interaction with context much further in the direction of broader social context, where the focus shifts significantly from the textual output to the features of context, such as the changing identities of the participant, the social structures or professional relationships the genres are likely to maintain

3 The Annual Reports corpus consists of 282,476 words whilst the European Council Conclusions simply amount to 57,857 words.

> or change, and the advantages or disadvantages such genres are likely to bring to a particular set of readers. (Bhatia 2004: 20)

4. Textual analysis of the Annual Reports

As previously highlighted, through the Reports the Commission plays the role of the mediator, trying to 'round off the corners' through the use of hedging strategies to mitigate criticism and tone down comments on Turkey's negative performance. Hedging is the process whereby the author reduces the strength of what he is writing and has been defined as "the means by which the writer can present a proposition as an opinion rather than a fact" (Hyland 1996: 478). Hedging "can be achieved in an indefinite number of surface forms" (Brown/ Levinson 1987: 146). In our analysis, we chose to focus on the following surface forms of hedging concerning the Commission texts:

- downtoners,
- contrast/concessive adverbials,
- modals.

4.1. Downtoners

Some hedges are represented by downtoners, which Biber *et al.* (1999: 555) describe as "degree adverbs which scale down the effect of the modified item". From an analysis carried out on our corpus the downtoners that have frequently emerged are: *almost*, *quite* and *partial/ partially*. These adverbs are used in relation to actions carried out by Turkey in the attempt to comply with the required conditions. In particular, although the objectives have not been thoroughly accomplished, the Commission tends to draw the attention on the efforts made by Turkey and the positive results attained so far:

(1) Turkey has *almost* completed the alignment with the Common Custom Tariff and the customs legislation is largely aligned with the Community customs legislation. (Annual Report 2001, italics added)

(2) The Turkish Constitution has been *partially* amended in respect of fundamental rights and freedoms, and a number of legislative amendments have been introduced. (Annual Report 2002)

4.2. Contrast/concession adverbials

The Commission seems to 'tame down' criticism by presenting it in the form of a suggestion. Syntactically, criticism is subordinated to praise by preceding a negative comment with a positive one:

(3) Some provisions preventing the enjoyment of these rights such as the ban on broadcasting and education in languages other than Turkish have been abolished. *Nevertheless*, there has been limited improvement in practice in the ability of members of ethnic groups, to express their linguistic and cultural identity. (Annual Report 2002)

But the most common path of criticism that can be found in our corpus is the praise–criticism–suggestion triad. This strategy serves to mitigate the criticism and to encourage a better performance in the longer term. This is achieved through the use of contrast/concessive adverbials (Biber *et al.* 1999: 878-879) like *however*, *but*, *though*, *although* or *despite*:

(4) *Though* it is beginning to make progress in some areas, Turkey does not yet meet the Copenhagen political criteria and is therefore encouraged to intensify and accelerate the process of reform to ensure that human rights and fundamental freedoms are fully protected [...]. (Annual Report 2001)

Thus criticism ("Turkey does not yet meet the Copenhagen political criteria"), anticipated by praise ("it is beginning to make progress") and followed by suggestion ("is therefore encouraged to intensify"), is smoothed and conveys a message of encouragement to move towards further progress in the process of enlargement.

4.3. Modals

Modality is also used to present criticism in the form of a proposal. In the Annual Reports corpus, the first verbs are in fact the marginal modal NEED TO, in its inflected forms, and the modal SHOULD. Their relative occurrence, compared to their frequency in the BNC, proves how these two verbs are representative of the Commission Reports:

	AR frequency	AR percentage	BNC frequency	BNC percentage
Need to	824	0.29%	55,360	0.05%
Should	785	0.27%	109,156	0.11%

Table 2. Occurrence and relative frequency of NEED TO and SHOULD in the Annual Reports (AR) and the British National Corpus (BNC).

The modal auxiliary SHOULD is often used in extremely mitigated assertions that, acknowledging the efforts so far carried out, encourage Turkey to continue in its reforms. *Efforts* is also the first collocate in our corpus of the verb SHOULD, whose most common constructions are:

(5) Turkey *should focus further efforts* on completing the legislative, administrative and economic framework. (Annual Report 2002)

(6) Turkey *should continue its efforts* to achieve full harmonization with the aquis. (Annual Report 2003)

(7) Turkey *should concentrate further efforts* on aligning its legal framework. (Annual Report 2002)

There is also a frequent use of the marginal modal NEED TO, as well as of the verb NEED and the noun NEED, which build a non-assertive context. These are often used with an impersonal construction (8) or with agent deletion (9). In (10) Turkey is a hidden agent:

(8) […] *there is still a need for* enhancing transparency. (Annual Report 2002)

(9) Civilian control over the military still *needs to be improved.* [italics added]. (Annual Report 2000)

(10) The actual human rights situation as it affects individuals in Turkey *needs improvement.* [italics added]. (Annual Report 2002)

5. Textual analysis of the European Council Conclusions

The Reports analyzed in the previous section are not binding documents. The Commission recommendations can be endorsed or not by the European Council which officially, legally and politically decides on the opening of negotiations. While the Commission is generally encouraging towards a possible accession of Turkey, the relations between the European Council and this country have "always been characterized by a discrepancy in the respective aspirations of the partners" (Kramer 1994: 192). The European Council seemed prepared to invest only the minimum amount of 'closeness' in the relationship, without taking any steps in the direction of a lasting and irreversible integration of this country into the EU.

However, we must not forget that the enlargement is a highly sensitive issue in terms of external relations and that the European Council is a political summit where language has to be used very cautiously. In this respect, the wording used in the Conclusions of the European Council is aimed to avoid, on the one hand, any direct confrontation with an applicant country that could raise diplomatic problems (e.g. the European Council never explicitly denies Turkey's possible accession) and, on the other, any contractual commitment that could bind Europe to a promise of future membership. In order to do so, different techniques are used in the Conclusions of the European Council. In particular our analysis concentrates on two strategies:

- 'not saying' (vague or 'hidden' reference),
- conditionality.

5.1. 'Not saying'

As previously remarked, until the Helsinki summit Turkey was never called 'candidate country'. From the Ankara Agreement to the Helsinki meeting, the word 'membership' was never directly mentioned with reference to Turkey. In the text of the Luxembourg European Council, the verbs referring to Turkey indicate 'strengthening of the links' with the EU as in (11) or a 'movement' towards membership as in (12), which, however, never imply membership itself and serve to avoid any promise of a tangible and final result:

(11) The European Council recalls that *strengthening Turkey's links* with the European Union also depends on that country's pursuit of the political and economic reforms [...]. (Luxembourg Council Conclusions 1997, Paragraph 35)

(12) The European Council considers that it is nevertheless important for a strategy to be drawn up to prepare Turkey for accession by *bringing it closer* to the European Union in every field. (Luxembourg Council Conclusions 1997, Paragraph 31)

As analyzed in Section 2, due to historical and political circumstances, the label 'eligible' was transformed into 'candidate' in the 1999 Helsinki Conclusions. In the text, the strategy of 'not saying' is carried on. It is interesting to point out that, although the whole Paragraph 4 of the document is entirely addressed to Turkey, this country is never directly mentioned:

(13) The European Council reaffirms the inclusive nature of the accession process, which now comprises 13 candidate States within a single framework. (Helsinki Council Conclusions 1999, Paragraph 4)

Although this is the first time that Turkey is listed among candidate states, reference is simply made to a number of 13 countries without direct reference to Turkey itself. Later on, the same section of the document reads:

(14) [...] the European Council recalls that compliance with the political criteria laid down at the Copenhagen European Council is a prerequisite *for the opening of accession negotiations* and that compliance with all the Copenhagen criteria is the basis for accession to the Union. (Helsinki Council Conclusions 1999, Paragraph 4)

The Copenhagen conditions are imposed once again as the preconditions to open negotiations. The significant detail is that, in 1999, Turkey was the only country not to have opened accession negotiations yet, so this formulation represented a subtle way of referring to this country only indirectly.

5.2. Conditionality

Another strategy used by the European Council to avoid an open commitment is conditionality. As highlighted earlier on in the paper, conditionality has historically been a fair instrument, applicable to all candidate States on an equal footing. Thus, the granting of membership is made conditional upon certain external criteria (the Copenhagen criteria) that are independent of the European Council's power to intervene: all candidate states are unilaterally responsible for proving their ability to become members:

(15) Membership *presupposes* the candidate's *ability* to take on the obligations of membership including adherence to the aims of political, economic and monetary union. (Copenhagen Council Conclusions 1993, Paragraph 7)

(16) Accession will take place as soon as the associated country *is able to assume the obligations of membership* by satisfying the economic and political conditions required as set out in the conclusions of that meeting. (Essen Council Conclusions 1994, Introduction)

The same is obviously true for Turkey, which for many years has been refused the opening of negotiations on the basis of external and objective conditions lying outside the European Council's competence. However, as shown in this section, a contrast emerges between how conditionality is presented and how it is actually applied with respect to Turkey. From the documents analyzed, one condition in particular appears to be less objective than others and applied inconsistently: the settlement of border disputes between Turkey and the Republic of Cyprus. The European Council manages to present this issue as a fair parameter applicable to all candidate states but, thanks to a complex and subtle formulation, it turns out to be a burden for Turkey alone and a clear obstacle to its accession.

The 1999 Helsinki Conclusions are a clear example of this strategy. In Paragraph 12, while reaffirming that "Turkey is a candidate State destined to join the Union on the basis of the same criteria as applied to the other candidate States", the European Council also subordinates the accession to the fulfilment of "political criteria for accession with particular reference to the issue of human rights, as well as on the issues referred to in paragraph 4" (Paragraph 12, Helsinki Council Conclusions 1999). So far, terms of fair conditionality seem entirely respected in the document. But once the intertextual reference to "paragraph 4" is disclosed, it unveils an additional commitment for Turkey, which resembles an imperceptible but adverse caveat within a contract:

(17) […] the European Council stresses the principle of *peaceful settlement of disputes* in accordance with the United Nations Charter and *urges candidate States to make every effort to resolve any outstanding border disputes* […] The European Council will review the situation relating to any outstanding disputes, […] at the latest *by the end of 2004*. (Helsinki Council Conclusions 1999, Paragraph 4)

Thus, in such an indirect way, the burden to solve the problem is placed on Turkey's shoulders and the resolution of borders becomes the essential prerequisite to open the European doors. As Smith (2003: 131) remarks, "the EU has put pressure on Turkey: the Helsinki European Council's declaration on good neighbourliness certainly places pressure on Turkey to contribute to a resolution of the issue". A further sign that these conditions were aimed at Turkey alone is also the time reference. "End of 2004" is the official date when the European Council finally had to pronounce itself on the possible opening of negotiations with Turkey. On the other hand, as shown in (18), the same condition ("peaceful settlement of border disputes") is presented a few paragraphs later only as a 'desirable solution' for Cyprus:

(18) The European Council underlines that a *political settlement will facilitate the accession of Cyprus* to the European Union. *If no settlement has been reached* by the completion of accession negotiations, the Council's decision on *accession will be made without the above being a precondition.* (Helsinki Council Conclusions 1999, Paragraph 9(b))

In confirmation of the above statement, the December 2002 European Council concluded negotiations with Cyprus in the absence of a settlement and, on 1 May 2004 Cyprus became a fully-fledged member of the EU. The European Council thus made use of its discretionary power behind a façade of fairness and objectivity. The language used proved to be an efficient tool to reach its final aim: diplomatic ties with Turkey have been maintained but the final concession is still far from being granted.

6. Conclusions

Our analysis has shown how the language used by the Commission and the European Council expresses their different roles in the EU enlargement process and their different attitude towards Turkey as a future member. The Commission is a supportive player as the recommendations it presents to the Council tend to highlight the positive steps undertaken towards future integration. But its role is simply advisory: it is the European Council that has the final say and therefore a more assertive voice. However, diplomacy is never overlooked in the wording of both documents. While the Commission plays down criticism, the Council avoids unconditional statements on future membership, which is postponed as much as possible thanks to the official but not so impartial rules of conditionality.

References

Agreement establishing an Association between the European Economic Community and Turkey (Ankara Agreement), 1963. <http://www.deltur.cec.eu.int/kitap/e-ankara.rtf>.

Bhatia, Vijay K. 2004. *Worlds of Written Discourse.* London: Continuum.

Biber, Douglas *et al.* 1999. *Longman Grammar of Spoken and Written English*. London: Longman.

Brown, Penelope / Levinson, Stephen C. 1987. *Politeness: Some Universals in Language Usage.* Cambridge: Cambridge University Press.

Declaration on Democracy, European Council of 8 April 1978, EC Bulletin No. 3 (1978) 5.

Hyland, Ken 1996. Nurturing Hedges in the ESP Curriculum. *System* 24/4, 477-490.

Kramer, Heinz 1994. EC-Turkish Relations: Unfinished Forever? In Ludlow, Peter (ed.) *Europe and the Mediterranean.* London: Brassey's, 190-249.

Maresceau, Mark 2001. The EU Pre-Accession Strategies: a Political and Legal Analysis. In Maresceau, Mark / Lannon, Erwan (eds) *The EU's Enlargement and Mediterranean Strategies. A Comparative Analysis*. Houndmills, Basingstoke: Palgrave Macmillan.

Scott, Mike 1998. *WordSmith Tools 3.0*. Oxford: Oxford University Press.

Smith, Karen E. 2003. The Evolution and Application of EU Membership Conditionality. In Cremona, Marise (ed.) *The Enlargement of the European Union*. Oxford University Press: Oxford.

Treaty establishing the European Community, 1957 (Treaty of Rome). <http://europa.eu.int/abc/obj/treaties/en/entoc05.htm>.

CRISTINA PENNAROLA

How EU Secondary Legislation Encodes Humanitarian Aid Policies

1. Introduction

Although the European Union has been involved in humanitarian aid operations since the late sixties, the legal basis of EU humanitarian policy is relatively recent as it was set out only in 1996 in the 1257/96 Regulation, which provides the following definition of humanitarian assistance:

> The Community's humanitarian aid shall comprise assistance, relief and protection operations on a non discriminatory basis to help people in third countries, particularly the most vulnerable among them, and as a priority those in developing countries, victims of natural disasters, man-made crises, such as wars and outbreaks of fighting, or exceptional circumstances comparable to natural or man-made disasters.

Humanitarian aid is explicitly identified according to two key features: alongside its charitable pain-relieving aim, its extra-Community destination. This apparently matter-of-fact distinction – in line with the common assumption that the disasters that originate humanitarian assistance programmes mostly happen outside Europe – proves to be a highly loaded lexicalisation, unmistakably pointing to the EU's different attitudes towards home disasters and third-country catastrophes.

The aims of this chapter are to explore the linguistic features of EU legislative writing related to humanitarian aid and to investigate the nation-bound character of Community support through the semiotic framework of Critical Discourse Analysis, which regards language as both reflecting and shaping social practices. The present research work is based on EU secondary legislation, derived from the Treaties and consisting of Regulations, Directives, Decisions and

Framework Decisions, published in the Official Journal of the European Union and also available through Eur-Lex, the electronic archive of EU legislation in all the official languages. The analysis was carried out on a thematic corpus of EU legal documents concerned with humanitarian aid policies (named H in the paper), drawn from the reference corpus (named E) consisting of all the EU legal documents issued by the Council and the Parliament from 1st of July 1999 to 31st December 2002.[1] In the second section of this chapter, the selection of the EU humanitarian documents has been further divided into two groups depending on whether the recipients of the humanitarian aid policies are third countries or Member States (cf. Figure 1).

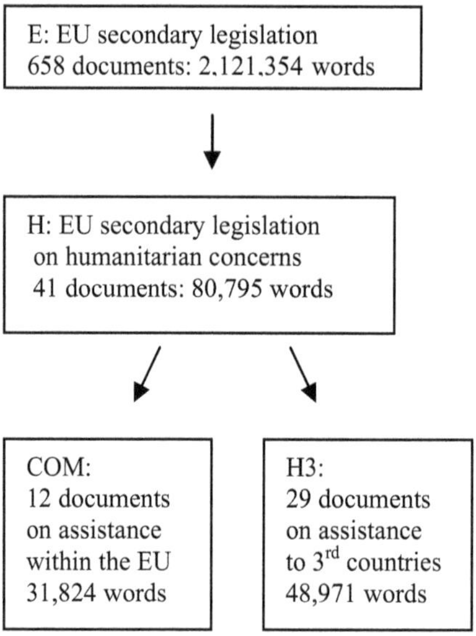

Figure 1. The EU secondary legislation corpus and subcorpora.

1 The corpus was set up by the Local Research Unit of Naples coordinated by Gabriella Di Martino within the MIUR National Research Project 'Intercultural Discourse in Domain-specific English'. As the collection, editing and classification of such a relatively large number of documents has proved a highly time-consuming task despite being divided between the Research Unit members, I am grateful to my husband Libero Cavaliere for his interested participation in the various phases of the EU legislation corpus research.

The low proportion of the humanitarian documents (approximately 4% of the whole corpus), resulting from the relatively recent advent of EU humanitarian lawmaking, may reflect the intricacies of the Community's international action as well as its reluctance to legislate on humanitarian policies so as to maintain the freedom to intervene according to the evolving socio-political situations of the assisted countries and to the often hidden agendas of the relieving nations (Collins 2001: 44-45; Smith 2001: 294-296).

2. The characteristics of EU humanitarian legislation

As pointed out by Bhatia (1993: 102), "legislative writing is highly impersonal and decontextualized, in the sense that its illocutionary force holds independently of 'whoever' is the 'speaker' (originator) or the 'hearer' (reader) of the document." Some of its prominent features, technical vocabulary and impersonal constructions (Gibbons 2003: 36) could be regarded as indicators of the style characteristic of EU legal documents and be used to verify whether the humanitarian documents would comply with the impersonal strain of legal discourse or, to the contrary, they might present a personal, 'human touch' (cf. Tessuto 2004: 199-200).

2.1. Keywords

The wordlists of the two EU corpora have been compared using Wordsmith Tools to draw a list of keywords, i.e. lexical items unusually frequent in the smaller corpus in comparison with the reference corpus. The keyness value of an item is calculated by a statistical procedure which takes into account the frequency of each word and the number of all the running words in both the small and the reference wordlists. The 40 most significant occurrences in the humanitarian corpus according to the Wordsmith Tools tabulations are shown in Table 1.

N	*Word*	*Keyness*	*N*	*Word*	*Keyness*
1	ASSISTANCE	782.8	21	LANDMINES	168.3
2	OPERATIONS	336.3	22	DEMOCRATIC	167.0
3	ACTION	336.3	23	IMPLEMENTATION	166.3
4	AND	328.7	24	PROTECTION	164.0
5	FUND	304.4	25	ACTIONS	163.8
6	EUROPEAN	286.2	26	DECISION	162.0
7	PERSONS	277.1	27	PARTNER	158.6
8	UNION	272.9	28	RIGHTS	142.0
9	SUPPORT	262.9	29	PROGRAMME	139.2
10	DISCRIMINATION	255.3	30	REFUGEES	138.5
11	MINE	245.2	31	HUMANITARIAN	126.7
12	TEMPORARY	235.3	32	ETHNIC	120.6
13	FINANCIAL	220.0	33	ECONOMIC	120.4
14	DISPLACED	211.4	34	WEAPONS	119.5
15	HUMAN	208.8	35	COOPERATION	118.2
16	FINANCING	200.1	36	CIVIL	116.8
17	RECONSTRUCTION	194.0	37	FINANCED	116.3
18	ANTI-PERSONNEL	191.7	38	PROGRAMMES	115.5
19	POLITICAL	176.5	39	RACIAL	115.1
20	MILITARY	172.2	40	VIOLENCE	111.7

Table 1. The most significant occurrences in the EU humanitarian corpus.

On the basis of the list of keywords, three main semantic fields can be identified:

a) one related to ASSISTANCE, with words such as *support, protection, cooperation, reconstruction,* which evoke a nurturing environment,
b) one related to VIOLENCE, with words denoting aggression, either man-oriented or environment related, for example: *emergency, military, weapons, discrimination*,
c) one related to POLICY, with words such as *fund, financing, democratic, implementation, programme,* which refer to economic and political concerns.

All these words appear to have a very high visibility in the humanitarian corpus not only on account of their frequency, but also as they systematically occur in the titles of the documents (See Appendix). Their emotive/affective connotations, either positive or negative, mark a significant deviation from the restrictedness and impersonality of legal vocabulary:

(1) Discrimination based on racial or ethnic origin may undermine the achievement of the objectives of the EC Treaty, in particular the attainment of a high level of employment and of social protection, the raising of the standard of living and quality of life, economic and social cohesion and solidarity. It may also undermine the objective of developing the European Union as an area of freedom, security and justice. (Council Directive 2000/43/EC)

The idea of conflict evoked by some keywords is also reinforced by the fight metaphor as the inflected forms of *fight* and *combat* frequently collocate with discrimination and violence. The recurrent lexical patterns highlight the militant role of the Community within and beyond its borders and the fierce opposition to any potentially subversive breach of human rights:

- *Combat* racism and xenophobia,
- Implement action programmes to *combat* such violence,
- Address different forms of discrimination and *combat* them,
- *Combat* trafficking in human beings and sexual exploitation,
- Strengthen the visibility of the *fight* against discrimination,
- Disseminate the values and practices underlying the *fight* against discrimination,
- Emphasise the European dimension of the *fight* against discrimination.

It is also worth noting the kind of negative keywords in the humanitarian corpus, i.e. unusually infrequent words in comparison with the reference corpus (Table 2).

WORD	*FREQ.*	*H.LST %*	*FREQ.*	*E.LST %*	*KEYNESS*
EXPORT	0		1,452	0.07	108.6
EEC	16	0.02	2,672	0.13	109.7
COMPANY	0		1,535	0.07	114.8
EXPORTING	0		1,624	0.08	121.5
INVESTIGATION	1		1,782	0.08	122.9
SALES	0		1,737	0.08	129.9
DUTY	0		1,918	0.09	143.5
PRICE	1		2,168	0.10	151.4
DIRECTIVE	64	0.08	5,859	0.28	154.5
PRODUCERS	0		2,084	0.10	155.9
PRICES	1		2,237	0.11	156.5
PRODUCTION	7		2,861	0.13	162.1
PRODUCT	4		2,637	0.12	163.8

Table 2. The most significant negative keywords in the EU humanitarian corpus.

The frequencies of these words expressed in numbers and in percentages present a distinct discrepancy between the reference and the target corpus. Most of these words are related to the domains of economy and industrial production which seem to be prominent in EU secondary legislation as it usually deals with the economic and financial aspects of the various Community policies (Smith 2001: 290), but seem oddly absent in the EU humanitarian documents apparently more concerned with ethical and moral issues.

2.2. Modal values

Impersonal constructions are a typical trait of legal discourse since by its very essence the law is seen as transcending individuals (Gibbons 2003: 76). Some typical constructs in EU legal documents present a distinct epistemic value as they introduce data or relate to previous argumentation:

(2) *It is a reasonable assumption* that benefits under subsidy programmes which are intended to benefit[2] […].

(3) *it is a fact* that the provisions of the abovementioned Articles of TERCL are further designed to restrict […].

(4) *it is accepted* here that concluding that dumping exist cannot in itself justify maintaining the measures […].

(5) *It is acknowledged* that duty drawback systems can allow for the refund or drawback of import charges […].

(6) *It is clear* that employment in these areas would also be jeopardised should injurious dumping be allowed […].

(7) *it is concluded* that the expiry of the measures on these imports is likely to lead to a recurrence of injury […].

(8) *it is underlined* that the subsidised imports must have significantly worsened the price pressure exerted […].

---

2 In all the examples included in the article, italics have been added to emphasize the relevant expressions.

(9) *It is understood* that this does not entail that a design must have an aesthetic quality [...].

(10) *it is very likely* that the closure of production lines manufacturing RBMs would affect the viability [...].

(11) *it is well known* that the variety is not suitable for cultivation in any part of its territory [...].

By contrast, deontic expressions conveying underlying ethical concerns appear remarkably more frequent in the target corpus of the EU humanitarian documents:

(12) *It is necessary* to ensure that these actions are coherent with the European Union's foreign policy [...].

(13) *It is fair* to allocate resources proportionately to the burden on each Member State by reason of its efforts [...].

(14) *It is important* to protect all natural persons against discrimination on grounds of racial or ethnic origin [...].

(15) *It is appropriate* that the Commission be assisted in the implementation of Community aid [...].

(16) *it is very urgent* to adopt this instrument; therefore, *it is necessary* to grant an exception to the six-week period [...].

(17) *it is desirable* to support efforts to sustain political and economic stabilisation in Bosnia and Herzegovina [...].

The list of impersonal *it* concordances produced by Wordsmith Tools for the two corpora shows that the EU reference corpus has twice as many occurrences as the target corpus (Table 3).

	IT Freq.	IT %	Main modal value
Humanitarian (H)	52	0.06	Deontic
Reference (E)	2,992	0.14	Epistemic

Table 3. Impersonal constructions in the two EU corpora.

This data seems to confirm the hypothesis that a humanitarian-based discourse, however embedded in legal language, would mostly favour a personal tone by identifying the agents or source of information:

(18) *It is important* to protect all natural persons against discrimination on grounds of racial or ethnic origin. *Member States should* also provide, where appropriate and in accordance with their national traditions and practice, protection for legal persons where they suffer discrimination on grounds of the racial or ethnic origin of their members. (Council Directive 2000/43/EC)

Beside SHALL, one of the most common modals in legal discourse (Garzone 2001), WILL is indicated by the Keywords Tool in Wordsmith as a significant occurrence. The WILL percentage seems rather high especially when compared to the reference corpus (Table 4).

	WILL freq.	WILL %	SHALL freq.	SHALL %
Humanitarian (H)	153	0.19	1,031	1.28
Reference (E)	1,561	0.07	23,477	1.11

Table 4. The frequencies for *will* and *shall* in the two corpora.

As pointed out by Palmer (1987: 138), "*will* is used to express volition or willingness on the part of the subject. It is clearly 'subject-oriented' and dynamic". Together with the affectively connoted keywords, and with the impersonal deontic forms, this feature may contribute to characterise the legal documents dealing with humanitarian policies as 'personal' or subject-oriented:

(19) The European Union will closely follow developments in Zimbabwe and would once again like to emphasise its desire to pursue the dialogue with Zimbabwe. (Council Decision 2001/179/EC)

(20) The Community Action Programme will continue to help to develop cooperation in this field even more effectively. (Council Decision 1999/847/EC)

(21) In the implementation of the programme, the Community will seek, in accordance with the Treaty, to eliminate inequalities and promote equality between men and women. (Council Decision of 27 November 2000)

3. Humanitarian legal discourse inside and outside the Community

Language is used differently depending on the status of the humanitarian assistance recipients: whether belonging to the Member States or to third countries. The very wording used to encode this distinction is significant: in fact, while the term *Community* and even to some extent the collocation *Member States* denote inclusion and also connote a host of related positive feelings such as communion, companionship, union and solidarity, the terms *third countries* and *non-Eu nationals* both point to exclusion and refer to separate socio-cultural identities. By definition, according to Council Regulation No 1257/96 of 20th June 1996, humanitarian help is exclusively directed at third countries either with a preventive aim or to provide help to the victims of natural or man-made disasters and structural crises. The aid policy is then planned, encoded and realized differently depending on where it takes place. The very opposition between non-EU nationals and Union citizens on grounds of their social rights, testifies to the EU's dilemma: the idealistic objective of acting as a beacon of equality and justice for all, on the one hand, and, on the other, the realistic fear of compromising the delicate balance between the social forces, including the growing group of the migrants inside the Community (Balibar 2001; Guiraudon 1998).

However, despite the narrow scope of humanitarian aid according to the Eurolanguage definition, humanitarian assistance does also cover Member States as several EU legal documents set up action programmes to be implemented within the Community in case of emergencies mostly in the field of civil protection or to defend minorities from discrimination and potential crises. Moreover, some EU policies aimed at relieving third countries may significantly affect the Community itself as in the case of refugee emergencies, when Member States may agree "on an alert and emergency procedure for *burden-sharing* with regard to the admission and residence of displaced persons on a temporary basis" (Council Directive 2001/55/ EC, italics added).

3.1. Word connotations

The legal documents aimed at humanitarian assistance within the European Union (indicated as COM) have been compared to the larger corpus of humanitarian assistance documents concerning third countries (named H3), in order to verify whether EU humanitarian assistance programmes may be presented differently according to the recipients and, more specifically, whether any bias can be traced in the language encoding of such policies. The two corpora's wordlists have been compared to find the keywords in the documents concerning aid in the European Union. Rather surprisingly, beside words such as *protection* and *solidarity*, the semantic field of conflict also seems well represented with words such as *racial*, *discrimination*, and *violence*. This means that words associated with prejudice and aggression are more representative of the Community-based humanitarian assistance than of the humanitarian policies directed at third countries, which can indeed appear surprising given the notoriously unstable socio-political situations in many non-EU countries favoured by Community aid policies. The large occurrence of such 'loaded' words conveys the contradictory nature of assistance within the EU, subject to a series of precautionary measures (cf. Guiraudon 1998):

(22) Member States should also provide, where appropriate and in accordance with their national traditions and practice, protection for legal persons where they suffer discrimination on grounds of the racial or ethnic origin of their members. [...] (18) In very limited circumstances, a difference of treatment may be justified where a characteristic related to racial or ethnic origin constitutes a genuine and determining occupational requirement, when the objective is legitimate and the requirement is proportionate. (Council Directive 2000/43/ EC)

The frequency wordlist also shows that humanitarian aid is defined differently depending on the target: in the community-driven humanitarian policies it is preferably referred to as *protection*, while in the third-country relieving programmes it is mostly identified as *assistance* (Table 5).

	PROTECTION freq.	%	ASSISTANCE freq.	%
COM	119	0.89	83	0.26
H3	27	0.06	246	0.50

Table 5. The frequencies for *protection* and *assistance* in the two sub-corpora.

This lexical differentiation unmistakably points to the diverse political and economic standing of the nations involved, the ones that offer and receive "shelter, defence, or preservation from harm, danger, or evil" in disasters under control and the others which receive "aid, support, relief" as their only means of salvation (*OED online*):

(23) The individual actions undertaken by the Community to implement the programme contribute to the *protection* of persons, environment and property in the event of natural and technological disasters, and a greater awareness of the interrelationship between human activities and nature, which in the future may make it possible to prevent many disasters, including floods. (1999/847/ EC: Council Decision)

(24) The Community *assistance* shall inter alia be for: (a) reconstruction, aid for the return of refugees and displaced persons, and stabilisation of the region; (b) the creation of an institutional and legislative framework to underpin democracy, the rule of law and human and minority rights, reconciliation and the consolidation of civil society, the independence of the media and the strengthening of legality and of measures to combat organised crime; (c) sustainable economic development and market-economy-orientated economic reform; (d) social development, with particular reference to poverty reduction, gender equality, education, teaching and training, and environmental rehabilitation. (Council Regulation (EC) No 2666/2000)

The European Community may appear to enact different strategic policies depending on the scope and recipients of the humanitarian policies, something which is in a way also conveyed by the collocational pattern 'Fortress Europe', a Eurojargon expression often used to mean "an attitude that wants to defend Europe from outside influences [...] and which often appears in discussions about asylum and immigration regulations", <http://europa.eu.int/abc/eurojargon/index_en.htm>. The Community can be conceptualised as an institutional subject responsible for a series of EU policies and regulations:

(25) The Community is determined to make a full contribution towards the goal of total elimination of anti-personnel landmines world-wide in the coming years.

(4) The Community and its Member States have provided the largest contribution to the wider international effort to overcome the tragedy of anti-personnel landmines. (Council Regulation (EC) No 1725/2001)

It can be also regarded as a physical space where a multitude of displaced persons and refugees can be offered 'temporary protection':

(26) 'mass influx' means arrival in the Community of a large number of displaced persons, who come from a specific country or geographical area, whether their arrival in the Community was spontaneous or aided, for example through an evacuation programme. (Council Decision 2001/792/EC)

It can be perceived as a status or quality as in the recurrent collocations such as *Community aid, Community action* etc., in which the adjectival function of *Community* can obscure its specific institutional meaning and liken it to any of the *community actions* successfully undertaken by charities or other well-meaning organizations:

(27) Community aid should be complementary to the efforts of the States concerned and be used to cover a share of the public expenditure committed to dealing with the damage caused by a major disaster. (Council Regulation No 2012/2002)

If the Community occurrences are grouped according to these lexicogrammatical distinctions, it becomes apparent that in the legal documents focusing on third country humanitarian help, the institutional role enacted by the European Community is much stronger and that the spatial conceptualisation of the EU is absent (Table 6).

	Agent %	Place %	Quality %	TOT %
COM	0.20	0.07	0.34	0.61
H3	0.41	0	0.38	0.79

Table 6. The roles and meanings of *Community* in the two sub-corpora.

However, even when the word has approximately the same frequency across the two corpora as in the case of the Community quality occurrences, the implicit ideological meanings may drastically differ depending on the context of occurrence. The highest lexical collocates associated with *Community* are *action* in the documents on the Community-based aid and *assistance* in those addressing disasters in third countries:

(28) A programme of *Community action* to fight violence towards children, young persons and women, is hereby adopted for the period 1 January 2000 to 31 December 2003. 2. This programme aims to contribute towards ensuring a high level of protection of physical and mental health by the protection of children, young persons an women against violence. (Decision No 293/2000/EC of the European Parliament and of the Council)

(29) *Community assistance* will be focused mainly on building up an institutional, legislative, economic and social framework directed at the values and models subscribed to by the European Union. (Council Regulation (EC) No 2666/2000)

If, as Firth pointed out, a word has to be judged by the company it keeps, the *Community programme* appears to be a neutral lexicalisation of the EU humanitarian actions; by contrast, the *Community assistance* collocation would unmistakably point to the subordinate status of the recipient countries, receiving aid but apparently unable to return the favour.

4. The 'measures' of assistance: a sample analysis

The linguistic analysis carried out in the two humanitarian sub-corpora has been narrowed down to two legal documents representative of the relief policies concerning Member States and third countries:

a) Council Directive 2001/55/EC of 20 July 2001 on minimum standards for giving temporary protection in the event of a mass influx of displaced persons and on measures promoting a balance of efforts between Member States in receiving such persons and bearing the consequences thereof,

b) Regulation (EC) No 2130/2001 of the European Parliament and of the Council of 29 October 2001 on operations to aid uprooted people in Asian and Latin American developing countries.

Although they differ in text-type – one being a Directive, the other being a Regulation – they are associated by a common theme, the aid to refugees either offered within the EU's borders or in their own territories. The genre differences, which concern the recipients and scope of the legal documents, have not been considered influential to the ends of the present analysis and have consequently been overlooked as extra-textual procedural features (Caliendo 2004: 245-246). It is worth noting that the refugee emergency is confronted differently in the two documents: through the EU Member States' hospitality in one case, and through displaced aid in Asian and Latin American developing countries in the second. This logistic difference, which obviously entails a varying degree of involvement on the part of the European Union, appears to mark parallel but antithetic relief policies either based on "minimum standards for […] temporary protection" (Council Directive 2001/55/EC) or on "effective, flexible and expeditious procedures […] for aid operations" (Regulation (EC) No 2130/ 2001): in fact, if the humanitarian aid may affect the orderly functioning of the Member States, the focus is on the self-defensive measures of *burden-sharing* (cf. Collins 2001: 442), whereas an economically and politically rewarding wide-scope humanitarian policy seems more likely to favour the intervention of the international Community, whatever its declared or concealed intent (Balibar 2001; Chomsky 1999). The very lexical encoding of the titles suggests the discrepancy between the Community's internal and external aid through pairs of opposites:

- *temporary protection* vs. *aid,*
- *measures* vs. *operations,*
- *displaced persons* vs. *uprooted people.*

As compared with the subdued, cautious words used to refer to the EU's intervention within its own borders, the terms denoting humanitarian help outside the Community seem to carry a strong dynamic connotation, vividly suggesting both the refugees' severe predicament and the EU's swift response. Also the keywords in the body of the documents reinforce these oppositions as *protection* and *measures,* contrasted with *aid* and *operations,* evoke a pre-emptive rather than proactive response (Table 7).

	PROTECTION freq.	PROTECTION %	AID freq.	AID %
Directive	107	1.83	2	0.03
Regulation	1	0.03	19	0.64

Table 7. The frequencies for *protection* and *aid* in the two documents.

Not only are the refugees in the Community offered protection rather than aid, but also such protection is inevitably temporary as the balance of efforts by the Member States seems bound to come to an end: the very list of concordances shows that the adjective *temporary* pre-modifies protection in 92 out of 107 strings, to the point that *temporary protection* may be regarded as a fixed expression in the document. The Community appears to be more 'present' in the development policies beyond its borders, at least from a quantitative survey of the word occurrences in the Regulation (Table 8); and the very collocates – from *financing* to *assistance* and *support* – mostly point to the philanthropic aspect of the Community policies.

	COMMUNITY freq.	%	MEMBER STATE/S freq.	%
Directive	13	0.22	132	2.26
Regulation	28	0.95	6	0.20

Table 8. The frequencies for *Community* and *Member State/s.*

By contrast, in the Directive, the European Community mostly acts as the sum of its Member States since the humanitarian assistance provided by each Member must be carefully checked and weighed to guarantee the 'balance of efforts'. It seems also worth noting that in nearly half the occurrences the Member States are the subject of the action (61 out of 132 strings) in charge of "provid[ing] necessary medical or other assistance" in accordance with Community law:

(30) *The Member States shall* receive persons who are eligible for temporary protection in a spirit of Community solidarity [...].

(31) *A Member State shall* communicate requests for transfers to the other Member States [...].

(32) *The Member States shall* make provision for persons enjoying temporary protection to receive necessary assistance [...].

(33) *The Member States shall* lay down the rules on penalties applicable to infringements of the national provisions […].

(34) *Member States shall* register the personal data referred to in Annex II, point (a), with respect to the person […].

(35) *Member States shall* apply temporary protection with due respect for human rights and fundamental freedom […].

(36) *The Member States shall* send the Commission all the information that is appropriate for drawing up this report […].

The remarkable emphasis laid on the Member States' duties in the Directive is to be contrasted with the impersonal strain of moral obligations laid down in the Regulation, mainly expressed through nominalization and passive voice and virtually minimising the European Community's active role during emergencies:

(37) An integrated, consistent and effective strategy must be devised for Community action in respect of humanitarian aid […].

(38) Aid must be coordinated at Community level and with other donors, non-governmental organizations (NGOs) and United Nations bodies […].

(39) This programme must provide for the basic needs of those persons from the time a humanitarian emergency subsides […].

(40) The effectiveness and consistency of Community, national and international prevention and intervention mechanisms should be ensured […].

(41) The measures necessary for the implementation of this Regulation should be adopted in accordance with Council Decision 1999/468/EC […].

(42) Effective, flexible and expeditious procedures need to be guaranteed for aid operations in this sphere […].

(43) It is particularly necessary to integrate aid for uprooted people and development cooperation […].

Although deontic modals present roughly the same frequencies across the two documents (Table 9), the ideological connotations drastically differ as do the very subjects bound by humanitarian obligations: Member States in the Directive and the somehow indefinite Community action in the Regulation. Despite the relationship of inclusion, these institutional labels are not identical as *Member States* point to the variety of countries and suggest a sort of confederacy, while *Community* highlights the sense of union, somehow concealing the single individualities and responsibilities of its components.

	SHALL %	SHOULD %	MUST %
Directive	1.68	0.31	0.09
Regulation	1.43	0.31	0.17

Table 9. Deontic modality in the two EU documents.

If the aid recipients are explicit in both documents, the senders may appear on purpose blurred in the Regulation as the assistance outside the Union may be felt less urgent and consequential than inside-Community help. Thus, the EU's concern with third-country humanitarian emergencies, conveyed by the affectively connoted keywords such as *aid*, *operations* and *Community* as well as by the prominence of deontic modals, appears perplexingly ambiguous in the light of deleted agency, especially if contrasted with the explicit acknowledgement of the Member States' duties in domestic emergencies put forward in the Directive.

5. Concluding remarks

The controversial concepts of European apartheid and neo-colonialism within the EU policies framed by Balibar (2001) as well as the theory of imperialism-grounded humanitarian assistance elaborated by Chomsky (1999) and Boltanski (1999) can be used to explain the differences in language encoding in the legal documents related to aid either within the EU or directed at third countries. The politics of pity connected with humanitarian help is based on political and economic asymmetry, geographical and cultural distance and on benevolent if not patronising concessions. As pointed out by Boltanski (1999: 189),

> In the case of the humanitarian movement, however, the mutual otherness of those who offer their aid and those who receive it is accentuated by their membership of different states: donors in rich democracies and recipients in poor countries with authoritarian regimes.

By contrast, the politics of justice that can only take place when all the parties are equal, centres on the constructive and empowering forces of dialectics, conflict and negotiation, which the prosperous states in the European Union may still be wary of activating.

References

Balibar, Etienne 2001. *Nous citoyens d'Europe?* Paris: La Découverte.

Bhatia, Vijay K. 1993. *Analysing Genre*. London: Longman.

Boltanski, Luc 1999. *Distant Suffering. Morality, Media and Politics.* Cambridge: Cambridge University Press.

Caliendo, Giuditta 2004. Modality and Communicative Interaction in EU Law. In Candlin, Christopher N. / Gotti, Maurizio (eds) *Intercultural Aspects of Specialized Communication.* Bern: Peter Lang, 241-259.

Chomsky, Noam 1999. *The New Military Humanism. Lessons from Kosovo.* London: Pluto.

Collins, C.D.E ^{2}2001. Social Policies. In El-Agraa, Ali (ed.) *The European Union. Economics and Policies.* Pearson: Harlow, 414-445.

Garzone, Giuliana 2001. Deontic Modality and Performativity in English Legal Texts. In Gotti, Maurizio / Dossena, Marina (eds) *Modality in Specialized Texts.* Bern: Peter Lang, 153-163.

Gibbons, John 2003. *Forensic Linguistics. An Introduction to Language in the Justice System.* Oxford: Blackwell.

Guiraudon, Virginie 1998. Multiculturalisme et droit des etrangers dans l'Union Européenne. In Kastoryano, Riva (ed.) *Quelle identité pour quelle Europe? Le multiculturalisme à l'épreuve.* Paris: Presses de Sciences Po, 143-166.

Oxford English Dictionary online. <http://dictionary.oed.com>.

Palmer. F. R. [1]1985. [2]1987. *The English Verb*. London: Longman.
Scott, Mike 1998. *Wordsmith Tools 3.0*. Oxford: OUP.
Smith, Michael [2]2001. The EU as an International Actor. In Richardson, Jeremy (ed.) *European Union. Power and Policy-making*. London: Routledge, 283-301.
Tessuto, Girolamo 2004. Language and Meaning in European Discourse of Human Rights. *Textus*, 17/1, 197-216.

Appendix

EU Secondary Legislation Humanitarian Documents

1. 1999/190/CFSP: Council Decision of 9 March 1999 adopted on the basis of Article J.4(2) of the Treaty on European Union on the implementation of the joint action concerning a contribution by the European Union to the re-establishment of a viable police force in Albania.
2. 1999/282/EC: Council Decision of 22 April 1999 providing macro-financial assistance to Albania.
3. 1999/320/CFSP: Council Decision of 10 May 1999 adopted by the Council on the basis of Article 14 of the Treaty on European Union, on a European Union contribution to the collection and destruction of weapons in Albania.
4. 1999/730/CFSP: Council Decision of 15 November 1999 implementing Joint Action 1999/34/CFSP with a view to a European Union contribution to combating the destabilising accumulation and spread of small arms and light weapons in Cambodia.
5. 1999/733/EC: Council Decision of 8 November 1999 providing supplementary macro-financial assistance to the former Yugoslav Republic of Macedonia.
6. 1999/786/EC: Council Decision of 29 November 1999 granting a Community guarantee to the European Investment Bank (EIB) against losses under loans for projects for the reconstruction of the earthquake-stricken areas of Turkey.
7. 1999/847/EC: Council Decision of 9 December 1999 establishing a Community action programme in the field of civil protection.
8. 2000/140/EC: Council Decision of 14 February 2000 providing exceptional Community financial assistance to Kosovo.
9. Decision No 293/2000/EC of the European Parliament and of the Council of 24 January 2000 adopting a programme of Community action (the Daphne programme) (2000 to 2003) on preventive measures to fight violence against children, young persons and women.
10. 2000/354/CFSP: Council Decision of 22 May 2000 setting up a Committee for civilian aspects of crisis management.

11. 2000/355/EC: Council Decision of 22 May 2000 providing exceptional financial assistance for Montenegro.
12. 2000/421/EC: Council Decision of 13 June 2000 on the conclusion, on behalf of the European Community, of the Food Aid Convention 1999.
13. 2000/596/EC: Council Decision of 28 September 2000 establishing a European Refugee Fund.
14. 2000/750/EC: Council Decision of 27 November 2000 establishing a Community action programme to combat discrimination (2001 to 2006).
15. 2000/786/EC: Council Decision of 27 November 2000 on the grant of funds to the Hellenic Republic in order to compensate partially for the interest paid on European Investment Bank loans for the reconstruction of the region which was devastated by the earthquake of September 1999.
16. 2001/79/CFSP: Council Decision of 22 January 2001 setting up the Military Committee of the European Union.
17. 2001/131/EC: Council Decision of 29 January 2001 concluding the consultation procedure with Haiti under Article 96 of the ACP-EC Partnership Agreement.
18. 2001/179/EC: Council Decision of 26 February 2001 setting the terms for financial support to Guinea-Bissau in the fisheries sector.
19. 2001/511/EC: Council Decision of 27 June 2001 on further exceptional financial assistance to Kosovo.
20. 2001/792/EC, Euratom: Council Decision of 23 October 2001 establishing a Community mechanism to facilitate reinforced cooperation in civil protection assistance interventions.
21. 2001/824/EC, Euratom: Council Decision of 16 November 2001 on a further contribution of the European Community to the European Bank for Reconstruction and Development for the Chernobyl Shelter Fund.
22. Decision No 36/2002/EC of the European Parliament and of the Council of 19 December 2001 concerning the Community contribution to the Global Fund to fight HIV/AIDS, tuberculosis and malaria.
23. 2002/148/EC: Council Decision of 18 February 2002 concluding consultations with Zimbabwe under Article 96 of the ACP-EC Partnership Agreement.
24. 2002/274/EC: Council Decision of 25 March 2002 concluding consultations with Liberia under Articles 96 and 97 of the ACP-EC Partnership Agreement.
25. 2002/463/EC: Council Decision of 13 June 2002 adopting an action programme for administrative cooperation in the fields of external borders, visas, asylum and immigration (ARGO programme).
26. 2002/647/EC: Council Decision of 12 July 2002 adopting the rules of procedure of the European Development Fund Committee.
27. 2002/842/CFSP: Council Decision of 21 October 2002 concerning the implementation of Joint Action 2002/589/CFSP with a view to a European Union contribution to combating the destabilising accumulation and spread of small arms and light weapons in South East Europe.
28. 2002/882/EC: Council Decision of 5 November 2002 providing further macro-financial assistance to the Federal Republic of Yugoslavia. Official Journal L 308, 09/11/2002 P. 0025 – 0027.

29. 2002/883/EC: Council Decision of 5 November 2002 providing further macro-financial assistance to Bosnia and Herzegovina.
30. 2002/1010/EC: Decision of the European Parliament and of the Council of 21 November 2002 on the mobilisation of the EU Solidarity Fund according to point 3 of the Interinstitutional Agreement of 7 November 2002 between the European Parliament, the Council and the Commission on the financing of the European Union Solidarity Fund, supplementing the Interinstitutional Agreement of 6 May 1999 on budgetary discipline and improvement of the budgetary procedure.
31. Council Directive 2000/43/EC of 29 June 2000 implementing the principle of equal treatment between persons irrespective of racial or ethnic origin.
32. Council Directive 2001/55/EC of 20 July 2001 on minimum standards for giving temporary protection in the event of a mass influx of displaced persons and on measures promoting a balance of efforts between Member States in receiving such persons and bearing the consequences thereof.
33. Council Regulation (EC, Euratom) No 99/2000 of 29 December 1999 concerning the provision of assistance to the partner States in Eastern Europe and Central Asia.
34. Council Regulation (EC) No 975/1999 of 29 April 1999 laying down the requirements for the implementation of development cooperation operations which contribute to the general objective of developing and consolidating democracy and the rule of law and to that of respecting human rights and fundamental freedoms.
35. Council Regulation (EC) No 976/1999 of 29 April 1999 laying down the requirements for the implementation of Community operations, other than those of development cooperation, which, within the framework of Community cooperation policy, contribute to the general objective of developing and consolidating democracy and the rule of law and to that of respecting human rights and fundamental freedoms in third countries.
36. Council Regulation (EC) No 2666/2000 of 5 December 2000 on assistance for Albania, Bosnia and Herzegovina, Croatia, the Federal Republic of Yugoslavia and the Former Yugoslav Republic of Macedonia, repealing Regulation (EC) No 1628/96 and amending Regulations (EEC) No 3906/89 and (EEC) No 1360/90 and Decisions 97/256/EC and 1999/311/EC.
37. Council Regulation (EC) No 2667/2000 of 5 December 2000 on the European Agency for Reconstruction.
38. Regulation (EC) No 1724/2001 of the European Parliament and of the Council of 23 July 2001 concerning action against anti-personnel landmines in developing countries.
39. Council Regulation (EC) No 1725/2001 of 23 July 2001 concerning action against anti-personnel landmines in third countries other than developing countries.
40. Regulation (EC) No 2130/2001 of the European Parliament and of the Council of 29 October 2001 on operations to aid uprooted people in Asian and Latin American developing countries.
41. Council Regulation (EC) No 2012/2002 of 11 November 2002 establishing the European Union Solidarity Fund.

MARCHILIA VOLINI

Phrasemes in EU Framework Decisions*

1. Introduction

This chapter provides a contrastive semantic and lexicographic analysis of phrasemes in the field of EU Framework Decisions from 1st July 1999 to 31st December 2002. Framework Decisions represent a key legal instrument introduced by the Amsterdam treaty to approximate the laws and regulations of the Member States in order to improve cooperation under the third pillar (Police and Judicial Cooperation in Criminal Matters). Proposals are made on the initiative of the Commission or of a Member State and they have to be adopted unanimously. They are binding on the Member States as for the result to be achieved, but leave the choice of form and methods to be used to national authorities. Therefore, from a linguistic point of view they have a flexible wording that can be adjusted to national contexts and different legal systems and they are a cross-border instrument of communication that mediates between Community law and each national legal system.

After an introductory definition and classification of phrasemes, this chapter analyses their occurrence in Framework Decisions in contrast with the rest of secondary legislation, and finally focuses on the use and abuse of English phrasemes in the transfer of their meaning or connotation to a different language, namely Italian.

* This research is part of a larger national research project on interculturality in Language for Specific Purposes coordinated by Prof. Maurizio Gotti.

2. Definition and classification of phrasemes

Over the past twenty years, phraseology has become a major field of investigation for many lexicographers. This is due to different factors: (1) "the existence of so many odd coming-together-of-words" (Palmer 1933: 13) which are technically called 'collocations' – ready-made, memorised word groups in which one word has meaning only in combination with another word; (2) the enormous development of corpus linguistics which has enabled linguists to inquire and analyse lexical patterns of written and spoken language by using computational devices; (3) a deeper awareness that language is a crucial mechanism contributing to the formation and reinforcement of cultural identity.

Before analysing the phenomenon of phrasemes, it is important to clarify the concept of collocation. Sinclair (2001: 16) wrote that if a few words appear "more frequently together than chance would predict, they are collocations" and before him, J.R. Firth (1951) defined collocations as "lexical solidarities". Nowadays the availability of large corpora, together with powerful statistical software tools, which are increasingly quick, flexible and precise, give this statement a scientific value, by showing that words in a text do not occur at random and that collocations are a statistically significant phenomenon. Van Roey's (1990) definition of collocation as "the linguistic phenomenon whereby a given vocabulary item prefers the company of another item rather than its synonyms because of constraints which are not at the level of syntax or conceptual meaning but at the level of usage" seems more exhaustive. However, even this is still unsatisfactory since it says nothing about the number of elements involved, the degree of frequency of occurrence and the classes of words which can be combined. Collocations belong to the macro-category of Set Combinations established by Zgusta (1971), i.e. combinations whose single constituent elements cannot be exchanged with or substituted by others and to which nothing can be added.

Nevertheless, we cannot neglect the relations existing between words and realia, the connotation of the words used and their range of application i.e. when each word is used in a certain context. Therefore when we have a two-word set combination whose "meaning […] includes 'intact' the meaning of one of its constituents, but the other component of its meaning is expressed by an element contingent on the first" (Mel'čuk 2001: 34), we face a different phraseological phenomenon. The latter is so complex that in the past many linguists have given it different names: 'compound lexical item' (Halliday 1971), 'multiword lexical unit' (Zgusta 1971), 'phraseological unit' (Gläser 1986), 'phrasal lexeme' (Moon 1998), 'compound lexical word' (Coates 1999), or 'multiword unit' (Fontenelle 2001). Recent phraseology studies use the term 'phraseme' (Mel'čuk 2001, Montero-Martinez *et al.* 2002, Meyer/Mackintosh 1996, Römer 2003). As shown in Figure 1, phrasemes are within the category of set combinations, suspended between the status of free combinations and set phrases. What makes them different from collocations is their higher degree of "setness". As a consequence, phrasemes can be defined as set combinations that speakers learn to use as single complete units because they underwent a complete process of 'crystallization'.

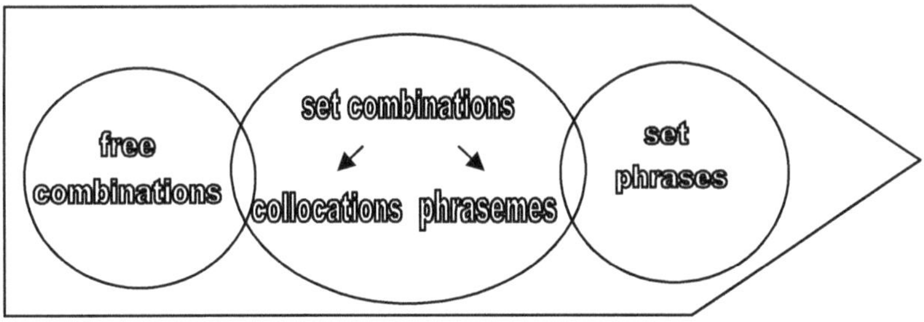

Figure 1. Set Combinations: collocations and phrasemes.

An example of phraseme is the expression *enter into force* which cannot be changed into *enter into action*, nor into *enter into immediate force* without severely compromising the meaning of the expression and affecting its acceptability as a phraseme. The combination of the words *enter* + *into* + *force*, therefore, proves to have a lexical meaning only as a whole. The programme WordSmith Tools 3.0 was used to extract word clusters having a significant co-occurrence in the selected texts by counting the span of words which appeared to the left or to the right of the selected keyword. In fact, two words are considered to co-occur if in a single sentence they are separated by fewer than five words. But the actual identification of phrasemes in EU Framework Decisions was particularly difficult because not all the strings of words are suitable for this study; most of them cannot be considered phrasemes but simple free combinations of words. In addition, despite any scientific method, phrasemes are by no means as fixed as some dictionary or inventories appear to suggest. Indeed, it is very difficult to establish a boundary since they are marked by different degrees of 'setness' and the categories often overlap. For these reasons the study of phrasemes still represents a major challenge in the field of phraseology. The basic criteria used to identify phrasemes have been set out by Zgusta (1971: 119-163):

1) *Substitution is impossible.* The 'Commutation test' is probably the most important criterion of a multiword lexical unit,
2) A phraseme *doesn't need to be continuous*, provided its meaning doesn't change,
3) Different semantic phenomena are criterial or at least indicative; therefore, the meaning of the whole *combination is not fully derivable from that of the single parts*,
4) A constituent part of a set combination of words may be severely or exclusively *restricted to it*,
5) It may have a *one-word synonym*,
6) It may have *the same status* as other multiword lexical units or single words,
7) It may have a *one-word equivalent in a foreign language*,
8) It may have *special formal and grammatical properties*. It would be a mistake to assume that set combinations must be continuous,
9) It could have the same *syntactic function as a morphologically simpler unit* which frequently coincides with the word.

From this point of view, the cluster *joint investigation team* is not a set combination because the terms can be substituted by other alternatives or eliminated without compromising the general understanding of the sentence. Instead *take part in* is a phraseme, because the 'Commutation test' shows that it is impossible to use a different particle with *take part* (*take part on* or *take part up*, for instance) without totally compromising the meaning. In addition, it would be a mistake to assume that set combinations must be contiguous; in fact the expression '*take* a major *part in*', is absolutely correct. Moreover, *take part in* has a one-word equivalent in a foreign language i.e. *partecipare a* in Italian, *participer à* in French. Finally, in English, this complex syntactic unit has a morphologically simpler unit bearing the same meaning i.e. *participate in.*

3. Analysis of phrasemes in EU Framework Decisions

The identification of phrasemes in Framework Decisions is rather complex because of problems related to their stability, which is linked to their frequency of occurrence, and to the cultural background they refer to. The English and the Italian Corpora examined in this research consist of 24,798 words for each language; the analysis of the English corpus shows evidence of the instability of some of the forms of phrasal lexemes. Some common phrasemes differ in type and in degree of stability, although they show some sort of regularity or what could be called 'predictability'. Because of the lexicalisation process, it takes some time before phrasemes can be considered as terminographic formalizations of a conceptual structure. For instance, phrasemes with *non* like *non-cash*, *non-criminal*, *non-execution* and *non-governmental* can be considered as terminology-in-the-making, since they become lexical units only when they are permanently linked to a concept. As a matter of fact, almost 30% of the phrasemes analysed have not yet frozen into a fixed canonical form probably because of their low frequency occurrence and their being virtually 'new'. This is especially true for phrasemes composed of adjective or noun plus noun such as *legal person* ('persona giuridica') and *requested person* ('persona ricercata'). These two can be considered phrasemes as the result of the lexicalisation of free phrases which enter into legal language to designate a specific concept. The frequency of occurrence of the phraseme *legal person* in Framework Decisions has been compared with the rest of EU secondary legislation and the resulting percentage is much higher in Framework Decisions: 0.29%. It was also noticed that out of 179 cases in Directives, Regulations and Decisions, 78 occurrences are in opposition to another phraseme: *natural person*. *Requested person*, instead turned out to be a phraseme only in English because in the Italian version of the corpus merely 16 occurrences of *persona ricercata* were found, while the remaining 26 occurrences in Framework Decisions are translated by a periphrasis. Table 1 shows the number of occurrences of Noun or Adjective + Noun Phrasemes.

Phraseme	*Frequency out of 24,798 words*	*Percentage in Framework Decisions*	*Frequency out of 2,078,552 words*	*Percentage in Directives, Regulations and Decisions*
In full awareness of	3	0.02%	0	0
A legal person/s	74	0.29%	179	0.008%
A requested person	42	0.16%	41	0.002%

Table 1. Occurrences of Noun or Adjective + Noun Phrasemes.

By contrast, phrasemes with a grammatical or operational function tend to be relatively stable because they are already lexicalised in everyday language and have been imported into legal language. Table 2 presents some examples of Phrasemes with a grammatical or operational function found in Framework Decisions as compared to other EU legal documents together with their frequency of occurrence.

Phraseme	*Frequency out of 24,798 words*	*Percentage in Frame-work Decisions*	*Frequency out of 2,078,552 words*	*Percentage in Directives, Regulations and Decisions*
In order to	22	0.08%	2.053	0.09%
In so far as	10	0.04 %	157	0.007%
As far as	7	0.02%	193	0.009%
In accordance with	56	0.22%	5.361	0.25%
Without prejudice to	9	0.03 %	850	0.04%

Table 2. Phrasemes with a grammatical or operational function.

Phrasemes are governed by rules that are partly individual, as determined by single speakers, and partly universal, because they are linked with a common background. The EU is a multicultural community of 25 states with different backgrounds, consequently phrasemes in EU Framework Decisions express values and concepts that cannot express a single culture but are representative of EU legal culture. Therefore, lexical patterns can betray cultural patterns, as in the case of the phraseme *Fundamental Freedoms* which in American culture represents a whole set of freedoms being bound to the First Amendment of the U.S. Constitution. which refers to the Freedom of Speech, Press, Religion, Petition and Assembly. Conversely, in the EU, this same phraseme involves the whole set of liberties guaranteed under the founding Treaties i.e. "the freedom of movement for workers, freedom of establishment, freedom to provide services, free movement of goods and freedom of capital movements and [...] freedom of competition" (*The ABC of Community Law)*. In light of this, phrasemes are the materialisation of various conceptual relations that are created between lexical units in a specific domain in a given culture.

4. The use and abuse of English phrasemes in Italian

Legal language in general is characterised by technical terminology, precision and legal background. Therefore, in EU law the translation of all the legislation in different languages can create some confusion. The phraseme *the commission of*, for instance, which commonly refers to "an official group of people who have been given responsibility to control sth or to find out about sth" or to "an amount of money that is to be paid to sb for selling goods and which increases with the amount of goods that are sold", according to the definitions given in the *Oxford English Dictionary*, in a legal context acquires a specific connotation if it is accompanied by the words *offence* or *infringement*, e.g. "to decide whether the victim may make a statement immediately after the commission of an offence" or "the commission of the infringements referred to in Article 1(1)". Moreover, it is interesting to notice that, in the Italian version of the corpus taken into consideration, the occurrences in the source text were not directly translated with "la commissione del crimine"[1] but were rendered in many different ways, as shown in Table 3.

1 As suggested in Picchi's (2003) dictionary.

Framework Decision	*Source text*	*Target text*
32000F0383	Article 8 – as well as for involvement as accessories or instigators in such offences or *the* attempted *commission of the offences* referred to…	Articolo 8 – nonché essere dichiarate complici o istigatori di tali reati o responsabili *del tentativo di commettere i reati* di cui …
32001F0220	Article 11 – its authorities should, in particular, be in a position: - to be able to decide whether the victim may make a statement immediately after *the commission of an offence*, …	Articolo 11 – dette autorità devono essere in grado, in particolare: - di poter decidere sulla possibilità di raccogliere la deposizione della vittima subito dopo *che è stato commesso il reato*,
32001F0413	Article 4 – instruments, articles, computer programmes and any other means peculiarly adapted for *the commission of* any of *the offences*.	Articolo 4 – strumenti, articoli, programmi di computer e altri mezzi appositamente allestiti per *la perpetrazione degli illeciti* …
32002F0475	Article 2 - "Structured group" shall mean a group that is not randomly formed for *the* immediate *commission of an offence* …	Articolo 2 – Il termine "associazione strutturata" designa un'associazione che non si è costituita fortuitamente per *la commissione* estemporanea *di un reato* ...
32002F0946	Article 2 – each Member State shall take the necessary measures to ensure that a legal person can be held liable where the lack of supervision or control by a person referred to in paragraph 1 has made possible *the commission of the infringements* referred to …	Articolo 2 – ciascuno Stato membro adotta le misure necessarie per garantire che le persone giuridiche possano essere dichiarate responsabili quando la carenza di sorveglianza o controllo da parte del soggetto di cui al paragrafo 1 abbia reso possibile *la perpetuazione degli illeciti* di cui …

Table 3. Translations of the phraseme *the commission of* into Italian.

On the other hand, from the analysis of Framework Decisions in Italian, it emerged that the calque of this English phraseme i.e. *la commissione di* also exists in Italian, but it is used where in English there is the passive voice, e.g. "il divieto di esercitare direttamente o per interposta persona l'attività professionale esercitata in occasione *della commissione del reato*" (32002F0946, article 1) translates "a prohibition on practising directly or through an intermediary the occupational activity in the exercise of which *the offence was committed*". In this example, the use of the nominalization in Italian is a good device to make the sentence structure simpler and to take the distance from the event, while the same function in English requires the use of the passive.

At times, in the translation from English into Italian there can be 'cross-cultural deafness' i.e. a barrier that could create serious problems in the transposition of EU secondary legislation into the different Member States' languages. In legal English the use of expressions like *custodial sentence* or *detention order* referring to the concept of 'going to prison' is very widespread, and in Italian they have an exact equivalent: *condanna a pena detentiva* and *ordine di arresto* respectively (Picchi 2003). However, EU jargon also introduced the phraseme *deprivation of liberty*, which sounds more 'politically correct'.

What is, however, extremely striking is the fact that the Italian version made a calque of this phraseme either from the English "penalties including the deprivation of liberty" or from the French "peines privatives de la liberté" and is overused. As a matter of fact *pene o misure di sicurezza 'privative della libertà'* occurs 0.12% in the Italian texts against 0.02% in the English texts. The tendency to overuse this calque in the Italian corpus is clearly illustrated in Figure 2 where the diagram shows how the calque *Pene privative della libertà* in Italian is translated into English by different formulas: 'deprivation of liberty' in 19% of the instances, 'custodial sentence' in another 37%, and 'terms of imprisonment' in the remaining 3%; while *misure di sicurezza privative della libertà* is translated in 41% of the cases by 'detention order'.

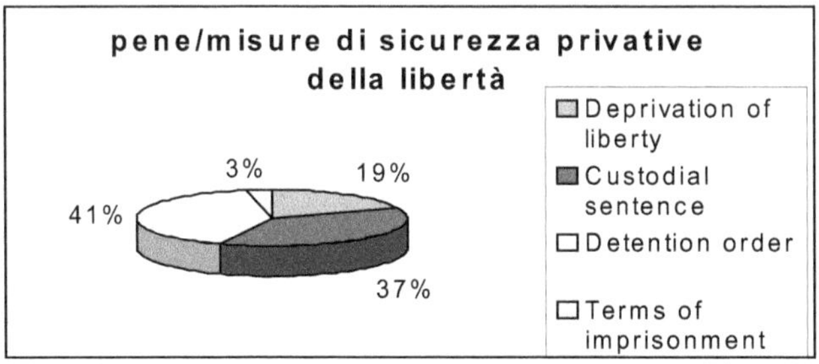

Figure 2. Use of *Pene/misure di sicurezza privative della libertà* in the Italian corpus.

Even if the concept of 'repeatability' or rather of 'frequency of co-occurrence' is welcome in the formation of new phrasemes, and the common usage of a certain phraseme gives it a higher chance of institutionalisation, the abuse of the same expression results in an evident phenomenon of loss in the translation which flattens the style of the text and makes it repetitive and redundant.

5. Conclusions

In this chapter a linguistically-oriented approach to concept analysis was followed, whereby terminological phrasemes are seen as potential indicators of conceptual meaning. In particular, the importance of concept identification in the interpretation of phrasemes in a legal context has been underlined. The innovative remark emerging from this research study is that, although phrasemes provide important conceptual footholds for terminologists in the field of law, they might also be their point of weakness. Indeed, it is vital that phrasemes are treated coherently throughout EU legislation in order to avoid misinterpretations or overgeneralization in the cross-cultural transposition of EU legislation into the legal systems of the different Member States.

References

Beccaria, Gian Luigi 1994. *Dizionario di Linguistica.* Torino: Einaudi.

Biber, Douglas / Conrad, Susan / Reppen, Randi 2000. *Corpus Linguistics: Investigating Language Structure and Use.* Cambridge: Cambridge University Press.

Bolognesi, Giancarlo 1987. Linguistica e Filologia. In Bolognesi/Pisani (eds), 13-36.

Bolognesi Giancarlo / Pisani, Vittore (eds) 1987. *Linguistica e filologia: atti del VII convegno internazionale di linguisti, Milano, 12-14 September 1984*. Brescia: Paideia.

Coates, Richard 1999. *Word Structure*. London: Routledge.

Cowie, Anthony P. 1999. *English Dictionaries for Foreign Learners: A History*. New York: Oxford University Press.

Cowie, Anthony P. (ed.) 2001. *Phraseology: Theory, Analysis, and Applications*. Oxford: Oxford University Press.

De Franchis, Francesco 1984. *Dizionario Giuridico*. Milano: Giuffré.

Firth, John Rupert 1951. Modes of Meaning. In *Papers in Linguistics 1934-51*. London: Oxford University Press.

Fontenelle, Thierry 2001. Conclusion. In Cowie (ed.), chapter 9.

Gläser, Rosemarie 1986. *Phraseologie der englischen Sprache*. Tübingen: Max Niemeyer.

Klajn, Ivan 1972. *Influssi Inglesi nella Lingua Italiana*. Firenze: Leo S. Olschki.

Longman Dictionary of Contemporary English 2003. London: Longman.

Martinet, André 1972. *La Linguistica – Guida alfabetica*. Milano: Rizzoli.

Martinet, André 1967. *Elementi di Linguistica Generale*. Bari: Laterza.

McEnery, Tony / Wilson, Andrew ²2001. *Corpus Linguistics*. Edinburgh: Edinburgh University Press.

Montero Martínez, Silvia 2003. Estructuración conceptual y formalización terminográfica de frasemas en el subdominio de la oncología. *Estudios de Lingüística Española*. Universidad de Valladolid, Volume 19.

Moon, Rosamund 1998. *Fixed Expressions and Idioms in English: A Corpus-based Approach*. Oxford: Clarendon Press.

Morani, Moreno 1987. *Linguistica, Filologia e Traduzioni*. In Bolognesi/Pisani (eds), 397-403.

Oxford Advanced Learner's Dictionary of Current English 2000. Oxford: Oxford University Press.

Oxford English Dictionary 1989. Oxford: Oxford University Press.

Picchi, Fernando 2003. *Grande Dizionario di Inglese*. Milano: Hoepli.

Sinclair, John M. 1987. *Looking up: An account of the Cobuild Project in lexical computing*. London: Collins.

Sinclair, John M. 1991. *Corpus, Concordance, Collocation*. Oxford: Oxford University Press.

Thomas, Jenny / Michael Short 1996. *Using Corpora for Language Research*. London: Longman.

Zgusta, Ladislav 1971. *Manual Of Lexicography*. The Hague: Mouton, 119-163.

Lo Zingarelli 2004. Bologna: Zanichelli.

Internet Websites

<http://www.fi.muni.cz/gwc2004/proc/120.pdf>. *Language to Logic Translation with PhraseBank*, Adam Pease and Christiane Fellbaum, 2 Princeton University, Department of Psychology, Green Hall, Princeton, NJ 08544, 20 May 2004.

<http://www.benjamins.nl/cgi-bin/t_articles.cgi?bookid=TERM%203:1 &artid=10026323>. *Refining the terminographer's concept-analysis methods: How can phraseology help?* (article summary), in Terminology 3:1 (1996), Ingrid Meyer e Kristen Mackintosh, John Benjamins Publishing Company, 22 May 2004.

<http://www.benjamins.nl/cgi-bin/t_articles.cgi?bookid=TERM%208:2 &artid= 290021289>. *Terminological phrasemes in OntoTerm®: A new theoretical and practical approach* (article summary), in Terminology 8:2. 2002. (pp. 177–206), Silvia Montero-Martinez, Mercedes Garcia de Quesada e Pedro A. Fuertes Olivera, John Benjamins Publishing Company, 22 May 2004.

<http://www.personal.uni-jena.de/~xcr/IVP-Web/idioms-berlin.html>. *Grammaticalization and lexicalization processes of phrases with verbs*, Christine Römer (24.9. 2003), 18 May 2004.

<http://www.dirk-siepmann.de/Links/SpecialLanguage/Minutes1.htm>. *Special-purpose Language in Theory and Practice*, Ruhr-Universität Bochum / Englisches Seminar, 24.10.02/31.10.02 Session 1, Siepmann, 22 May 2004.

<http://citeseer.ist.psu.edu/cache/papers/cs/14047/http:zSzzSzwww.csi.uottawa.cazSz~ingridzSzeurlex.pdf/meyer94phraseme.pdf>. *Phraseme Analysis and Concept Analysis: Exploring a Symbiotic Relationship in the Specialized Lexicon*, Ingrid Meyer and

Kristen Mackintosh, School of Translation and Interpretation, University of Ottawa, Canada K1N 6N5, 23 May 2004.

<http://www.benjamins.nl/jbp/additional/term.gloss.pdf>. *Glossary of Terms used in Terminology*, Bruno De Besse', Blaise Nkwenti-Azeh and Juan C. Sager, 23 May 2004.

<http://europa.eu.int/eur-lex/accessible/en/about/abc/abc_06.html>. *The ABC of Community law, the Fundamental freedoms*, Klaus-Dieter Borchardt, 4 June 2004.

<http://europa.eu.int/scadplus/leg/en/cig/g4000d.htm#d1a>. *SCADplus: Glossario*, *decisione quadro*, 7 June 2004.

<http://europa.eu.int/scadplus/leg/it/cig/g4000p.htm#p>. *SCADplus : Glossario, Pilastri dell'unione Europea*, 7 June 2004.

<http://europa.eu.int/scadplus/leg/it/cig/g4000t.htm#t2>. *SCADplus : Glossario, Titolo VI del Trattato UE*, 7 June 2004.

<http://europa.eu.int/eurodicautom/Controller>. *Eurodicautom*, 7 June 2004.

<http://www.house.gov/Constitution/Amend.html>. *First Amendment to the U.S. Constitution*, 9 June 2004.

<http://www.oed.com/>. *Oxford English Dictionary online*, 2 February 2005.

PAOLA CATENACCIO

Implementing Council Directive 1993/13/EEU on Unfair Terms in Consumer Contracts in Great Britain: A Case for Intra-linguistic Translation?

1. Introduction

One of the aims of the European Union, right from its inception as European Community, has been "the approximation of the laws of Member States to the extent required for the functioning of the common market" (*Consolidated Version of the Treaty establishing the European Community*, art. 3h). Such approximation, however cautiously worded, has not failed to generate heated debates about the need for – and indeed the desirability of – what has sometimes been perceived as the encroaching of Europe upon national legislation. Nonetheless, the harmonisation of the legal systems has made steady progress through the implementation of the *acquis communautaire* in the various member states, and is the main condition for the accession of new members.

The implementation of the *acquis* at national level can sometimes make it necessary to change existing laws, introducing concepts derived from other legal systems and previously alien to the legislation in question. Moreover, as the language in which EU legal instruments are worded – 'Eurolanguage', or 'Eurolect' (Goffin 1994) – is the result of a linguistic compromise between different traditions, it is often by its very nature different from the language traditionally used in the local legal systems both in terms of terminology, discursive organisation and textual structure. Thus, linguistic difficulties build upon legal difficulties.

This chapter looks at the debate surrounding the implementation of Council Directive 1993/13/EEU on Unfair Terms in Consumer

Contracts in Britain in a linguistic perspective, with a view to assessing the impact of European legal language on this area of English law. The discussion is framed within the wider context of the development of a European contract law designed to gradually replace national legislations, and investigates the articulation of resistant discourses within official English documents.

2. Language, law and harmonisation in the European Union

As the result of the harmonisation of the legal traditions historically present in Europe, the law and language of the European Union share many of the features of most international legal tools – 'hybrid texts' "produced in a supranational multicultural discourse community where there is no linguistically neutral ground" (Trosborg 1997: 145-146). Conceived not only as instruments for bridging the gaps between different legal systems, but as steps towards the creation of a new system encompassing (though not necessarily replacing) the existing ones, they entail the creation of a new legal language (Robertson 2001) which, although ideally neutral, is nonetheless subject to cultural constraints (Bhatia/Candlin/Gotti 2003, Bathia/Candlin/Engberg/Trosborg 2003). In turn, the language of international law 'reflects back' on the national systems (Giannoni 2003: 222; cf. also Garzone 2003), potentially modifying – or at least redefining – both the language and the concepts on which they are based.

This is particularly true of European law: since the Union requires the member states (with varying degrees of flexibility) to implement European laws, national governments are faced with the task of integrating into their legal systems laws which are the result – both in normative content and linguistic expression – of a compromise between traditions (Campana 1999). Although these texts come in a variety of national language versions, all of which are legally binding, their terminology and textual organisation may be very far from the local standard legal use.

The gap between the language variety used at European level and the one used locally can be especially wide in the area of terminology, where the European Union has made "painstaking efforts to create a more natural lexicon for the ever-growing multilingual jurisdiction" (Šarčević 1997: 260-261). This has entailed, on the one hand, the careful avoidance of existing national legal terms, and, on the other, the creation of "terms which are reasonably transparent and can be easily translated", with priority being given to literal equivalents (Šarčević 1997: 261) as opposed to natural equivalents, i.e. terms that already exist in the target language system(s). As is customary with international law, these new legal terms are often terms from ordinary language to which a legal meaning has been assigned; as such, they are not always immediately recognisable as 'terms of art', and it is frequently necessary to provide definitions which specify their meaning against common usage. Thus, a terminology mainly made up by core language words to which domain specific meanings are attached ('Eurospeak') is used at European level, whereas at the national level the traditional legal terminology continues to be in use.

The coexistence of two legal sub-codes of the same language may not in itself represent a problem in so far as their domains of applicability remain discrete. But what happens when – as is the case with European Directives – a legal instrument originally conceived at supra-national level and then re-drafted in national language versions is to be implemented in national legislation? What variety should prevail – the European or the local one? The issue is particularly relevant for European Directives because, of all European secondary legislation,[1] they are the only ones which require implementation in national law; however, the member states may choose the form and methods for adaptation into their national legal systems, which implies that the formulation and wording of the Directives needn't be preserved, pro-

1 "Regulations [...] are directly applicable and binding in all EU Member States without the need for any national implementing legislation. Directives [...] bind Member States as to the objectives to be achieved within a certain time-limit while leaving the national authorities the choice of form and means to be used. Directives have to be implemented in national legislation in accordance with the procedures of the individual Member States. Decisions [...] are binding in all their aspects for those to whom they are addressed. Thus, decisions do not require national implementing legislation. A decision may be addressed to any or all Member States, to enterprises or to individuals. Recommendations and opinions [...] are not binding." (The EUR-Lex website, http://europa.eu.int/eur-lex/en/about/pap/process_and_players2.html).

vided the end-result – normatively speaking – stays the same. In other words, national governments can choose whether to opt for a strategy of 'domestication' of the EU Directives involving, amongst other things, intra-linguistic translation possibly resorting to functional equivalents (where available) in order to avoid discourse transfer, or to adopt their form and language, thus introducing a 'foreignising' influence. The issue is even more problematic when the EU Directive contains concepts which are alien to the target legal culture: the insertion into a legal system of "a new rule expressed in alien concepts [and language] without it being integrated into the existing doctrinal fabric" may result in "an imaginative reconstruction of legal doctrine"; on the other hand, any "attempt to tame the new principles by equating them with existing national legal doctrine" (Collins 1997: 409) would imply a simplistic reduction of the concepts themselves – either way, hardly a satisfactory solution.

In the case of EU legislation belonging to the contract law *acquis* (in itself a controversial area, as contract law is a domain in which the divergence between different traditions is particularly evident) this already complex issue is further complicated by the existence of a much publicized ongoing project aimed at going beyond the Directives ('functional' pieces of legislation designed to tackle individual problems) and establishing what is frequently referred to as "a more coherent European contract law" (COM(2003) 68 final) complete with its own terminology and textual conventions,[2] for use not only in supra-national commerce, but also internally in the member states. This development would significantly reduce the flexibility now granted to national government in the implementation of Directives, especially in the area of terminology. The timeframe for the execution of this long-term plan (as stated in European Parliament Resolution on the Approximation of the Civil and Commercial Law of

2 Official documents and academic studies on this issue abound. Besides the documents issued by the Lando Commission (PELC – Principles of European Contract Law) and the Pavia Group, cf. also COM(2001) 398, COM(2003) 68 final, Heutger (2003, 2004), Grundmann/Stuyck (2002), Hesselink (2001, 2002a, 2002b), Schmidt (1999), Faure (2002). An extensive bibliography can be found on the website of the Commission on European Contract Law, <http://frontpage.cbs.dk/law/commission_on_european_contract_law/>.

the Member States 2001 – COM(2001) 39) includes the following steps (emphasis added):

> from 2005: consistent application of the common legal concepts and solutions in legal terminology by all EU institutions involved in legislative drafting and implementing procedures;
> from 2006: European legislation implementing the common legal principles and terminology for cross-border or *national* contractual relations;
> beginning of 2008: review of how far the common legal principles and uniform terminology in European law have proved their value in practice, and consideration of whether uniform European provisions should be laid down in respect thereof, so as to lead, in the longer term, to *uniformity in contract law* within the EU and *as regards the laws of its Member States.*

This suggests that, despite misgivings on several parts,[3] the now optional adoption of European terminology for use within the legal systems of the member states is likely to become compulsory within the next few years. In this context, the choices made by national governments with respect to the implementation of European Directives on contract-related topics can shed some light on their cultural and political attitude towards the assimilation of this new legal language.

3. The implementation of Council Directive 1993/13/EEC: between compliance and resistance

The harmonizing policy described above suggests that there appears to exist a strong thrust, on the part of the European Union, in favour of the adoption within national legislations of a common terminology agreed at European level (at least as concerns contract law), in spite of the fact that most legal acts of the EU concerning this area of law are Directives, and therefore binding in their result, but not in their form. In a long-term perspective of compliance with EU guidelines, this

3 Cf. in particular the response of the UK government to the Commission Consultation Process for the development of an European contract law, which shows its reluctance to acknowledge the need for a unified system (COM(2003) 68 final, p. 22).

would seem to argue in favour of the introduction of the terminology (if not necessarily all the textual features) of EU Directives in national legal instruments implementing it. However, local (not least political) circumstances must be taken into account when assessing the desirability or suitability of integrating in the local legal system language and possibly concepts at odds with the legal culture of the member state concerned.

Council Directive 1993/13/EEC on Unfair Terms in Contracts is part of the contract law *acquis*; as such, its implementation in national (and particularly in English) legislation is subject to the kind of pressures pointed out above. This makes it an interesting test case, especially since the various phases of its integration into the English legal system are clearly documented in a number of legal acts and proposals.

3.1. Unfair terms in contracts in English law

Council Directive 1993/13/EEC on Unfair Terms in Consumer Contracts was implemented in Britain in 1994 through the promulgation of the Unfair Terms in Consumer Contracts Regulations (1994), later replaced by a slightly different version (1999). The new law was not meant to supplant but rather co-exist with the pre-existing English legislation regulating unfair terms in contracts, the Unfair Contract Terms Act (1977). However, clashes in the provisions made by these legal instruments[4] prompted a discussion on the way in which they could be better reconciled, which resulted in a Consultation Paper on Unfair Terms in Contracts (2003) containing – amongst other things – a proposal for a new Act bringing together the 1977 Act and the 1999 Regulations.

In the rest of this chapter the lexical, textual and discursive features of these legal documents will be looked at in order to identify similarities and differences between the legal language used at na-

4 This phenomenon is called "double banking": according to the Davidson Review (2006: 37) "double-banking arises when European legislation covers similar ground to that covered in existing domestic legislation and the two regimes have not been coherently merged in the implementation process".

tional level prior to the Introduction of the Directive (as exemplified in the Unfair Contract Terms Act 1977) and its European counterpart (as exemplified in Council Directive 1993/13/EEC on Unfair Terms in Consumer Contracts). The aim of this analysis is to verify whether the implementation of the European Directive in Britain by means of the Unfair Terms in Consumer Contracts Regulations (1994, 1999) involved discourse transfer, and – further – whether the approach followed by the Joint Consultation Paper in its proposal for an Act combining the English and European provisions showed evidence of discourse merging.

3.1.1. Textual and discursive features: a comparison of Unfair Contract Terms Act (1977) and Council Directive 1993/13/EEC

The Unfair Contract Terms Act (1977) and Council Directive 1993/13/EEC on Unfair Terms in Consumer Contracts are examples, respectively, of the native English legal discourse on unfair terms and of the European legal discourse in English on the same area of law. If one compares the two documents, one is immediately aware of a number of differences between them, starting from macro-structural aspects such as layout and textual organisation. Besides the obvious divergences in the standardised parts and formulae framing the two documents, deriving from their differing traditions and normative status (primary *vs* secondary legislation),[5] the textual organisation of the provisions themselves shows a much greater complexity in the 1977 Act, with numbered and individually titled sections characterised by multiple subsectioning (marked not only by numbers, but by subsequent, hierarchically ordered points identified by letters – a structure

5 In particular, the Unfair Contract Terms (1977) includes the short customary formula used in English law Acts of Parliament ("Be it enacted by the Queen's most Excellent Majesty, by and with the advice and consent of the Lords Spiritual and Temporal, and Commons, in this present Parliament assembled, and by the authority of the same, as follows:"), whereas the opening sections of EU Directives, which serve a paratextual function, consist of a much longer (but varying in length), more articulated, less formulaic but equally standardised portion of text, comprising, among other things, the 'citation' and the 'recital', which set respectively the legal basis and the general motivation for the document.

that has been likened to a game of chess – Wagner 2002) signalling complex conceptual and syntactic articulation, as shown below:

(1) *3. Liability arising in contract*
1) This section applies as between contracting parties where one of them deals as consumer or on the other's written standard terms of business.

2) As against that party, the other cannot by reference to any contract term—
(a) when himself in breach of contract, exclude or restrict any liability of his in respect of the breach; or
(b) claim to be entitled—
(i) to render a contractual performance substantially different from that which was reasonably expected of him, or
(ii) in respect of the whole or any part of his contractual obligation, to render no performance at all,
except in so far as (in any of the cases mentioned above in this subsection) the contract term satisfies the requirement of reasonableness.

On the other hand, Council Directive 1993/13/EEC is structured (as is customary with this type of documents) in a series of numbered articles subdivided, where necessary, into numbered paragraphs, but with no further subdivision:

(2) *Article 1*
1. The purpose of this Directive is to approximate the laws, regulations and administrative provisions of the Member States relating to unfair terms in contracts concluded between a seller or supplier and a consumer.
2. The contractual terms which reflect mandatory statutory or regulatory provisions and the provisions or principles of international conventions to which the Member States or the Community are party, particularly in the transport area, shall not be subject to the provisions of this Directive.

As far as syntactic articulation is concerned, the 1977 Act displays all the features which have been identified as typical of native legal English (Malinkoff 1963; Hiltunen 1990), among which hypotaxis, left branching and multiple embedding are the most common, whereas the European Directive displays a much lower incidence of the same.

In terms of cognitive processing, the English legal instrument features several internal and external references which are far from being transparent, as shown in the examples below:

(3) *Scope of Part I*
1) For the purpose of this Part of this Act, 'negligence' means the breach—

> [...]
> (c) of the common duty of care imposed by the Occupiers' Liability Act 1957 or the Occupiers' Liability Act (Northern Ireland) 1957.
> 2) This Part of this Act is subject to Part III; and in relation to contracts, the operation of sections 2 to 4 and 7 is subject to the exceptions made by Schedule 1.
> 3) In the case of both contract and tort, sections 2 to 7 apply (except where the contrary is stated in section 6(4)) only to business liability.

On the contrary, cross-referencing is virtually absent from the European Directive, where only once reference is made to the Appendix attached to the main text. The most striking differences, however, are to be found in the lexicon of the two documents, which shows extremely little overlapping. In particular, key concepts and terminology of the Unfair Contract Terms Act (1977) such as 'liability' and 'negligence' do not occur in the body of the provisions in Council Directive 1993/13/EEC on Unfair Terms in Consumer Contracts ('liability' occurring twice in the recital, but never in the provisions), whereas a key concept of Council Directive 1993/13/EEC such as 'good faith' is not found anywhere in the English 1977 Act.

3.1.2. Unfair Terms in Contracts Regulations (1994; 1999)

Council Directive 1993/13/EEC was implemented in English law through the promulgation of the Unfair Terms in Contracts Regulations (1994, 1999).[6] The most evident feature of the new English legal instrument introduced in compliance with European law is the extent to which it adopts the terminology of the Directive. No attempt is made to adjust the language or 'translate' exogenous expressions and concepts (such as the above mentioned 'good faith') into the local va-

---

6 Both Regulations report almost to the letter Articles 1-6 of Directive 1993/13/EEC, which establish the key concepts and principles, as well as reproducing the Annex containing a list of terms which may be regarded as unfair. However, Articles 7-11, which assign the member states the task of finding the most suitable means to achieve certain targets (such as preventing the continued use of unfair terms, or ensuring that legal action may be taken against the use of unfair terms), deal with the practical means of enforcing the principles stated in the first part of the Directive, and are left deliberately vague. The 1999 Regulations differ from their previous version in the provisions designed to deal with the second part of the Directive, extending their scope and modifying them with the introduction of new qualifying bodies.

riety of legal English. In fact, the 1999 version of the Regulations displays a resolve to erase even the slight formal changes (especially in the definitions of key terms and in the arrangement of the provisions) discernible in the 1994 version, as explicitly stated in the 'Explanatory note' attached to them (emphasis added):

> (4) These Regulations revoke and replace the Unfair Terms in Consumer Contracts Regulations 1994 [...].
> Those Regulations implemented Council Directive 93/13/EEC [...]. Regulations 3 to 9 of these Regulations re-enact regulations 2-7 of the 1994 Regulations *with modifications to reflect more closely the wording of the Directive.*

The few points of divergence are confined to the different structuring of the information (often resulting in the text of the Regulations displaying a greater number of sections and subsections), and, occasionally, syntactical changes. The following example shows how an instance of negative construction (typical of European legal language) is restructured so as to make it easier to process, reducing the distance between the subject and the negative verb form, and separating two logically distinct components of the provision itself:

> (5) *Directive 1993/13/EEC*
> Article 1
> [...]
> 2. The contractual terms which reflect mandatory statutory or regulatory provisions and the provisions or principles of international conventions to which the Member States or the Community are party, particularly in the transport area, shall not be subject to the provisions of this Directive.

> (6) *Regulations (1999)*
> Terms to which these Regulations apply
> 4. [...]
> 2) These Regulations do not apply to contractual terms which reflect
> (a) mandatory statutory or regulatory provisions (including such provisions under the law of any Member State or in Community legislation having effect in the United Kingdom without further enactment);
> (b) the provisions or principles of international conventions to which the Member States or the Community are party.

In addition, Regulation 4.2. also shows some expansion (reference to provisions under non-English laws having an effect in the United Kingdom) and reduction (reference to transport is omitted).

Another example of sentence restructuring aimed at simplifying negative structures while involving the fronting of a secondary clause is the following:

> (7) *Directive 93/13/EEC*
> Article 4
> 1. [...]
> 2. Assessment of the fair nature of the terms shall relate neither to the definition of the main subject matter of the contract nor to the adequacy of the price and remuneration, on the one hand, as against the services or goods supplied in exchange, on the other, insofar as these terms are in plain, intelligible language.

> (8) *Regulations (1999)*
> Assessment of fair terms
> 6. – 1) [...]
> 2) Insofar as it is in plain, intelligible language, the assessment of fairness of a term shall not relate-
> (a) to the definition of the main subject matter of the contract, or
> (b) to the adequacy of the price or remuneration, as against the goods or services supplied in exchange.

The fronting of the secondary clause emphasises the condition for the validity of the provision, whose two components are separated into subsections and linked by the disjunctive conjunction *or*, thus transferring the negation from the conjunction to the verb. Again, the result of this operation is syntactic and cognitive simplification, as well as an increase in visual immediacy.

Elsewhere the changes affect the subdivision into paragraphs, multiplying the number of logically distinct subsections:

> (9) *Directive 93/13/EEC*
> Article 3
> 1. A contractual term which has not been individually negotiated shall be regarded as unfair if, contrary to the requirement of good faith, it causes a significant imbalance in the parties' rights and obligations arising under the contract, to the detriment of the consumer.
> 2. A term shall always be regarded as not individually negotiated where it has been drafted in advance and the consumer has therefore not been able to influence the substance of the term, particularly in the context of a pre-formulated standard contract.
> The fact that certain aspects of a term or one specific term have been individually negotiated shall not exclude the application of this Article to the rest

of a contract if an overall assessment of the contract indicates that it is nevertheless a pre-formulated standard contract.
Where any seller or supplier claims that a standard term has been individually negotiated, the burden of proof in this respect shall be incumbent on him.
3. The Annex shall contain an indicative and non-exhaustive list of the terms which may be regarded as unfair.

(10) *Regulations (1999)*
Unfair Terms
5. – (1) A contractual term which has not been individually negotiated shall be regarded as unfair if, contrary to the requirement of good faith, it causes a significant imbalance in the parties' rights and obligations arising under the contract, to the detriment of the consumer.
(2) A term shall always be regarded as not having been individually negotiated where it has been drafted in advance and the consumer has therefore not been able to influence the substance of the term.
(3) Notwithstanding that a specific term or certain aspects of it in a contract has been individually negotiated, these Regulations shall apply to the rest of a contract if an overall assessment of it indicates that it is a pre-formulated standard contract.
(4) It shall be for any seller or supplier who claims that a term was individually negotiated to show that it was.
(5) Schedule 2 to these Regulations contains an indicative and non-exhaustive list of the terms which may be regarded as unfair.

In this example, Art. 3.2 of Directive 93/13/EEC is subdivided into three sections; the long-winded prepositional phrase 'the fact that' introducing a left-branching secondary clause is replaced by 'notwithstanding', a negative preposition typical of legal English which allows the drafter to avoid the negative construction in the main sentence. Finally, in Regulation 5.4., a left-branching hypothetical clause is replaced with an embedded relative clause; although this results in multiple embedding, it facilitates the connection between claiming and proving, while the use of a marked cleft structure draws attention to the subjects ("any seller or supplier") whose responsibility it is to perform the action described.

The conclusion that can be drawn from this brief discussion is that the text of 1999 Regulations closely resembles the text of the Directive, operating changes only for the sake of simplification (in accordance with the several sets of guidelines and recommendations issued from the mid-seventies onwards – cf. Cutts 1995). In particular, this involves changes in the layout of the text, with a greater number of subdivisions; changes in syntax, aimed mainly at reducing the incidence of negative constructions (thus facilitating cognitive processsing); and modifications to the thematic structure, designed to give salience to certain parts of the text. From the point of view of textual organisation, especially as regards *dispositio*, this results in the 1999 Regulations displaying a partial similarity with existing English legislation (as in the 1977 Act above) in terms of recursive sectioning of the text, albeit exhibiting much simplified linguistic and organisational features (especially as regards syntax and the incidence of internal and external references). This simplification cannot, however, be put down to the influence of the language of the Directive (which, in fact, the Regulations further clarify), but is rather the result of endogenous trends (Cf. Cutts 1995, Cutts 2000).

Whereas the textual structure of the 1999 Regulations suggests an at least partially 'domesticating' approach, as far as the lexicon is concerned a 'foreignising' attitude is apparent. The terminology of the Directive is consistently maintained, even where this entails the introduction of a concept – such as the concept of good faith – traditionally alien to English contract law, with consequences for the English legal system which, while not necessarily causing its 'disintegration' (Whilelmsson 1996: 74, quoted in Collins 1997: 409), have indeed raised many issues and prompted a heated debate.[7]

3.2. *Domesticating European Contract Law*

With the coming into force of the Unfair Terms in Consumer Contracts Regulations (1999), two different types of legislation, establishing different provisions, involving different concepts and drafted in different languages became simultaneously applicable in the United Kingdom. This state of affairs led to the establishment of a committee to discuss the issue whose efforts found expression in the Joint Con-

7 Literature on the difficulties raised by attempts to integrate the concept of good faith into the common law system abounds. Cf. especially Bridge (1984), Goode (1992), and, with particular reference to good faith in contracts and Directive 93/13/EEC, Teubner (1998), de Moor (1995), Brownswood (1994; 1996), Joerges (1995); see also Zimmermann/Whittaker (2000).

sultation Paper on Unfair terms in Consumer Contracts (2001), an attempt at combining the two legislations which provides extensive commentary on their overlapping and divergences, and puts forward the proposal for a new Bill which should replace the 1977 Act and the 1999 Regulations, merging their contents into a single legislative instrument.

The Joint Consultation Paper is a 200-page document containing much doctrinal debate on various aspects of English and European law. What is of particular interest for the linguist, however, is the way in which the problem of integrating Directive 93/13/EEC is framed in linguistic terms. When considering the language of the new Bill, for instance, the Discussion Paper insists on the need that it be 'clear and accessible'. To this purpose, the potential advantages of incorporating the language of the Directive are described in a heavily hedged statement:

> (11) Even though the UK is not required to employ the language of the Directive when implementing it, there may be an advantage in doing so. It seems likely that there will be cases in the ECJ on whether Member States have properly implemented the Directive, and whether their Courts have applied it correctly. Such cases might give authoritative interpretations on the words of the Directive, for example the meaning of 'contract' or of 'contrary to the requirement of good faith'. If the UK legislation is in similar terms to the Directive, it will be easier to apply the jurisprudence of the ECJ to the interpretation of the UK legislation than if that legislation uses different terminology.

Not surprisingly, the Joint Consultation Paper goes on to argue that

> (12) the price to be paid, however, is the relative unfamiliarity of the terminology of the Directive and the fact that some of the concepts do not form part of English or Scots legal traditions. The point of European legislation in the form of Directives rather than Regulations is to allow Member States to implement the legislation in accordance with their own legal traditions. We would go so far as to say that the parts of the Directive, in particular the indicative list of terms which may be unfair, are very difficult for even a lawyer from the UK to interpret. It cannot be said that all the examples are "clear and accessible". Keeping to the precise wording of the Directive would mean abandoning the third limb of this project [*making the law clear and accessible*]. (71-72)

Later on, when discussing the indicative list of unfair terms which the Directive provides for inclusion in the legislation of the Member States, the following passage is to be found (again, hedging in the formulation provides a clear sign of the writers' attitude):

> (13) UTCCR [Unfair Terms in Consumer Contracts Regulations] contain an indicative list, or 'grey' list, copied from the Annex to the Directive, It appears that legislation needs to contain such a list in order to comply with the Directive. In any event the indicative list appears to have been found useful, at least by the OFT in its work in seeking to eliminate unfair terms, and we are not aware of any call to remove it. Two questions may be asked. First, should the indicative list be expanded to include other clauses which have been found to be unfair? Secondly, not all the examples on the indicative list are easy to understand. *The language is complex* and the examples sometimes refer to concepts from other legal systems which seem to have no exact equivalent in the laws of England and Scotland. Should the list be reformulated, 'translating' the examples into terms which are recognisable to readers from the UK and, if it is permissible to do so, omitting altogether any that are not?
> [...]
> To 'translate' the list into UK terms, while ensuring that it complies with the Directive, is not easy. Moreover [...] some of the existing paragraphs have no relevance to UK law, or seem to cover terms that, in UK law, do not seem unfair. (99-101; emphasis added)

Hence, members of the Law Commission "provisionally propose that the indicative list should be reformulated in terms which are more directly applicable to UK law and more readily comprehensible to UK readers" (101). As for the alleged complexity of the language of the Directive, the Joint Commission does not explain in detail where the difficulties lie. In particular, these difficulties cannot be put down to the use of obscure specialised terminology (which the Directive carefully avoids, strictly adhering to the principle that words should be used in their most common meaning), or because of syntactic complexity (which, as in the case of the provisions, could be easily simplified). Rather, they appear to be related to the inherent vagueness – hardly a problem unique to the Directive (cf. Bhatia/Engberg/Gotti/Heller 2005).

The suggestion to rewrite the list providing examples of unfair terms put forward by the Commission would likely result in the stylistic aligning of the resulting document with English legislation also in the detailed listing of cases and exceptions, as exemplified in the Unfair Contract Terms Act (1977). This suggests that the difficulties detected by the Commission may have more to do with the lack of domain specificity of both language and format, neither of which fits in with the tradition-sanctioned conventions of the community of practice called upon to interpret and use it, and of which the members of the Commission are eminent representatives.

In line with this 'translational' approach, but on a more clearly conceptual basis, the phrase 'good faith' as it is used in the Directive is also extensively discussed in the paper[8]. Significantly enough, it is not the concept which is criticised, but its wording. As a matter of fact, after putting forward several proposals for its interpretation, it is finally found that it can be conflated with the concept of fairness and reasonableness – in tune with common law tradition and with the wording of the 1977 Act. In particular, it is stated that the wording 'good faith' may be "a bow to the German tradition", and that anyway not even the Germans take it into consideration any more (44). Hence, the discussion paper proposes the elimination of the wording 'good faith' and the re-introduction of the expression 'fair and reasonable' (39-51), on the assumption that, in respect of the topics covered by the regulations, there is no difference in substance: in fact, the main point in the discussion of the 'good faith principle' is not that it *means* the same as 'reasonable and fair', but that *for the purpose of a contract*

8 The concept of good faith in contract law is generally said to be alien to the Common Law system, although it is certainly present in certain types of contract, such as insurance contracts (cf. Solly this volume), contracts to subscribe for shares in a company, family settlements, contracts for the sale of land, contracts for suretyship and partnerships (Chitty on Contracts 2004: para 6139). In general terms, however, there is widespread reluctance on the part of English scholars to accept the introduction of the good faith principle in contract law based on the belief that "the introduction of a standard of uncertain content with strong moral overtones" would cause uncertainty, potentially damaging "the commercial practices which have provided the bedrock of English contract law" (MacQueen 1999: 5). The development of a European contract law in which the concept of good faith plays an important role has caused a spate of scholarly articles on the difficulties raised by attempts to integrate this concept into the common law system. Cf. especially Bridge (1984), Goode (1992), and, with particular reference to good faith in contracts and Directive 93/13/EEC, Teubner (1998), de Moor (1995), Joerges (1995); see also Zimmermann/Whittaker (2000).

the two definitions reach the same results when assessing whether a term was unfair.

When coming to the new proposal, the Discussion Paper – wary to mitigate criticism with a compliant attitude – concludes that it should not be based on either the 1977 Act or the 1999 Regulations. From the point of view of its contents, the careful consideration given to issues of interpretation most likely ensures that the requirements of the Directive are included in the Bill. However, in terms of textual and discursive structure, as well as in the choice of terminology, the Bill proposal clearly shows a desire to conform to the tradition of English law, albeit in its 'clarified', post-1980s form:

> (14) *Part 1*
> Business liability for negligence
> *1 Contract terms or notices excluding or restricting business liability for negligence.*
> 1) Business liability for death or personal injury which results from negligence cannot be excluded or restricted by a contract term or notice.
> 2) Business liability for other loss or damage which results from negligence cannot be excluded or restricted by a contract term or notice unless (as the case may be) –
>   (a) the term is fair and reasonable, or
>   (b) it is fair and reasonable to allow reliance on the notice.
> 3) 'Business liability' means liability for breach of an obligation or duty that arises –
>   (a) from anything that was done or should have been done for purposes related to a business, or
>   (b) from the occupation of premises used for purposes related to the business of the occupier.
> 4) "Anything done for purposes related to a business" includes anything done by an employee of the business which lies within the scope of his employment.

The example shows many of the features which had been identified as typical of the Unfair Contract Terms Act 1977: multiple subdivision (to a greater extent than the 1999 Regulations), repetition, specific exemplification of cases and exceptions covered by the provisions. Later in the text, internal and external references are also used. This has the effect, on the one hand, of making the Act less self-explanatory and transparent, but also, on the other, of integrating it into a body of pre-existing law, effectively making it part of that tradition.

As concerns the lexicon, the re-introduction of the term 'negligence' at the very beginning of the Bill sets the pace for a terminological use (including doubling, as in 'fair and reasonable', but see also 'possession or ownership') which is in line with English usage, while differing substantially from the usage which has become consolidated in European legal language.

4. Conclusions

Whereas the integral adoption in the UK of the wording of the European Directive on Unfair Terms in Consumer Contracts in 1999 suggested the integration of both lexis and concepts (especially the concept of 'good faith' – a concept which is alien to English contract law, but features prominently in recent European documents on contract law and presumably will make its way into a future European Civil Code), more recent developments suggest that there is significant resistance, within the English legal environment, to this kind of integration. European legal English is in many ways macroscopically different from the legal English of the UK. As the result of the convergence of the legal systems of Europe, its terminology is neither typically 'continental' nor English. Its emphasis on words being used in their common sense also presents potential problems for their utilisation in domain-specific texts and situations, as domain-specific meanings are bound to develop (through definitions, for instance) which may clash with local meanings – whether British or other – both specialised or in the core language. Because of this, it appears to be escaping the control of traditional gatekeepers of legal discourse (lawyers and judges, but also politicians) thus creating tensions and misunderstandings.

The debate surrounding the implementation of Directive 93/13/EEC confirms that finding a compromise between the opposing pulling factors of tradition and Europeanisation is a difficult task. Linguistic choices come fraught with cultural, but above all political implications. In the area of contract law especially, 'translating' European Directives into local languages will not be an option for much longer. In this perspective, the work of the Joint Commission may be seen as futile. In endeavouring to maintain a local identity (in terms of law, but also of discursive conventions), however, it brings to the fore the crux at the heart of Europe – how to value diversity, and still promote uniformity.

References

Bhatia, Vijay 1983. Simplification v. Easification – the Case of Legal Texts. *Applied Linguistics* 4/1, 42-54.

Bhatia, Vijay 1994. Cognitive Structuring in Legislative Provisions. In Gibbons, John (ed.) *Language and the Law*. London and New York:: Longman, 136-155.

Bhatia, Vijay / Candlin, Christopher N. / Gotti, Maurizio (eds) 2003. *Legal Discourse in Multilingual and Multicultural Contexts: Arbitration Texts in Europe*. Bern: Peter Lang.

Bhatia, Vijay / Candlin, Christopher N. / Engberg, Jan / Trosborg, Anna (eds) 2003. *Multilingual and Multicultural Contexts of Legislation: An International Perspective*. Frankfurt am Main: Peter Lang.

Bhatia, Vijay / Engberg, Jan / Gotti, Maurizio / D. Heller (eds) 2005. *Vagueness in Normative Texts*. Bern: Peter Lang.

Bridge, Michael G. 1984. Does Anglo-Canadian Contract Law Need a Doctrine of Good Faith? *Canadian Business Law Journal* 9, 385-434.

Caliendo, Giuditta 2004. EU Language in Cross-Boundary Communication, *Textus* 17/1, 159-178.

Campana, Marie-Jeanne 1999. Vers un langage juridique commun en Europe? In Sacco, Rodolfo / Castellani, Luca (eds) *Les multiples langues du droit europèen uniforme*, Torino: L'Harmattan, 7-29.

Chitty on Contracts 2004. 29th Edition. London: Sweet and Maxwell.

Collins, Hugh 1997. The Voice of the Community in Private Law Discourse. *European Law Journal* 3/4, 407-421.

COM(2001) 398 C5-0471/2001 2001/2187(COS), European Parliament resolution on the approximation of the civil and commercial law of the Member States, *OJ* C140E/538-542, 13.06.2002.

COM(2003) 68 Final, Communication from Commission to the European Parliament and the Council, *A More Coherent European Contract Law. An Action Plan*, *OJ* C63/1-44, 15/03/2003.

Consolidated Version of the Treaty establishing the European Community, *OJ* 24.12.2002, C325/33-183.

Council Directive 93/13/EEC of 5 April 1993 on unfair terms in consumer contracts, *OJ* 21.04.1993, L093/29-34.

Cutts, Martin 1995. *The Plain English Guide*. Oxford: Oxford University Press.

Cutts, Martin 2000. *Lucid Law*. High Peak: Plain Language Commission.

Cutts, Martin 2001. *Clarifying Eurolaw*. High Peak: Plain Language Commission.

Davidson Review 2006. *Implementation of EU legislation. Final Report*. London: The Stationery Office.

de Moor, Anne 1995. Common and Civil Law Conceptions of Contract and European Law of Contract: The Case of the Directive on Unfair Terms in Consumer Contracts. *European Law Review of Private Law*. 3, 257-270.

Garzone, Giuliana 2003. Arbitration Rules across Legal Cultures. In Bhatia, Vijay / Candlin, Christopher N. / Gotti, Maurizio, *Legal discourse in Multilingual and Multicultural Contexts*. Bern: Peter Lang, 177-220.

Giannoni, Davide Simone 2003. The UNCITRAL Model and Italian Statute Law. In Bhatia, Vijay / Candlin, Christopher N. / Gotti, Maurizio (eds), *Legal Discourse in Multilingual and Multicultural Contexts: Arbitration Texts in Europe*. Bern: Peter Lang, 221-246.

Gibbons, John (ed.) 1994. *Language and the Law*. London and New York: Longman.

Goffin, Roger 1994. L'Eurolecte: Oui, Jargon Communautaire: non. *Meta* 39/4, 636-642.

Goode, Royston M. 1992. *The Concept of 'Good Faith' in English Law*. Roma: Centro di studi e ricerche di diritto comparato e straniero.

Grundmann, Stefan / Stuyck, Jules (eds) 2002. *An Academic Green Paper on European Contract Law*. The Hague: Kluwer Law International.

Hesselink, Martin W. 2001. The Principles Of European Contract Law: Some Choices Made By The Lando Commission. *Global Jurist Frontiers* 1/1, Art. 4. <http://www.bepress.com/gj/frontiers/vol1/iss1/art4>.

Hesselink, Martin W. 2002a. The Politics of European Contract Law: Who Has an Interest in What Kind of Contract Law for Europe?, *Global Jurist Frontiers* 2/1, Art. 3. <http://www.bepress.com/gj/frontiers/vol2/iss1/art3>.

Hesselink, Martin W. 2002b. The Structure of the New European Contract Law. *Electronic Journal of Comparative Law* 6/4 <http://www.ejcl.org/64/art64-2.html>.

Heutger, Viola 2003. Law and Language in the European Union. *Global Jurist Topics* 3/1, 1-15.

Heutger, Viola 2004. A More Coherent European Wide Legal Language, *European Integration Online Papers* (EioP) 7/2, <http://eiop.or.at/eiop/pdf/2004-002.pdf>.

Hiltunen, Risto, 1990. *Chapters on Legal English:Aspects Past and Present of the Language of the Law*. Helsinki: Suomalainen tiedeakatemia.

Joerges, Christian 1995. The Europeanisation of Private Law as a Rationalisation Process and as a Contest of Legal Disciplines – An Analysis of the Directive on Unfair Terms in Consumer Contracts. *European Review of Private Law* 3, 175-192.

MacQueen, Hector L. 1999. Good Faith in the Scots law of contract: an undisclosed principle? In Forte, Angelo D.M. (ed.) *Good Faith in Contract and Property Law*. Oxford: Hart Publishing, 5-37.

Mellinkoff David, 1963. *The Language of the Law*. Boston: Little, Brown and Co.

PECL Parts I and II 1999. *Principles of European Contract Law Parts I and II*, ed. by Ole Lando / Hugh Beale. Prepared by the Commission on European Contract Law, The Hague: Kluwer Law International.

PECL Part III 2003. *Principles of European Contract Law, Part III* ed. by Ole Lando, Eric Clive, André Prüm and Reinhard Zimmermann, The Hague: Kluwer Law International.

Robertson, Colin 2001. Multilingual Law: A Framework for Understanding LSP within the EU. In Mayer, Felix (ed.) *Language for Specific Purposes. Perspectives for the New Millennium*. Vol. 2. Tübingen: Gunter Narr Verlag, 697-703.

Šarčević, Susan 1997. *New Approaches to Legal Translation*. The Hague: Kluwer Law International.

Schmid, Christoph U. 1999. The Emergence of a Transnational Legal Science in European Private Law. *Oxford Journal of Legal Studies* 19, 673-689.

Tiersma, Peter M., 1999. *Legal Language*. Chicago: The University of Chicago Press.

Teubner, Gunther 1998. Legal Irritants: Good Faith in British Law or How Unifying Law Ends Up in New Divergences. *The Modern Law Review* 61, 11-32.

Trosborg, Anna 1997. Translating Hybrid Political Texts. In Trosborg, Anna (ed.) *Text Typology and Translation*. Amsterdam: Benjamins, 145-158.

Unfair Terms in Contracts. A Joint Consultation Paper, The Law Commission Consultation Paper no 166 / The Scottish Law Commission Discussion Paper no 119. London: TSO (available online at <http://www.lawcom.org.uk; http://scotlaw.org.uk>).

Wagner, Anne 2002. The Legal Discourse of the Common Law: A Game of Chess. *International Journal for the Semiotics of Law.* 15, 345-360.

Wilhelmsson, Thomas 1996. Legal Integration as Disintegration of National Law. In Wilhelmsson, Thomas (ed.) *Twelve Essays on Customer Law and Policy*. Helsinki: Helsinki University Press.

Zimmermann, Reinhard / Whittaker, Simon (eds) 2000. *Good Faith in European Contract Law*. Cambridge: Cambridge University Press.

Part 3:
Translating Legal Discourse

GIROLAMO TESSUTO

Legal Concepts and Terminography: Analysis and Application

The aim of this analysis is to highlight descriptively the terminological implications found in two differing systems of language and law – English and Italian. This analysis is divided into four sections. The first section is an introductory approach to word meaning regarded as conceptual in nature, assuming that the most direct and complex connections of linguistic forms are with their conceptual structures. The second section deals with the distinctive features of legal concepts, regarded as socio-culturally embedded and subject to a number of constraints by the law system. The third section discusses the implications and constraints arising from the previous two sections and which affect the process of intercultural communication for a variety of language users. This third section provides a conceptual and linguistic analysis of *mens rea* terms extracted from a corpus of English/Italian texts of criminal law. The fourth section argues for the potential benefits arising from a comparative method of descriptive terminography. The issues examined from different integrated perspectives and principles in modern terminology culminate in the proposed standardised format of data entry in terminographical applications.

1. Introduction

1.1. Mapping forms and concepts in the language of criminal law

The prima facie motivation for a useful approach to meaning is to consider it as being represented by the links between linguistic forms and concepts, whether in the general or specialist use of language. This approach can be considered as being primarily conceptual in nature in that conceptual categories[1] classify experience in human cognition via the medium of language. These conceptual categories allow for a set of semantic as well as grammatical features and are crucial to our daily communication. Let us examine the structure of the conceptual system underlying the term 'Intention', by illustrating how linguistic forms are specifically linked with concepts (see Fig. 1). We shall draw on a plain model of linguistic forms and associated concepts and consider the conceptual level of structure (cognition) in language as advanced by Jackendoff (2002).[2]

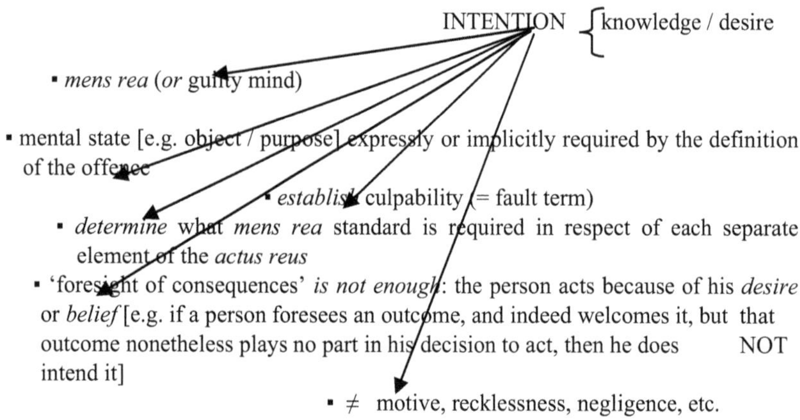

Figure 1. Mapping linguistic forms and concepts.

This model clearly consists of interconnected parts belonging to a category (Intention). The model exemplifies a complex set of variations

1 The cognitive function (ideational), coming immediately after a textual and a communicative (interpersonal) function, is well known in language (Halliday 1985). However, the prototype theory of meaning (Rosch 1977) demonstrates that the human being has a prototype (for each linguistic category) in his/her mind, and that classification takes place in this manner.

2 In his influential theory of Conceptual Semantics, Jackendoff (2002) proposes three levels of structure: phonological, syntactic, and conceptual. Together they provide a complete description of a (natural) language.

linking linguistic forms to concepts much more than the ordinary meaning would reveal. This ordinary meaning unsatisfactorily confines the concept to a set of sufficient semantic features. Therefore, interconnected parts are rich enough to represent the subtle meanings expressible in the language of Intentionality. The rule under the English criminal law on Intention clarifies the model further. The concept of Intention *is only one of* the main forms of *mens rea* and *requires* 'knowledge' of certain circumstances as part of the *mens rea*. The concept *denotes* a 'mental state' and *is used to establish* 'culpability' and *to determine* what *mens rea* standard is required in respect of each separate element of the 'actus reus'. Its *near subordinate* concept of 'mere foresight of consequences', which does not necessarily imply an Intention,[3] is then *different from* 'motive', 'recklessness', and a great variety of other possible states of mind. Thus, we understand that in the language expressing criminal states of mind, linguistic forms of Intention map directly onto conceptual structures at variable degrees of complexity so that they categorize experience and facilitate stored knowledge. The conceptual structure outlined above can also be seen in a wider perspective, by considering intrinsic dimensions (semantic properties) of 'descriptive' meaning[4] (Lyons 1977): quality, intensity and specificity. Each of them in turn will be examined.

In this context of discussion, quality is simply variation of meaning between *intention(ally)*, *reckless(ly)*, *negligence(-tly)* or *knowledge (-ingly)* as criteria to designate a person acting in different, and therefore specific levels of mental states under the criminal law. While it is true that *intention(ally)* and *reckless(ly)* designate the same area of semantic quality, they nonetheless differ in intensity. In our example, it is the feature of variation in intensity which produces culpability in the person acting, as in the following commonly used linguistic forms:

- The defendant acted *intentionally* in the circumstances.
- The defendant acted *recklessly* in the circumstances.

---

3 'Foresight' as a category has a relatively low level of distinctness from Intention.

4 This is not to deny that other labels have been given to this type of meaning, e.g. 'referential', 'logical', 'ideational', or 'propositional', each being characterised in its own way by different authors.

- The defendant *knew* that he had acted dishonestly in the circumstances.

The law concludes from these examples that *intentionally* is more intense than *recklessly*, which is in turn more intense than *knowingly*. It is therefore the gravest form of *mens rea* taken progressively in the paradigm. Variation of descriptive meaning may also be detected in specificity through a variety of logical properties. For example, in clauses like *He acted with intent to*... and *He acted with mens rea* (or *guilty mind*) *to*..., the former differentiates the exact type of specificity from the latter more general type.

1.2. The nature of legal concepts

The question now is: how are legal concepts to be regarded when they are placed within discursive practices of the criminal law in which they bear implications and constraints? The answer lies initially in the inherent features of legal concepts and terms, whose semantic evolution derives very often from ordinary word meanings acquiring specialist use over time. Legal concepts are intrinsically bound up with the national legal systems and principles in which they are formulated. As well as being socio-culturally determined, they are subject to moral values and traditions of the country concerned at a particular point in time. Apart from these self-evident constraints, there are others less evident which compromise semantic explicitness and certainty. This is further complicated by terms expressing indeterminate, evaluative concepts of ordinary language, which are not defined either by the law or in reference materials in a uniform way.

Concepts are continually re-defined by the legal community, making it more difficult for language users (e.g. lawyers, translators, technical writers, language planners, etc.) when a word and concept with an established core of meaning is stretched beyond its ordinary use. The result is ambiguity and inconsistency. Thus far, it would not seem unreasonable to develop a systematic method of descriptive terminography (see § 2) to identify and analyse concept-term behaviour in legal document collections.

2. Method

According to Sager (1990) a definition of terminography[5] as a discipline deals with:

(a) building specialized dictionaries and term banks;

(b) the "set of practices and methods used for the collection, description and presentation of terms" (Sager 1990: 3); and

(c) "a theory [...] required for explaining the relationships between concepts and terms" (Sager 1990: 3).

Our proposed method is to describe the use and function of concepts and their designated terms in a single specialized domain such as Criminal Law, in both intralingual and interlingual contexts, and to establish degrees of equivalence of concepts. The tenor of the text producing a meaning for equivalence system purposes is also taken into account. Conceptual and linguistic analysis of the term *mens rea* (*intention* and *recklessness*) is carried out using definitions extracted from a corpus of English and Italian criminal law texts as found in draft-codes, case law, as well as legal theory in both Common Law and Civil Law systems. The types of legal texts for comparison correspond roughly to those established by Bhatia (1983: 2) – i.e. legislative writing with a prescriptive function, academic writing, and juridical writing. The present analysis is based on definitions and accounts for the established positions in literature that "[s]pecialized definitions describe a concept within a special subject field" (e.g. Sager 1990: 39), as well as the extent to which equivalence of concepts can be established between variable systems.

The descriptive concept-centred method (Sager) is widely established in scholarly literature on terminology (eg, Cole 1991; Wright/Budin 1997; Cabré 1998, 2000a), and is an important feature on which terminography is based (eg, Picht/Draskau 1985; Meyer/Eck

5 A comprehensive name (terminology) is also used to refer to the "vocabulary of a special subject field" (Sager 1990: 3), which is further reiterated as the "set of terms representing the system of concepts of a particular subject field" (ISO 1087: 1990), and "the scientific study of the concepts and terms found in special languages" (ISO 1087: 1990).

1996). The method has an onomasiological rather than semasiological component, which describes and contrasts terms and their paradigmatic relations with other subordinate concepts (eg, Picht/Draskau 1985; Meyer/Eck 1996). The method draws on the principles advanced by Wüster (1979), Arntz/Picht (1989) and Koller (1992), for whom equivalence is defined as 'conceptual correspondence' of terms (Arntz/Picht 1989: 159), which assumes that, for legal concepts to bear comparison, they must have the same intension(s)[6], i.e. the condition which includes the characteristics determining the comparability and applicability of the concept in interlingual contexts. If the descriptive method identifies and analyses conceptual categories, it follows that the method also gains benefit from cognitive linguistics and computational linguistics, which both affect the theory of terminology and specialized language studies.

2.1. Analysing mens rea *concepts*

The central case of wrongdoing occurs when the defendant's crime is intentional (intended consequence), which takes on the linguistic form of 'direct intention'. Where the defendant's aim is not prohibited by the particular crime (unintended consequence) because he *believes* or *realises* that in order to achieve his purpose he will have to commit the prohibited act, the defendant is said to possess 'oblique intent'. The ordinary dictionary definitions of 'intention' confine the meaning to "an act of intending; a volition that you intend to carry out" (*WorldNet Hyperdictionary*, 2003) and "a thing intended; an aim or plan, or the action or fact of intending" (Pearsall 1998). The definitions are meant to describe what the law qualifies as 'direct intention'.

---

6 The International Standardization Organization distinguishes between intension and extension of a concept. The former is a "set of characteristics which makes up the concept" while the latter is the "totality of objects to which a concept corresponds" (ISO 1087-1:2000, Terminology work – Vocabulary – Part 1: Theory and application).

Legal theorists (Simester/Sullivan, 2001: 115) attach a stretched meaning to 'intention' to describe cases where the defendant *intended* the *actus reus* in the ordinary, paradigm sense of 'intention', or recognised that the *actus reus* was a *virtually certain* consequence of his actions. While the former case embraces the standard ordinary language meaning of 'intention', in the latter case the defendant does not act in order to bring about the intended outcome.[7] The Law Commission has offered the following plain definition of a person acting 'intentionally':

(1) a person acts intentionally with respect to a result when it is his purpose to cause it; or although it is not his purpose to cause it, he knows that it would occur in the ordinary course of events if he were to succeed in his purpose of causing some other result. (Draft Criminal Code, Report 218/1993: clause 1)

By comparison, Italian legal theory uses the terms *dolo intenzionale* (or *dolo diretto/di primo grado*) and *dolo indiretto* (or *di secondo grado*):

(2) *dolo intenzionale*
il soggetto ha di mira proprio la realizzazione della condotta criminosa (reato di azione), ovvero la causazione dell'evento (reato di evento), sia esso stato previsto dall'agente come certo o anche soltanto come possibile. (Fiandaca/ Musco 1995: 320)

(3) *dolo indiretto*
quando la realizzazione del reato non è l'obiettivo che dà causa alla condotta, ma costituisce soltanto uno strumento necessario perché l'agente realizzi lo scopo perseguito [...] l'evento lesivo rappresenta una conseguenza accessoria necessariamente (o assai probabilmente) connessa alla realizzazione volontaria del fatto principale. (Fiandaca/Musco 1995: 321)

The all-inclusive drafting format in text (1) embraces the distinct Italian concepts of *dolo intenzionale* in (2) and *dolo indiretto* in (3). Conceptual items in text (1) behave in the same way as those in texts (2) and (3): *dolo intenzionale* is described in the ordinary paradigm sense of a person acting *with respect to a result when it is his purpose to*

7 English legal theory and case law exemplify this case by considering that D knows (or believes, desires, or realises, all of which are used interchangeably as correlated *mens rea* words).

cause it, and *dolo indiretto* is described in the remaining clauses of the English text revolving around conditionality patterns (Perkins 1983) predicated on the agent (*he knows that it would... if he were*).[8] The two concepts (denoted hyponymously by the superordinate, adverbial term 'intentionally') describe a case of absolute equivalence by different linguistic and structural means. Clearly, both hyponymic Italian concepts, expressing conceptual relation of inclusion, are also the lexical reflex of the part-whole relation, as in the paradigmatic case *intention(ally): direct/oblique intention*, in which 'direct/oblique intention' stand as the meronym.

It is the linguistic information in the second part of the English text which raises discussion. The emphatic, hypothetical use of *would* expresses the need for something more than just foresight that the result is more likely than not, or requires some higher degree of probability, in order to specify the level of foresight required in the ambiguous phrase *in the ordinary course of events*. This would be a case of 'recklessness', which the Law Commission defines in (6) as requiring that the person "is aware of a risk that the outcome will occur as a result". The dynamic modal *will* expresses futurity and prediction (Palmer 1990: 36-37).[9] However, the ordinary dictionary definitions of 'recklessness' – "the trait of giving little thought to danger" (*WorldNet Hyperdictionary* 2003) or "without thinking or caring about the consequences of an action" (Pearsall 1998) – provide little guidance.

Traditionally, in case law (R v. Cunningham [1957] 2 QB 396, 399; R v. Caldwell [1982] AC 341, 354) recklessness has been taken to mean the deliberate and conscious taking of an obvious and unreasonable risk by the defendant; the risk being defined in terms of *reasonableness*.[10] Thus, the main difference between 'intention' and 'recklessness' is that, while in both cases the defendant must *foresee*

---

8 In both systems, the conceptual structure of 'intention' (*dolo*) encompasses two mental requirements: (1) 'knowledge' (*rappresentazione*) in the form of 'consciousness' (*coscienza*), 'awareness' (*conoscenza*), or 'foresight' (*previsione*); and (2) 'will' (*volontà*).

9 This dynamic modality can also include a case of 'extrinsic modality' in Biber's terminology to refer to "the logical status of events or states, usually relating to assessments of likelihood" (1999: 485).

10 Specifically, through the objective 'reasonable man test'.

the possibility of causing an event, in 'recklessness' he need not be *motivated* to bring it about. These concepts are illustrated periphrastically in case law definitions in (4) and (5) below:

(4) *Cunningham (or subjective) recklessness*
A person is reckless where:
– he is subjectively aware of the existence of the risk; and
– he nevertheless goes on to take that risk; and
– the taking of the risk is objectively unjustified in the circumstances. (R v. Cunningham [1957] 2 QB 396, 399)

(5) *Caldwell (or objective) recklessness*
A person is reckless where:
– the risk is a serious one; and either
– he is subjectively aware of the risk and goes on to take it ('Cunningham'); or
– he gives no thought to the possibility of the risk and the risk was an obvious one; and the taking of the risk is objectively unjustified under the circumstances. (R v. Caldwell [1982] AC 341, 354)[11]

The Law Commission has proposed the following plain, comprehensive definition of recklessness:

(6) A person acts recklessly with respect to: (i) a circumstance, when he is aware of a risk that it exists or will exist; and (ii) a result, when he is aware of a risk that it will occur, and it is unreasonable, having regard to the circumstances known to him, to take that risk. (Report 218/1993: Clause 1)

By comparison, we read about *dolo eventuale* and *colpa cosciente* in Italian legal theory:

(7) *dolo eventuale*
quando la volontà non si dirige direttamente verso l'evento, ma l'agente lo *accetta* come conseguenza eventuale, 'accessoria' della propria condotta. Sicchè egli, pur non 'intendendo' realizzarlo o anche sperando che non si verifichi, tuttavia ne accetta il verificarsi. [...] L'evento può dirsi accettato in tutti i casi in cui l'agente: a) si rappresenta almeno la *possibilità positiva* del verificarsi di esso; b) permane altresì nella *convinzione* o anche nel *dubbio* che esso possa concretamente verificarsi; c) tiene, ciononostante, la condotta quali ne

11 The law recognises that the definition of 'Caldwell recklessness' is an extension of the earlier companion of 'Cunningham recklessness'.

siano gli esiti: anche *a costo* di cagionare l'evento e, perciò, 'accettandone il rischio'. (Mantovani 1992: 320-321)

(8) *colpa cosciente* (or *con previsione dell'evento*)
quando l'evento, pur non essendo voluto, è tuttavia *previsto* dall'agente. (Mantovani 1992: 341)

Reading through the texts evidences a higher degree of comparable complexity than the 'intention' counterpart. Comparing the two texts we notice that text in (6) overlaps with corresponding and differing characteristics denoted by the conceptual structures of *dolo eventuale* and *colpa cosciente*. While it is true that the three texts revolve around the agent's subjective perception (foresight = awareness) of the risk occurring, the wording of 'degree of foresight' in recklessness shares with the meaning of *dolo eventuale*, but differs in intension from *colpa cosciente*. This is because Italian law treats the agent acting in *colpa cosciente* as when he believes that the event will *not* occur (Mantovani 1992: 342: "il soggetto ha il preciso convincimento che l'evento non si verificherà"). In *dolo eventuale* the agent is treated as believing or doubting that the event may occur, accepting the risk in a), b), or c) conditions in (7). This type of variability in constructing 'foresight' is also shown by the lexical patterning, describing 'recklessness': the meaning of the indicative verbal form *exists* and the modalized form *will exist* in clauses (6.i) and (6.ii) both suggest foresight of 'a consequence as virtually certain'. Hence, English 'recklessness' and Italian *dolo eventuale* share the same conceptual characteristics, but overlap with some differing features in *colpa cosciente*.

3. Results and Discussion

The foregoing analysis is illustrative of the problems involved in the comparison of concepts. We have seen that the terms 'intention' and 'recklessness' convey a meaning which goes beyond what could be attributed in ordinary usage, so that any attempt to designate (still less without proper qualifiers) the concepts as *dolo*, *colpa* and, ordinarily, as *intenzione, indifferenza, inavvedutezza*, or other similar combinations as most ordinary bilingual dictionaries seem to suggest, will simply result in an exercise of style. The usefulness of the above comparative descriptive analysis is that it serves as a tool for computerised terminographical applications in criminal law. To realise such work the user's requirement for specific terminology data in specialised fields of knowledge should be identified pragmatically. The data should be analysed by describing and documenting concepts and terms[12] through corpus-based definitions in interlingual contexts. The data are complemented with other linguistic information, such as: grammatical, (near)synonymy, polysemy, homonymy, paradigmatic relations of inclusion and exclusion, etc. These are commented and visually represented below through a three-stage procedure and standardised data entry.

Stage 1

- Identification of users' requirements in their academic and/or professional settings (eg, legal academics/legal practitioners, (legal) translators, technical writers, LSP students).
- Documentation of concepts/terms (in single specialised subjects and subfields) from each national system.
- Co-operative work (with law and language experts).

Stage 2

- Description of concepts and terms in numerical or alphabetical enumerative systems, and their classification according to legal branches and text sources.
- Pronunciation, Parts of speech, Acronym, Geographical use, Origin.
- Definition.
- (Near)Synonyms, Polysemes, Homonyms : Hypronyms, Hyponyms.
- Phraseology: idioms/fixed phrases, maxims of law, collocations (grammatical, lexical).
- Context examples from case law: these are concepts ranked through short paragraphs. These are of particular value since many concepts are expanded to demonstrate how the particular point of law operates. This expansion does not only help users to understand the concept more clearly, but also provides additional

12 A term is "a meaningful unit comprising one word (simple term) or several words (complex term) that represents a single specific concept within a concept field" (de Bessé 1997: 64).

linguistic material for the comprehension of aspects of meaning which have direct relevance in legal language syntax.
- Non-linguistic designations of concepts and terms, such as diagrams and flow charts.

Stage 3

- Equivalence system (absolute, relative, none, functional): the concept entries from one legal system are compared with the entries from another legal system and degrees of equivalence are established (co-operative work: linguist/law expert).
- If concepts only occur in the ST, the following strategies will apply: 1. borrowing; 2. calque; or 3. newly coined term (in TL) will apply.

Figure 2 visually represents a standardised model for single data entry ('recklessness'), the number and type of data being recorded (e.g., collocation) will obviously depend upon the requirements set by the individual entry. Cross reference entries (►) in *italics* and **bold-type** are also provided.

Subject: Law / Diritto
Subfield: Criminal Law / Diritto Penale
Main field: Public Law / Diritto Pubblico

Concept: *recklessness* ⟶ **Term:** *dolo eventuale*
(ai confini di *colpa cosciente*)

reck·less (rĕk'lĭs): *adj.*

1. (of a person or their actions) without thinking or caring about the consequences of an action (Pearsall 1998).
2. the trait of giving little thought to danger (WorldNetHyperdictionary 2003): *a reckless driver.*

recklessly **reck'less·ly** *adv.*
recklessness **reck'less·ness** *n.*

ORIGIN: [Old English *recceléas*, from the Germanic base (meaning 'care') of RECK]
Source: *The New Oxford Dictionary of English*, Pearsall, Oxford, 1998

Legal system: EN
Source: Law Commission (Report) No 218, *Legislating the Criminal Code: Offences Against the Person and General Principles*, 1993, London, HMSO.

Definition:

> • *Recklessness*
> A person acts recklessly with respect to: (i) a circumstance, when he is aware of a risk that it exists or will exist; and (ii) a result, when he is aware of a risk that it will occur, and it is unreasonable, having regard to the circumstances known to him, to take that risk.

Legal system: IT
Source: Mantovani F. *Diritto Penale*. Padova, Cedam, 1992, 320-341.

> • *dolo eventuale*
> […] quando la volontà non si dirige direttamente verso l'evento, ma l'agente lo *accetta* come conseguenza eventuale, "accessoria" della propria condotta. Sicchè egli, pur non "intendendo" realizzarlo o anche sperando che non si verifichi, tuttavia ne accetta il verificarsi. […] L'evento può dirsi accettato in tutti i casi in cui l'agente: a) si rappresenta almeno la *possibilità positiva* del verificarsi di esso; b) permane altresì nella *convinzione* o anche nel *dubbio* che esso possa concretamente verificarsi; c) tiene, ciononostante, la condotta quali ne siano gli esiti: anche *a costo* di cagionare l'evento e, perciò, "accettandone il rischio". (1992: 320-321)
> • *colpa cosciente* (or *con previsione dell'evento*)
> […] quando l'evento, pur non essendo voluto, è tuttavia *previsto* dall'agente. (Mantovani 1992: 341)

Synonyms: ▶ *heedless, inattentive to duty, gross negligence, wild carelessness and disregard for consequences, wilful blindness, wilfulness* → see ▶ for variant meanings

Hyperonyms, Hyponyms: recklessness is one of the three classes of mental states constituting ***mens rea*** (the Latin for **guilty mind**): **Intention** → **Recklessness** → (**Gross**) **Negligence** → see ▶ for variant (gradable) meanings
Recklessness shows less **culpability** than **intention**, but more culpability than **criminal negligence**. The most culpable *mens rea* elements have **foresight** and **desire** on a subjective test.

Homonyms: **specific intent**

Phrases: *to act recklessly* (*with respect to a material element of a criminal offence*), *to attract recklessness, to attract liability for recklessness* (*for reckless conduct/ behaviour*), *to impute recklessness, to be liable in recklessness* (*for reckless conduct*)

Context example:

> R v Caldwell [1982]
> D (Caldwell) set fire to a hotel where people were staying while intoxicated. D was charged with an offence against s. 1(1) of the Criminal Damage Act 1971, which makes it an offence to damage another's property "being reckless as to whether any such property would be destroyed or damaged". D claimed intoxication as a defence to the charge of *intention* to endanger life. This defence was upheld, but the court ruled that intoxication could not be raised as a defence against a charge of recklessness. The House of Lords held that, although D did not foresee the risk (and therefore could not be charged of recklessness under the Cunningham definition), recklessness included cases where a reasonable (not drunk) person would have seen that the risk was an obvious and serious one.

Flow chart

Recklessness
D *realises/aware of risk* [**subjective** recklessness
D *fails to realise/think of the risk*
BUT
ordinary prudent man *would realise risk* [**objective** recklessness]

Figure 2. Standardised Data Entry for Terminography: A Model,

The comparative concept-oriented terminography model, focuses more on information in the SL rather than in the TT context, providing previously identified language users with as much specialised information as possible. This information abides by the legal discourse practices of the system concerned, enabling language users to avoid an almost inevitable naïve attitude to concepts and terms. At the same time, the rationale should preserve the quality and integrity of legal information, promoting certainty and consistency of terminological applications. This leads to the immediate purposes of a comparative descriptive terminography, which are to establish and preserve monoreferentiality and precision of terms and to avoid semantic ambiguity (Gotti 2003 : 32-35; Scarpa 2002: 29-31). In our case of a legal domain-specific terminography, the precision requirement arising from the law demands that the terminological work be also prescriptive as well as descriptive in nature, as put forward in the scholarly literature in this field (Scarpa 2002: 29). For specialized knowledge and efficient communication to be promoted and to avoid the ambiguity of terms, standardisation should be applied. Standardisation will seek to remove:

1. synonymy as alternative representations of the same concept, such as in the instances of *recklessness, wilful blindness*, and *ordinary negligence*. However, *recklessness* transcends (therefore extends in meaning) *ordinary negligence* in law simply because, to be reckless, conduct must show indifference to consequences in circumstances involving peril to the life or safety of others, although no harm is intended;
2. reduce polysemy as the coexistence of many possible meanings for a concept: for example, polysemous senses have a linear relation if one is a specialisation of (i.e., a hyponym or meronym) the other, such as: *intention* (*dolo*) → *recklessness* (*colpa cosciente*) → *negligence* (broadly as *colpa*) taken linearly, and
3. reduce homonymy as one concept has the same pronunciation or spelling as another but different meanings, such as *specific intent* (and not *basic intent*) being different from Italian *dolo specifico*. However, because *basic intent* encompasses *recklessness*, we understand that the relation in the vocabulary of criminal law language is of hyponymy, since *basic intent* is a hyponym of *recklessness*, and conversely, *recklessness* is a superordinate (hyperonym) of *basic intent*.

4. Conclusion

As we have seen in the *mens rea* analysis, these and other terms, represent different concepts (in paradigmatic sense relations) with different extensional meanings and definitions. Thus, the terminographer's task will be:

- to borrow concepts (SL terms are transferred directly to TL);
- to transfer SL term in a literal translation directly to TL (calque); to propose new terms (neologisms).

For example, in translation-oriented terminography the concept of *ulterior intent*, which is practically non-existent in TT, will require a linguistic (semantic) calque to be applied for functional purposes. Thus, for example, *acting with ulterior intent* will be rendered as *agire dolosamente con fine ulteriore*. However, it should be remembered that standardisation purposes are not exclusively confined to communication practices involving two national systems of language and law as in the current analysis, but may extend to international contexts, e.g. the EU where international criminal law matters now stand high on the European agenda. In fact, it is not so easy to perceive whether concepts of international mutual assistance in criminal matters may have an obvious place in the legal 'categories' families common to Civilian, Common, or other lawyers. Yet, the need for an equivalence systems of concepts in this area will require terminographers (perhaps by co-operating with law experts) to standardise terminology throughout different law systems and cultures so as to aid international communication.

While we cannot escape from the above advantages of using any such descriptive work for terminography, common sense shows that they are not so easy to perceive when comparability and applicability of concepts are involved in the establishment of the equivalence system. In the analysis of 'recklessness' we have seen that conceptual identity proves to be difficult to attain because of the comparability and applicability standards, so that the case of 'recklessness' is one which overlaps with corresponding (*dolo eventuale*) and differing conceptual features (*colpa cosciente*) in comparable definitions. Therefore, the case is one of a *relative* equivalence. While this is true of concepts used in differing systems and traditions (Common Law v Civil Law), we must not deny that equivalence also implies sociological factors outside the law to be taken into account. When contrasting languages for terminographical applications, such as is required for the compilation of terminological resources and/or translation for law purposes, we notice that the main disagreement in the comparison of concepts is invariably raised by the tertium comparationis (TC). This is a variant on a common basis against which two concepts can be described and measured. In terminographical applications, such as the one being examined, variation may also be measured for cultural (epistemic) indeterminacy/inconsistency of concepts and terms (eg, *negligent, reasonable*) as we have already described.

Faced with similar constraints in the equivalent system, therefore, a descriptive terminographical data information which cannot satisfy complete conceptual correspondence, because of the systems primarily differing from each other, could at least provide a complete documentation of the use and function of concepts and terms in their national contexts. And it is at this point where the purpose of any such terminographical resource should alternatively be identified: i.e. "to inform the user" (Šarčević 1991: 619) and to provide a reasoned and systematic legal knowledge of national concepts seen as "knowledge units" (Dahlberg 1976: 83), which are part of a culturally and legally rooted knowledge system. We cannot deny that similar terminographical resource data may also bring advantages in a variety of applications and disciplines, such as:

- Legal Translation/Information Retrieval: translators may not be experts in the subject-field (which often results in incorrect or wrong translations); or research materials available in both TL and SL are inadequate in order to decide on priorities of the translation strategy in culture-specific contexts, or no easy access to subject-field specialists is available for translation.
- Computer-Aided Language Learning (CALL).
- Distance Learning.
- Technical Writing.

For a descriptive terminographical resource to rely also on integrated theory, it should take into account the insights of cognitive semantics mentioned before. In fact, the value of an integrated socio-cognitive model is easy to recognise since language has a cognitive (ideational) function (Halliday) and, many of the conceptual categories by which language users express their ideas in discourse via the medium of language are created in the mind which has prototype structure (Rosch). We have seen that examples of the category Intention can share different, subtle relations of variable complexity (*is one of* the main forms of mens rea, *is used to establish* culpability, *to determine* mens rea requirement, *is different from* motive, etc.). In such cases, the approach to meaning we saw before intuitively comes into play to associate the word with the mental representation of the type of object, so that it can be used to refer to, and to be acted upon, by the agent *intending*, or being *reckless*, to achieve a particular criminal consequence. These potentials of building together language, human mind, and world to elaborate cognitive semantics in terminology are further explained in empiricist position by Geeraerts (1993), who claims that "experience determines conceptuality" and that "conceptual knowledge determines experience" (1993: 58). Along these lines, a communication-oriented and discourse-centred approach to terminology is therefore gaining ground (Cabré 2000b; Temmerman 2000).

References

Arntz, Reiner / Picht, Heribert. 1989. *Einführung in die Terminologie-arbeit. Studien zu Sprache und Technik.* Hildesheim: Olms.

Bhatia, Vijay K. 1983. *An Applied Discourse Analysis of English Legislative Writing*. Birmingham: University of Aston.

Biber, Douglas *et al.* 1999. *Longman Grammar of Spoken and Written English*. London: Longman.

Cabré, Castellvì Teresa T. 1998. A propos de la notion de la notion de qualité en terminologie. *La banque des mots* 8. CILF: Paris, 7-34.

Cabré, Castellvì Teresa T. 2000a. La terminologia tra lessicografia e documentazione: aspetti storici e importanza sociale. *Forum del Seminario permanente 'Lessicologia, terminologia e metodi di classificazione*'. Roma, 6 aprile 2000. <http://www.isrds.rm.cnr.it/HyperDocs/assiterm/forum.htm>.

Cabré, Castellvì Teresa T. 2000b. Elements for a Theory of Terminology: Towards an Alternative Paradigm. *Terminology* 6/1, 35-57.

Cole, Wayne D. 1991. Descriptive Terminology: Some Theoretical Implications. *Meta* 36, 16-22.

Dahlberg, Ingetraut 1976. Über Gegenstände, Begriffe, Definitionen und Benennungen: Zur möglichen Neufassung von DIN 2330. *Muttersprache* 2, 81-117.

De Bessé, Bruno 1997. Terminological Definitions. In Wright Ellen S. / Budin Gerhard (eds) *Handbook of Terminology Management*, vol. 1. Amsterdam: Benjamins, 63-74.

Felber, Helmut / Budin, Gerhard 1989. *Terminologie in Theorie and Praxis*. Tübingen: Gunter Narr.

Fiandaca, Giovanni / Musco, Enzo 1995. *Diritto Penale* – Parte Generale. Bologna: Zanichelli.

Geeraerts, Dirk 1993. Cognitive Semantcs and the History of Philosophical Epistemology. In Geiger, Richard A. / Rudzka-Ostyn, Brygida. (eds) *Conceptualizations and Mental Processing in Language*, Berlin: Mouton de Gruyter.

Gotti, Maurizio 2003. *Specialized Discourse: Linguistic Features and Changing Conventions*. Bern: Peter Lang.

Halliday, Michael A.K. 1985. *An Introduction of Functional Grammar*. London: Edward Arnold.

Jackendoff, Ray 2002. *Foundations of Language: Brain, Meaning, Grammar, Evolution*. Oxford: Oxford University Press.

Koller, Werner 1992. *Einführung in die Übersetzungswissenschaft*, Heidelberg: Quelle & Meyer UTB.

Law Commission, (Report) No 218, *Legislating the Criminal Code: Offences Against the Person and General Principles*. 1993. London: HMSO.

Lyons, John 1977. *Semantics*. Cambridge: Cambridge University Press.

Maidahl Cristiansen, Lisbet / Duvå, Grete / Laursen, Anna-Lise 1994. Das Translationswörterburch für Fachsprachen. Ein integriertes Konzept. In Burkhard, S. / Henning, B. (Hrsg.) *Das Fachwörterbuch. Fachwissen und seine Repräsentation in Wörterbüchern.* Tübingen: Narr, 269-284.

Mantovani, Ferrando 1992. *Diritto Penale*. Padova: Cedam.

Palmer, Frank R. 1990. *Modality and the English Modals*. London: Longman.

Pearsall, Judy 1998. *The New Oxford Dictionary of English*. Oxford: Oxford University Press.

Perkins, Michael R. 1983. *Modal Expressions in English*. London: Pinter.

Picht, Herbert / Draskau, Jennifer 1985. *Terminology: An Introduction*. Guildford: University of Surrey.

Riggs, Fred W. 1989. Terminology and Lexicography: Their Complementarity. *International Journal of Lexicography* 2, 89-110.

Rosch, Eleanor 1977. Human Categorization. In Warren Neil (ed.) *Advances in Cross-Cultural Categorization*, vol. 1. New York: Academic Press, 1-49.

Sager, Juan C. 1990. *A Practical Course in Terminology Processing*. Amsterdam: Benjamins.

Šarčević, Susan 1991. Bilingual and Multilingual Legal Dictionaries: New Standards for the Future. *Meta* 36/4, 615.

Scarpa, Federica 2002. Terminologia e Lingue Speciali. In Magris, Marella / Musacchio, Teresa M. / Rega, Lorenza / Scarpa, Federica (eds) *Manuale di Terminologia – Aspetti Teorici, Metodologici e Applicativi*. Milano: Hoepli.

Simester, Andrew P. / Sullivan, Robert G. 2001. *Criminal Law. Theory and Doctrine*. Oxford: Hart.

Temmerman, Rita 2000. *Towards New Ways of Terminology Description. The Sociocognitive Approach*. Amsterdam: Benjamins.

WorldNet Dictionary 2003. Webnox Corp. <http://www. hyperdic tionary.com>.

Wright, Ellen S. 1997. Term Selection: the Initial Phase of Terminology Management. In Wright Ellen S. / Budin Gerhard (eds), 13-21.

Wright Ellen S. / Budin Gerhard (eds) 1997. *A Handbook of Terminology Management*, vol. 1. Amsterdam: Benjamins.

Wüster, Eugen 1979. *Einführung in die Allgemeine Terminologielehre und terminologische Lexikographie*. 2 Bde. New York: Springer.

Marta Chromá

Semantic and Legal Interpretation: Two Approaches to Legal Translation

1. Introduction

Motivations for researching the language of law[1] differ when considering those of the lawyer, the linguist and the translator. Lawyers usually engage in linguistic analysis in order to find the best way to formulate efficiently and persuasively what they wish to say or how to express the law so that it applies in the intended manner to the relevant recipients. Thus a lawyer's analysis of the language is pursued for the sake of his/her future better performance. Linguists usually examine the language 'as is' and 'where is' (to use the language of contracts) in order to identify building elements of the text and their relations and describe them in their linguistic metalanguage; no matter their conclusions, they scarcely (or only exceptionally) influence lawyers' writing. Translators create the third group of specialist professionals who engage in research into legal language. Translators′ methods should combine the approaches of both lawyers and linguists and be based on a comparison of the source and target languages, and source and target legal systems, so that the respective legal information may be effectively communicated to the ultimate recipient of the translated text in line with the purpose of translation. Unsurprisingly, translators can sometimes have a positive influence on the writing of

1 One of the oldest definitions of the English language of law can be found in Mellinkoff's bible of English legal linguistics (1963, 2004: 3) describing it as "the customary language used by lawyers in those common law jurisdictions where English is the official language. It includes distinctive words, meanings, phrases, and modes of expressions. It also includes certain mannerisms of composition not exclusive with the profession but prevalent to have formed a fixed association".

lawyers: frequent questions such as "what did you mean by that" or "does this phrase mean this or that?" asked by an in-house translator in a big international law firm may move some lawyers to start thinking about the way in which they express themselves and to start to formulate their ideas in clearer and more distinct language.

2. Translation of the legal text

The language of law, as emphasized many times before, is a quite formalized language at all levels: lexical, syntactic, textual, and genre. Traditionally its vocabulary has been regarded as the main distinctive feature, particularly with respect to the use of terminology, but it has also been stressed on many occasions that legal language is not just composed of terms of arts; these make up only about 25% of vocabulary, depending on the genre (cf. Chromá, 2008).

Since law belongs to a wider category of humanities, the vocabulary of which is based on abstract words and expressions which however bear quite a precise meaning, legal terminology consists primarily of abstract terms deeply and firmly rooted in domestic culture and intellectual tradition. Language represents culture because the words refer to culture, conceived as the beliefs and practices of a society, but the representation is never complete or perfect (Nida 2001: 27). Therefore legal translation has what Nord (1997: 41) calls a referential function depending on the comprehensibility of the source text. The function poses problems when source and target readers do not share the same amount of previous knowledge about the objects and phenomena which are referred to, as is often the case with source-culture realities or realia. Bergenholtz and Tarp (1995: 60) use the attribute 'culture-dependent' to denote subjects such as law that have historically and culturally developed their own specific features within delimited geographical areas. Obviously, the main task of the translator at the preparatory stage of his or her work is to 'decode' this "culture-dependence". Alcaraz and Hughes (2002: 3) explicitly say that the first stage in successful translation is to understand the source text fully; and only then can the production of a target text follow. Smith defines (1995: 181) three prerequisites for the successful translation of legal texts: (a) a basic knowledge of the respective legal systems, (b) familiarity with the relevant terminology, and (c) competence in the target language's specific legal style of writing. The first requirement, if satisfied by the translator, more or less represents the 'decoding' of the culture-specificity or culture-dependence of the source text: if familiar with both the source and target legal systems and the respective branch of law in both systems, the translator may identify in advance potential linguistic as well as legal (i.e. substantive) traps in which he or she otherwise might be caught. Knowledge of relevant terminology in both the source and target languages is the second requirement closely linked with, and resulting from the first prerequisite. The competence of the translator in using specific legal styles of writing in the TL builds upon the first two prerequisites and provides for the adequate genre formatting of the translated text; such competence results from the translator's sufficient knowledge of genres of legal texts.

Our experience suggests that the translation of legal texts should not be undertaken without an extensive knowledge of the respective legal topic in both the source language and the target language, i.e. the knowledge of concepts, terms denoting these concepts, sentence patterns visualizing the information, genre classification of the text, legal culture, and so on, in both languages and legal systems. Next, the legal translator should consider the purpose (or 'skopos', in Vermeer's terminology) of the translation and, in particular, of the target legal text, and furthermore, preferably, the expectations of the ultimate recipient. Consideration of such issues may help the translator decide whether a 'documentary' translation or an 'instrumental' translation, or their combination, should be produced (Trosborg 1997: 154-155 referring to Nord 1991: 72). The former serves as documentation of source culture communication between the author and the source text recipient; for example, a British act if translated into Czech will never have the same function in a Czech environment, i.e. the function of the law and the translation will only be documentary. The latter is a communicative instrument in its own right, which will focus on some features of the source text, while pushing others into the background, but which fully concentrates on the target text in order to serve the expectations of the target recipient. Using the example of legislation, secondary legislation adopted within the European Union is translated into all official languages and has the same function in all member states. The translation is instrumental, having the same effect in all member states, although in the case of European legislation it may be quite tricky to name any of the official languages as a source language (cf. Šarčević 2002).

Translation is a very complex activity. What happens in the process of translation of a legal text?

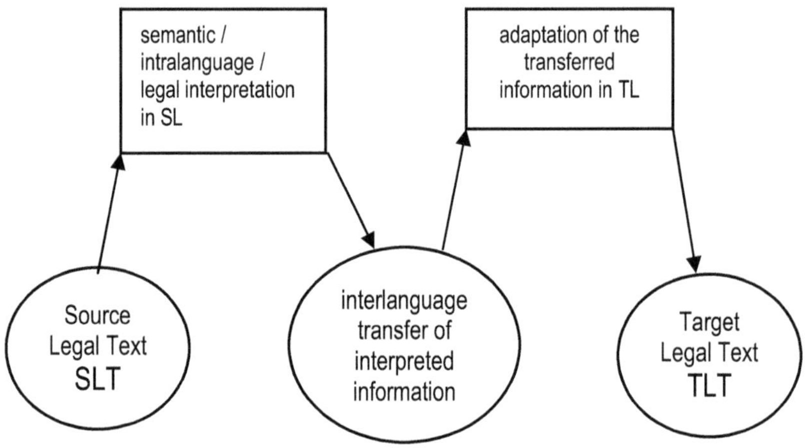

Graph 1. The process of legal translation.

The creation of a source legal text depends on many factors:
(a) the system of law and its branch or branches within which the text is framed, and the subject-matter the text deals with;
(b) the author's intention, which may determine the tenor of the text in question;
(c) the required degree of normativity of a legal text;
(d) the genre of text (text type), which usually requires a certain repertoire of linguistic structures including sentence patterns, etc; and
(e) the purpose of interaction between the producer and potential recipients of the source legal text, which may determine the choice of both linguistic and formal tools.

The translator tries to fully understand the source text, meaning that he or she decodes and interprets the information contained in the source text. Then the interpreted information is transferred into the target language. Finally, the transferred information is adapted according to the purpose of the translation, respecting the relevant genre and styles of legal writing in the target legal system, and possibly the needs and expectations of the ultimate recipient, for example by adding explanatory comments in footnotes. Thus the target legal text has been created. As the picture indicates, the most important part of legal translation is to understand the text fully, i.e. to correctly interpret legal information contained in the source legal text, so that the transfer of the information into the target language and target legal system is as precise and comprehensible as possible.

2.1. Interpreting as intralingual translation

Smith (1995: 180) mentions that 'intralingual translation', or translating the legal language into the standard language, can be extremely challenging whenever legal phrases or terms are imprecise or open to interpretation due to their semantic or legal indeterminacy. Intralingual translation in such an understanding is a component part of the interpretation of legal clauses and provisions. Tomášek (1990: 113) points out that legal translation is a procedure based on both linguistic and legal comparative approaches. He asserts that the content of legal information should be fully preserved and transposed into the target language so that the target legal text corresponds with usage in the target legal environment. What is denoted as 'intralingual' translation by Smith above, Tomášek (1991: 147) calls 'intrasemiotic' translation, and describes it as the transfer of information from the first to the second semantic level of the source language, i.e. the interpretation of law by means of transfer from the legal language to the legal metalanguage. 'Intersemiotic' translation is then understood by Tomášek as the translation of a legal text from the source language to the target language.

As can be assumed from the above, the quality of legal translation is fully dependent on the ability of the translator to adequately interpret the original text and to transpose it into the language and legal culture of the recipient. Šarčević (2000: 72) goes further, stating that the goal of legal translation is to produce a text that will preserve the unity of a single instrument by guaranteeing its uniform interpretation and application. Joseph (1995: 33-34), in his analysis of the practice of legal translation, concludes that translators should interpret rather than merely translate (for example, by interrupting the translation with an informed commentary); they should intervene in the text semantically, stylistically, and intellectually, to the extent called for. He adds:

> It should be insisted that where law is concerned, the desire to provide easy reading should not lead one to sacrifice fully interpretative translation in favour of the simple legal convention of the target language anytime the systems differ or anytime the original includes resonances and connotations that the simple target-language equivalent cannot capture.

Maintaining Joseph's requirements, we claim that the primary objective of legal translation is that the target recipient should be provided with as explicit, extensive and precise legal information in the target language as is contained in the source text, complemented (by the translator) with facts rendering the original information fully comprehensible in the different legal environment and culture.

Translators of legal texts in the Czech Republic are mostly linguists who do not have a law degree, with limited (layman's) experience of Czech law and familiar only to a limited extent, if any, with Anglo-American law. As explained above, a legal translator must mediate information between languages and between legal systems. Civil law (and Czech law as a derivative) and Anglo-American law, based on common law, share only a few legal concepts, mainly in those branches of law that are more international (trade, banking, insurance, public international law, etc). However, many more legal concepts differ between the systems or do not exist in the opposite system and thus no corresponding terminology may be found; moreover it may also happen that existing terms, although appearing close in meaning in both the source and target languages when semantically interpreted, denote slightly or greatly different legal concepts when interpreted legally.

There are several types of legal interpretation, such as *extensive* (or *liberal*, where the interpreter acts upon his or her own discretion considering all alternatives of interpretation), *logical* (based upon formal logic), and *strict* interpretation, which is the most frequently used (not allowing for more than one interpretation). Another is called *grammatical* and is based exclusively on decoding the meaning of words themselves.[2] This is the approach closest to semantic (in linguistic terms) interpretation. Every legal text can be interpreted in many ways, usually depending on the priorities and background of the person interpreting. In practice a combination of approaches are used, and, as Tiersma (1999: 132) points out, the nature of the document must be taken into account.

Semantic interpretation, as we understand the term for the purposes of translation, means that words or phrases are assigned their meaning regardless of any context. Where the legal context is to be considered when looking for an adequate meaning, legal interpretation is in question. Legal interpretation cannot dispense with a profound legal knowledge of the respective topic. What in fact happens when the translator 'interprets' the source text? He or she will try to identify the most likely meaning which can be transferred into the target language, as it is essentially impracticable to provide all possible meanings in the target text suggested (of a term, phrase, clause, sentence, an utterance) in the source text.

Moreover, the translator should consider how the target text, i.e. his or her product, may be interpreted by lawyers in the target legal system. The translator should avoid translational equivalents (at all levels of translation) that might lead to ambiguous interpretation. In order to do so he or she should know what may cause ambiguity, i.e. he or she should know the law.

The following three examples will indicate what the translator should take into account.

---

2 There has been quite intensive discussion on the role of dictionaries of general language in establishing the meaning of words in legal texts, as can be seen, for example, in Solan (2003).

2.1.1. 'And/or' conjunction

The combined conjunction *and/or* is very common in legal texts although experts in legal writing have persisted in condemning this 'hydra' among conjunctions. Solan (1993: 45) points out that when it comes to the interpretation of legal documents, *and* generally means conjunct *and*, and *or* is generally construed disjunctively, as meaning 'either/or'. When the combined conjunction *and/or* appears in a legal document of any sort, it may therefore cause problems in its interpretation. Garner (1995: 56) even asserts that many types of legal documents have been harmed by the lack of clarity of *and/or*. But he also claims that, no matter how clumsy it may be, the conjunction does have its specific meaning: 'x and/or y' means 'x or y or both'. Later Garner (2001: 112) contradicts himself stating that in about 50 percent of cases *and/or* means *and*, and in the other 50 percent it means *or*. Geoffrey Sellers, one of 16 lawyers working as Parliamentary Counsel in the UK Parliament, makes the following comment:

> The conjunction 'and/or' is recognised in English but is not regarded as acceptable usage in a literary or legislative context. It is sometimes referred to as the 'missing conjunction' because 'and' and 'or' are not adequate to express the whole range of logical possibilities. For instance:
> Does '*A and B may do X*' mean that only A and B acting together may do X, or that either or both of them may do X?
> Does '*A or B may do X*' mean that either A or B but not both may do X, or that either or both of them may?
> If the drafter is alert to this point it is always possible to make the position clear (by using more words), but it is still something of a trap. Ordinary colloquial English relies on the context to resolve possible misunderstandings, which drafters cannot always afford to do. What is meant by 'and/or' is the weak alternative – the second one in the two cases just mentioned. For those with a classical education, it can be explained as equivalent to the Latin 'vel', as opposed to 'aut' or 'et'. (Private email communication)

The Czech language lacks such a conjunction, but because it has been so often used in English documents, translators have coined its Czech literal 'equivalent', *a/nebo,* which is as unclear as its counterpart in English. Lawyers and Czech language experts continue to argue about its meaning and legitimacy whilst the conjunction continues to settle into legal Czech. Translators into Czech should ignore this innovation and should instead opt for a more wordy variant 'x or y or both'.

2.1.2. 'Subject to' phrase

Subject to may either be a part of a verbal phrase, *be subject to sth.,* or may stand alone, usually at the beginning of a provision in a contract or a statute. Whilst the former predicative function is unambiguous in all contexts the latter may cause interpretative problems. For example:

> Contracts may also *be subject to* conditions before performance is required, or they may be unconditional.

The predicate *be subject to* may be replaced by *be dependent upon* and as such translated into Czech. The following three excerpts are taken from authentic legal texts and illustrate four different meanings of the prepositional *subject to*:

> Our company is interested in purchasing the [name and address of business]. The purchase would include fixtures, equipment, furniture, stock in trade, parts, supplies, leasehold interests, and goodwill. *Subject to* a formal contract, we are prepared to offer $_______ for the business *subject to* the below listed terms: [...].

Subject to contract is a formulaic expression that has the effect of creating a preliminary contract of sale until a final or formal contract records the agreement (Garner 1995: 840). It suggests that the offer to pay money is only conditional and in the final contract the amount may differ. The second phrase *subject to the below terms* specifies that the offered amount in the preliminary contract will apply *according to* the listed terms.

> Employees' arrears of wages or salary [including commission and holiday remuneration] for 4 months prior to the relevant date *subject to* a financial limit to be set by delegated legislation.

Subject to a financial limit suggests that the arrears of wages may not exceed the statutory financial limit.

> *Subject to* the provisions of this Act, the memorandum and articles, when registered, bind the company and its members to the same extent as if they respectively had been signed and sealed by each member, and contained covenants on the part of each member to observe all the provisions of the memorandum and of the articles.

Subject to the provisions of this Act may be replaced by *if there are no contrary provisions in this Act* and should be translated as such.

2.1.3. The meaning of 'default'

The examples below show the use of the noun *default*.

> In the event of a *default*, the Seller may enter upon the premises of the Buyer and reclaim said goods. If the Seller retakes the goods he/she has the right to resell them for credit to the balance purchased, and the Seller may reacquire the same as further defined and set forth under state law.

Here the noun *default* suggests that the payment for goods is not made, i.e. that there is a delay in payment, for which there is a special translational equivalent in Czech law (which is *prodlení*).

> On a *default* of any obligation for which the security interest is granted, or the breach of any term of this security agreement, the secured party may declare all obligations immediately due and payable and shall have all the remedies of a secured party as set forth in the Uniform Commercial Code as enacted in the Debtor's state.

Default in the second example can be replaced by *non-performance* or *failure to perform* and translated as such into Czech (*neplnění*).

3. Implications for the training of translators

We have tried to show that even apparently minor issues in the interpretation of the source text may lead to imprecise or even incorrect and misleading translation. In our opinion, the only way for a translator to minimize difficulties in interpreting the source legal text and, as a result, to increase the clarity of their translational product for the final recipient, is to acquire over time a good knowledge of both legal systems.

Eight years ago, the Charles University Law School began a complementary two-semester training programme for practising translators and interpreters. Originally, the programme consisted of 150 contact hours; having considered the practical needs of translators, the duration was expanded to 162 hours of instruction over two semesters. One half is designed to introduce participants into Czech law (both private and public law branches) and the second half is devoted to linguistic and translational seminars on the same topic, based on a comparative linguistic and legal approach. Participants meet once a week[3] for six hours; a three-hour lecture on Czech law (delivered by a law teacher[4] specialized in the scheduled topic) is followed by a comparative linguistic seminar led by experienced teachers of legal English, legal German, legal French and legal Russian.[5] All participants who pass a comprehensive examination at the end of the course are awarded a certificate which is recognized by courts as a proof of their legal and linguistic competence to act in proceedings and all related activities.

Such a course is essential but represents only the first step in a legal translator's proficiency; everyday practice follows and the main issue is that a translator should always 'act with due diligence' at every stage of his or her translation. Where a translator is expected to translate an English sales contract into Czech, he or she, if inexperienced, should find similar contracts in the target language, look for basic vocabulary and phrases in both texts, and try to identify interlingual and interlegal matches. An efficient feedback tool for a translator in checking whether or not a phrase he or she intends to use exists in the target language is the Internet.[6] In addition to that, legal dictionaries, law textbooks and other written sources (such as authentic legal

---

3 Fridays between 12 and 18 o'clock are the teaching days, so as to enable translators from all over the country to arrive in Prague and participate in the course.

4 Selecting law teachers for such a course has been a difficult task: such a teacher should, in addition to extensive legal knowledge, understand linguistic issues in a specific area of law and be able to identify interpretive problems of legal terminology.

5 For more information on the schedule and content of the course please email chroma@prf.cuni.cz.

6 Google is quite helpful since it is possible to determine not only if the chosen phrase exists in the target language but also where it is used (through identification of the relevant websites listed) – whether it is preferred, for example, in British or American sources, or if it appears only in translations from other languages into English. Such information may become quite important when considering the final recipient of the translated legal text.

instruments) in both the source and target languages should be consulted in order to produce a good translation serving the intended purpose which is comprehensible to and useful for the final recipient.

References

Alcaraz, Enrique / Hughes, Brian 2002. *Legal Translation Explained.* Manchester: St. Jerome Publishing.

Bergenholtz, Henning / Tarp, Sven (eds) 1995. *Manual of Specialised Lexicography*. Amsterdam: Benjamins.

Chromá, Marta 2008. Translating Terminology in Arbitration Discourse: A Conceptual Approach. In: V. K. Bhatia / C. N. Candlin / J. Engberg (eds): *Legal Discourse across Cultures and Systems*. Hong Kong: Hong Kong University Press, 309-327.

Mellinkoff, David 1963, 2004. *The Language of the Law.* Eugene: Resource Publications.

Nida, Eugene A. 2001. *Contexts in Translating.* Amsterdam: Benjamins.

Nord, Christiane 1991. *Text Analysis in Translation.* Amsterdam: Rodopi.

Nord, Christiane 1997, 2001. *Translating as a Purposeful Activity.* Manchester: St. Jerome Publishing.

Šarčević, Susan 2000. *New Approach to Legal Translation.* The Hague: Kluwer Law International.

Šarčević, Susan 2002. Problems of Interpretation in an Enlarged European Union. In R. Sacco (ed.) *L'interprétation des texts juridiques rédigés dans plus d'une langue.* Torino/Paris: L'Harmattan/Isaidat, 239-272.

Smith, Sylvia 1995. Culture Clash: Anglo-American Case Law and German Civil Law in Translation. In M. Morris (ed.) *Translation and the Law*. Amsterdam: Benjamins, 179-200.

Solan, Lawrence M. 1993. *The Language of Judges.* Chicago: The University of Chicago Press.

Solan, Lawrence M. 2003. Finding Ordinary Meaning in the Dictionary. In M. Robinson (ed.) *Language and the Law*. Buffalo: William S. Hein & Co., 255-278.

Trosborg, Anna 1997. *Rhetorical Strategies in Legal Language. Discourse Analysis of Statutes and Contracts*. Tübingen: Gunter Narr.

Vermeer, Hans J. 2000. Skopos and Commission in Translation Action. In L. Venuti (ed.) *The Translation Studies Reader*. London: Routledge, 221-232.

STEFANO MARRONE

System-texts and Cross-system's Translation

1. Introduction

This paper analyses methodological and linguistic issues related to the translation into English of the *Regolamento* of Italy's *Camera dei deputati* (Lower House of Parliament) and its publication both in hard copy and on the Internet.[1] An attempt is made to contribute to a definition of this type of text, for which a categorisation as legal text may appear too restrictive. Some historical/political background is provided in order to identify the extra-linguistic factors which shaped the source text and which characterised the expected target context (Snel Trampus 1989: 107).

2. The political context

In the last fifteen years or so international relations between Parliaments have changed in scope and nature: before the fall of the Berlin wall they did not go beyond formalities, as the pluralist composition of Parliaments was thought to make them unreliable in foreign policy. Then what is currently referred to as 'Parliamentary diplomacy' began to take shape, and almost overnight Parliaments appeared as a flexible tool for establishing contacts with emerging or sensitive countries. This changing perception of the role of national Parliaments was also

1 The author is the Head of the Interpreting and Translation Unit at Italy's Camera dei Deputati. The translation project started in 1999 and was completed in 2000.

related to such factors as economic globalisation, ascendancy of the Executive branch, EU enlargement. The new scenario made it imperative for national Parliaments – traditionally the most inward-looking of state bodies – to adjust their procedures in order to keep up with the speed and effectiveness of decision-making processes taking place increasingly outside the realm of Parliaments. For Parliaments to keep abreast of this process was also viewed as a way of bridging the so-called democratic deficit in European and international affairs.[2]

Against this backdrop, the then President of the Chamber of Deputies announced in 1999 the geopolitical priorities for the Italian Parliament: the European Union, the Mediterranean in a broad sense (today's Greater Middle East), Central and Eastern Europe. This new stance entailed substantial linguistic activity, i.e. a multilingual website in Arabic, English, French, German and Spanish and the translation of the Chamber's *Regolamento* and Italy's Constitution into these five languages in hard copy and on the website itself. Understandably, given the cross-cultural status of English, the English version of the *Regolamento* was seen as being the most sensitive, as a sort of 'calling card' in the globalising political arena.

3. The 'force-field' around our translation work

Our Unit (see footnote 1) was thus faced on the one hand with a new momentum towards international openness, on the other with a deep-seated domestic legacy or embeddedness (Pym 2004). Let me stress already at this stage the powerful dynamic thrust of this outward-inward tension (the word 'conflict' does not seem appropriate), which had a profound impact on our Unit's 'strategic thinking'. As we shall see more closely, the text of the *Regolamento* had been shaped within a closed cultural system in a drafting process spanning over a century. To what time and space were we supposed to transfer it? The target

2 This need was acutely perceived by the Italian Parliament, Italy being under the Constitution a Parliamentary democracy, with Parliament playing a very significant role.

here was not a "given culture, a discrete system based on a concept of closed sovereignty" (Pym 1998). Our text was to be transferred to the de-materialised time and space of the Internet. We envisioned our multifarious target audience to consist mostly of non-native English-speakers, young and not necessarily specialised readers, while bearing in mind the specialist readership (Parliamentary officials, constitutional lawyers, and a few dedicated politicians) in different English-speaking countries. Being a unit within the administration of the Chamber also meant that another relevant 'audience' included fellow Parliamentary officials and political authorities.[3]

4. Text typology

The *Regolamento* is certainly a legal text and as such methodological issues related to the translation of legal texts apply here.[4] However, to the extent that it regulates the interplay of political forces, relations between Parliamentary authorities and Parliament's administration, as well as relations between Parliament and other state organs, this text is also an intricate web – spun in a time span of a century and a half – of culture- and system-bound legislative, political and administrative

3 We had ample access to the expertise of Parliamentary lawyers. In the early stages we consulted with individual Parliamentary officials. We soon became aware that a more structured method for consultation was required and proposed therefore that a working group be established, consisting both of Parliamentary officials and of three members of our unit, in order to minimise subjective interpretations of the text and debate general methodological issues.

4 Though not primarily concerned with theoretical issues, our Unit felt it increasingly necessary to underpin our professional activities with some selected readings. Besides authors explicitly cited in the paper, the following have substantially influenced our thinking: Adamopoulos (1989); Frosini (1992); Garzone (2000); Gémar (1988); Newmark (1982); Sacco (2000); Schena (1997); Snel Trampus (1989); Viezzi (1994).

concepts.[5] Moreover, in Italy the Rules of Procedure of the two Houses of Parliament have constitutional status and, together with the Constitution itself, provide the fundamental framework for Italy's legal system. In view of their original (in a legal sense) constitutive function and sweeping scope across time and space one might be tempted to define this kind of texts as system-texts embodying and epitomising a legal system as a whole.

The basic core of the text dates back to 1848, when the *Regolamento* of the Piedmontese Parliament (the *Parlamento Subalpino*) was adopted. The 1848 *Regolamento* drew heavily upon the Rules of the French and Belgian Parliaments (Galeotti 1900).[6] The *Regolamento* was subsequently amended on several occasions, in conjunction with major political developments. A first example is a Parliamentary crisis in 1900 which led to the introduction of speaking time limits. Another turning point was the introduction of universal suffrage in 1920. The suspension of the Rules by the Chamber of Fasces and Corporations in the Fascist period was a wound which was to be healed only by the Constituent Assembly which, after the war, revived the Rules of 1922. More recently, the transition to a first-past-the-post or majoritarian electoral system led to the introduction of new procedures to make government action more effective, such as stringent constraints on speaking times, the tabling of amendments and the recourse to secret ballots.

The drafting process, of necessity, lacked homogeneity in that the substantive input was provided by subsequent 'waves' of Members of Parliament, who set their own politico-procedural priorities – often the result of compromises among different political forces – while the drafting itself was the work of successive generations of

5 Parliamentary law is characterised by a marked political dimension, and perhaps the greatest difficulty, apart from the large number of technical terms, lay in interpreting and transposing ambiguous language reflecting partially unresolved political issues. For a comparison of different Parliamentary systems, see Cosentino (1958); Frosini (1988); De Franchis (1996).

6 This is the first Parliamentary handbook published in Italy. It was found to be of great help for a correct interpretation of the most ancient provisions – some containing French-inspired linguistic fossils that have survived subsequent revisions – and also for its surprisingly modern intercultural approach.

Parliamentary officials and constitutional lawyers.[7] Obviously, the genesis of this text made it imperative to carry out a diachronic analysis (Schena 1997: 23). To try and summarise the different dimensions involved in the Source Text, the *Regolamento* of a House of Parliament in a Parliamentary republic and, as already mentioned, the Constitution may well be defined as system-texts, combining at least:

a) a legal dimension (system-boundedness);
b) a politico-institutional dimension (culture-boundedness, changing over time as a function of political developments);
c) a diachronic dimension (different historical contexts for individual provisions or groups of provisions. In our case: historical core; post-war proportional representation; European Union; first-past-the post).

System-text A, as tentatively defined above, was thus to be transferred to what we could define as a 'diverse universe' B, consisting of native and non-native, specialist and non-specialist English speakers from a multiplicity of countries, systems and cultures.

5. The translation

The translation of this text into English in the era of globalisation and the Internet, and in view of the politico-institutional scenario described above, seemed to require our Unit to go beyond 'bilateral'[8] functionalist approaches broadly involving a quest for equivalents ensuring a "minimum common denominator" (Marrone 1990: 74) or, better, the "highest common meaning" (Šărčević 1997: 77), either in

7 The *Regolamento* has been compared to a living body, whose limbs grow or are stunted depending on political events. Others have compared it to a medieval text, which grows by accretion with unwritten glosses on the margins: it lives on and rules thanks to its interpretations, which constitute an implicit co-text.

8 I will return later to the notions of 'bilateral' or 'multilateral' in this context. Suffice it to note here that at the time of the translation (and traditionally, given Italy's geopolitical position as a medium-sized country), Italy's foreign policy was tilted strongly in favour of multilateralism.

the British or the American system. One of the main goals of the exercise was indeed to enable foreign interested parties to appreciate our Parliamentary culture, with its specific procedural solutions; to make available the experience of a powerful national Parliament to other countries with different systems.

After a first stage of trial and error,[9] our Unit finally opted for a cross-systems approach, even when one system seemed to offer several acceptable functional equivalents: as already alluded to, a multiplicity of authentic models appeared as a way to accurately reflect the political context of the translation work and the historic importance of the text, while ensuring the cultural relevance of the translated text.[10] A broad sample of models was selected, including the Parliamentary Rules of Procedure or Standing Orders of the United States, United Kingdom, Canada, India and South Africa, plus the European Parliament and NATO Parliamentary Assembly. Besides the actual texts of the Rules, often encumbered with culture-bound stereotyped formulae, the relevant literature (Parliamentary handbooks, public policy documentation, etc.) and the websites of the relevant Parliaments (links and discussion fora) were found to be of great help.

Let us now analyse some examples, starting from the title. In the examples, the Italian original term is provided first, followed by a number of possible equivalents and the relevant institutional reference; in brackets, comments or explanations, if any, are given when necessary; the final line, in bold italics, is our translation. Other relevant authentic expressions found in the corpus of sources are provided in the footnotes. In examples 1 to 5, where the institutional content of the Italian term was very 'domestic', the risk was adopting partial

---

9 The first draft was completed by an experienced British translator with a legal background. Our Unit was responsible for supervising and revising his work. However, we soon realised that the unconditional adoption of the British model, or of any other national model, for that matter, was not suited to the general purpose of the translation work. Moreover this task could not be handled by a single freelance translator as too much collective work had gone into the drafting of the ST. There was simply too much embedded, implicit knowledge. The first draft thus served as a linguistic skeleton, providing us with the basic structure.

10 This also serves to keep readers on the alert: a dynamic interplay of familiarity and estrangement or alienation ensures that a translated legal text is read with a critical mind, free from automatic associations.

functional equivalents, i.e. authentic terms identified by the specialist but which do not adequately reflect substantive differences. In these cases, priority was given to highlighting the specific features of the original and avoiding false 'institutional cognates'.

(1) *Regolamento della Camera dei deputati*
UK: *Standing Orders*
US Senate: *Standing Rules*
European Parliament (EP) and other international Parliamentary assemblies: *Rules of Procedure*
Rules of Procedure of the Chamber of Deputies
[The more general equivalent was chosen]

(2) *Legislatura*[11]
UK, Canada, Ireland: *Parliament*
US: *Congress*
Parliament
[Here too the more general equivalent was chosen]

(3) *Presidente della Camera*
US-UK: *Speaker of the House*
President of the Chamber
[The US-UK solution offers an only partial equivalence as in Italy the presiding officer wields considerably greater powers]

(4) *Gruppi parlamentari*
UK literature [not mentioned in the Rules]: *Parliamentary party*
US: *party caucus*
EP: *political groups*
Parliamentary groups
[In Italy *Gruppi parlamentari* have legal status, unlike political parties, and a strong administrative relationship to the Parliament]

(5) *Gruppo Misto*
UK: Cross-benchers
EP: Non-attached Members
US: Independents
Mixed Group

---

11 False friend: *Legislature* denotes a law-making body (*a democratic legislature; Acts of subordinate legislatures*), while *legislatura* means a Parliamentary term and is rendered in different ways depending on the 'name' of the Legislature in a given system (*during this Parliament; the 6th Parliament; in recent Congresses*).

[In all of the above the notion of 'Group' is lacking, whereas in Italy the *Gruppo Misto* may be very large and is often sub-divided into political sub-groupings: members of disparate affiliations join together to be entitled to the administrative privileges of Group status. Moreover, the Italian Chamber is a hemicycle, which renders the UK solution not applicable]

The following example concerns the adoption of politically correct criteria: a political decision turned out to be necessary here.[12]

(6) *Presidenti dei Gruppi*
UK, US, EP Rules: *Chairman, he/his*
US manuals: *Chairperson; he/she; his/her*
UK (Erskine May, 1989)[13]: *Chairman, he/his*
Group Chairpersons*; *he/she; his/her
[It was deemed appropriate to adopt a general criterion of political correctness with respect to gender – not found in the texts of the Rules of Anglo-Saxon Parliaments – in view of a number of factors, such as publication on the Internet and the policy of the then President to enhance the visibility of Women Parliamentarians]

The following examples, on the other hand, involve system-bound procedures whose rendering in English required some degree of interpretation:

(7) *disegni di legge di conversione di decreti legge*
UK (Erskine May, 1989): *To confirm*
government bills confirming decree-laws
[This is a procedure whereby Parliament endorses a regulatory instrument of the Executive. We found no satisfactory equivalents for *decreti-legge*, as the term *executive order*, for example, lacks a reference to the role of Parliament implied by the word *legge*]

The term *decree-law* is one case in which the 'pull' of the source system was felt to be so strong as to justify an odd and ugly calque to

---

12 One school of thought within the working group, including our Unit, maintained that there were many factors arguing for a politically correct approach; the others thought that it would make the text too cumbersome. Ultimately, the question was submitted to and decided by the President. It is open to question whether subsequent Presidents would have made the same choice.

13 Erskine May's Treatise on the Law, Privileges, Proceedings and Usage of Parliament, is generally held to be the most authoritative text on Parliamentary law in the UK.

render the specific Italian instrument, which combines government legislative action (decree) and Parliamentary intervention (law) in a single-term semantic condensation of a system of checks and balances. The transition to a majoritarian system (source of this term: US Parliamentary literature), with the emphasis shifting from participation to effective decision-making, had a major impact on the programming of Parliamentary business[14] and on voting procedures.[15]

(8) *Le ripartizioni in quote di tempi e di argomenti sono computate in via tendenziale e con riferimento alle previsioni formulate all'atto della predisposizione del calendario.*
The allotment of speaking time and subjects shall aim at an overall balance and reflect the forecasts underlying the order of business.

The term *in via tendenziale* was submitted to the working group as it suggested a measure of flexibility to allow for political contingencies. We translators feared, however, that possible translations such as *tentative* or *in principle* or *flexible* would have conveyed an impression of excessive looseness, inappropriate in Parliamentary Rules. It also emerged that underlying this clause there was a concern to reassure minorities: the political forces which had been shorthanded in the allotment of time and topics in a given order of business (spanning two to three weeks) would be compensated in the following order of business. We had to negotiate meaning (as the drafters had had to negotiate the substance). Eco (2003) defines the process of translating as a negotiating process. This perspective provides some very useful insights. In English the word 'negotiate' has value added: one negotiates hurdles. Our solution thus reflected the idea of aiming at an overall balance over time.

---

14 The allotment of speaking time and agenda items to different Parliamentary groups is the essence of Parliamentary politics.

15 Secret ballot was the normal mode of voting in the first decades after the war as a tool to protect the freedom of the members of the new democratic Parliament after a long dictatorship. Then, as democracy came to be perceived as more stable, the public ballot gradually gained ascendancy as it embodies modern values such as transparency, accountability and effective decision-making. This entailed changes to the Rules with respect to the admissibility of and voting on amendments to bills, thus streamlining the Parliamentary agenda, and the introduction of speaking time limits.

In hindsight our translation appears to be tilted explicitly in favour of the minorities. Was this due to the then predominant cultural climate within the institution (the President at the time belonged to the Democrats of the Left, a party that had been in the opposition for forty years)? Was the new majoritarian culture not yet as pervasive as it is now? Would we make the same choice again? Perhaps not, as the same provision may well be interpreted in such a way as to give the ruling majority more room for manoeuver in pushing through its programme. This ambiguity was probably due to problems of political acceptance in the transition from one electoral and political system to another. Another example of this politico-textual malaise is to be found in provisions on the voting of amendments. The power to amend government measures is an all important power of Parliament. Without limitations, however, it can turn into filibustering. The Italian classification of amendments turned out to be more detailed and abstract than corresponding formulations.

(9) *emendamenti interamente soppressivi, parzialmente soppressivi, modificativi, aggiuntivi*
US Senate: *motions to strike out and insert*
US House: *amendment in the nature of a substitute* (to completely replace a given clause) and *substitute amendment* (to be voted in lieu of another amendment).[16]
UK Commons: *1) amendments to leave out certain words, 2) to leave out certain words in order to insert or add others, 3) to insert or add certain words.*
EP: *an amendment may seek to change any part of a text, and may be directed to deleting, adding or substituting words or figures* [more straightforward, though not ensuring full correspondence]
amendments seeking to delete, to partially delete, to substitute, to add or insert [we maintained an element of redundancy as in the UK model]

(10) *Nel caso di votazione per appello nominale il Presidente indica il significato del sì e del no*
US and UK Rules and manuals: *ayes and nays*
In cases of roll-call votes the President shall indicate the import of Aye or Nay.[17]

---

16 As can be seen, authentic models were seen as carrying cultural connotations, probably because the power to amend belongs to the original core of Parliamentary powers.

17 This may well be the most ancient expression of Parliamentary decision-making. Those who are familiar with Anglo-Saxon Parliaments will have

How did the Italian Chamber address the question of 'filibustering' in the new majoritarian environment? As the President was given the power to select the amendments to be put to the vote, the residual freedom of Parliamentary groups (not individual members!) was textualised as follows:

(11) *I Gruppi possono segnalare [...] gli emendamenti [...] da porre comunque in votazione qualora si proceda [...] a votazioni riassuntive **[...].***
The Groups may announce [...] the amendments [...] to be in any case put to the vote if [...] voting is to be on selected amendments [...].

Here, in the process of translation, the powers of the President have become more explicit. A comparatively more modern section of the rules pertains to EU matters, where Parliamentary cooperation has focused on the quality of national legislation, on legislative simplification, and on new procedures meant to bridge the so-called democratic deficit. One should also bear in mind in this case that Parliaments are increasingly faced with regulatory competition, as it were, from different supranational (EU), national (regulatory or independent authorities, NGOs) and sub-national (regions) entities. The consequent demand for high-quality legislation led to the introduction of new procedures: law-making was to be based on a thorough preliminary assessment of the requirements of potential addressees.[18] As a consequence, a new procedural stage was textualised, that of the *istruttoria legislativa* in the reporting Committee.

(12) *Nel corso dell'esame in sede referente, [...] l'istruttoria prende [...] in considerazione i seguenti aspetti: a) la necessità dell'intervento legislativo, con riguardo alla possibilità di conseguirne i fini mediante il ricorso a fonti diverse dalla legge [...].*
During consideration of the bill by the reporting Committee [...] the pre-legislative scrutiny and consultation phase shall take the following aspects into consideration: a) whether the new legislation is necessary, or whether the

---

experienced the full House (*Hear, hear*; *Aye or Nay*) roaring with a sort of tribal echo. We relished the opportunity to leave a linguistic reminder of this primary expression of the will of a democratic body.

18 Italy's Chamber of Deputies spearheaded an EU-wide effort to improve the quality of legislation. See Proceedings of the Conference of EU Speakers, 2000, Volume 2, Roma, Camera dei Deputati.

same ends might be achieved through regulatory instruments other than an Act of Parliament [...].
[After looking in vain for a possible correspondence for the term 'istruttoria' – *Committees shall hold hearings* was not structured enough – we produced a collage including some OECD terminology.][19]

The term *fonti* is rendered in the literature as *sources of law*. In this case, however, the text leaves open the option of adopting government regulations instead of an Act of Parliament.[20] Another translation problem was how to deal with provisions pertaining to good Parliamentary manners. Do these differ across systems and cultures?

(13) *testi [...] formulati con frasi sconvenienti*
UK: ***couched in unparliamentary language***
US: *obscene or insulting* [this formulation is characteristically more explicit]
[The British formula, which we adopted, is the well-honed product of a long Parliamentary linguistic distillation]

(14) *l'essere intaccato nella propria condotta [...]*[21]
[Corresponding provisions in US or UK Rules sounded very weak. The Italian formula is powerful and culturally connotated. We feared this would be lost in a lexical translation. Where could we find the expression of a similar sense of 'honour'?

---

19 While doing research on the new Scottish Parliament, a couple of years after the translation had been completed, I came across the formula *pre-legislative scrutiny* in a description of its functions. Scotland, with its hybrid legal system and recent process of devolution may well come to act as a linguistic bridge between the two main bodies of Parliamentary law: the Continental, French-derived, and the Anglo-Saxon. The emergence of a Scottish Parliament may alter this dichotomy, but unfortunately this new linguistic reservoir was not available at the time of our translation. Scottish institutional English needs to differentiate itself from Westminster English; the Scottish Office stated explicitly that obscure or archaic procedures were to be avoided, in a general endeavour to win popular legitimacy. Scottish legal experts say in their website that they have consulted the Rules of several continental Parliaments before drafting their own Rules of Procedure. Did they read the English version of the *Regolamento* or did the same political priorities produce independently the same linguistic innovation?

20 Consider the paradoxical effect that translating *legge* with *law* would have had in this case.

21 This wording conveys a cultural connotation of the concept of honour now considered outdated.

The Rules of the Indian Parliament came to our aid:]
an unworthy or unbecoming conduct is imputed to […].

6. Conclusions

The translation project I have described involved a gradual re-thinking of the translation strategies of the Interpreting and Translating Unit of the Chamber of Deputies: our involvement, also as interpreters, in the new multilateral, indeed multipolar international policy of the Italian Parliament influenced our attitude vis-à-vis the *Regolamento* of our Institution. Faced with the task of transferring onto the Web this huge and authoritative linguistic material, reflecting different cultural contexts and political approaches, the notion of a multi-system approach gradually appeared to us as a deontological necessity. A measure of cultural relativism seemed the best way to achieve cultural relevance and authenticity. While trying to turn the new text into a comprehensible readable text, we made it permeable to multiple influences. Yet, 'under the spell' of its authoritative nature, we felt duty-bound to retain an underlying loyalty (Nord 1997: 123-128) to the Italian conceptual framework. Thus, no preordained criteria of equivalence were followed (cf. Frosini 1992: 117). Rather, a case-by-case assessment was conducted within the framework of clearly defined extra-linguistic priorities in a cross-systems' effort. As Garzone (2000: 9) puts it, there is no "single universally applicable concept of equivalence […]; the degree of equivalence […] depends first and foremost on the TT intended function as well as on the nature of the ST."

Avoiding cultural and linguistic monopolies was also a priority. While the EU system did provide a number of solutions,[22] notably where Anglo-Saxon equivalents appeared too heavily connoted,[23] an

22 The EU is our common European House. Therefore, in the few cases in which we had a choice among several acceptable institutional equivalents, preference was given to the EU model.

23 In a limited number of cases, we were able to use some hallowed formulae of Anglo-Saxon parliamentarism, common to several systems.

attempt was made to avoid the 'easy way out' of drawing solely upon handbooks or EU terminology. It was felt that this approach would have produced a bureaucratic, indeed a neuterised text, wholly lacking the lifeblood of cultural roots that could and should be found in Parliamentary Rules, as Parliaments ought to be the living embodiment of popular will. An attempt was also made, at least to some degree, to do justice to the diachronic dimension of the text, by retaining a few time-honoured formulae, while at the same time adopting some modern linguistic criteria, such as politically correct forms.

From a different and more general perspective, this analysis of the translation some years later led to the realisation that certain translation problems might have been resolved differently in a changed political scenario: individual cases such as *tendenziale*, or even basic methodological choices, such as the adoption of politically correct criteria or of a 'multilateral'[24] cross-systems' approach itself seem to have been fundamentally affected by political factors.[25]

This was a group effort, involving six people for a time span of over 18 months: among the many books that accompanied our work one that proved particularly useful was the first Italian Parliamentary handbook *Principi regolatori delle Assemblee* written by Ugo Galeotti in 1900, which we consulted when trying to understand the more ancient provisions. It is curious that as we were translating with an eye to the Internet and globalisation, we should have related so deeply to this insightful author, who appears to have shared some of our difficulties. This is a passage from his foreword:

> Mi diedi a rintracciare l'autorità che a me mancava là dove si temprano le umane cognizioni, nell'esperienza e nella ragione. Per la prima dovetti naturalmente ricorrere ai Parlamenti, fonte copiosa, perenne ed esclusiva [...]. Mi

---

24 It is conceivable that the choice between a bilateral versus a multilateral approach might fall in favour of bilateralism in an international context in which a specific political, legal and institutional system were to gain absolute predominance.

25 This raises general questions concerning the yardsticks to assess a translation's quality as well as a more specific ethical question – which can only be hinted at here – in relation to the professional responsibility of translators when confronted with texts whose authoring process spans several generations and which underlie a country's societal structures. Can the individual translator alone take on her/himself the huge burden of responsibility involved?

studiai poi di additare il fondamento razionale delle norme che venivo esponendo; ma le difficoltà incontrate mi sgomentarono e mi avrebbero indotto ad abbandonare il pensiero, se non avessi confidato che l'opera mia avrebbe potuto servire almeno come quella dell'esploratore di una landa fino ad ora vergine [...] facendo nascere in altri [...] il desiderio di approfondirne lo studio.
I set about tracing the authority I lacked there where human knowledge is forged, in experience and reason [...] For the former I resorted to Parliaments, the abundant, perennial and exclusive source [...]. Then I strove to point out the rational foundation of the rules of which I was expounding; yet I was utterly dismayed at the difficulties I encountered and I would have given up my endeavour had I not trusted that my work, akin to that of an explorer of virgin lands [...] , may arouse in others [...] the desire to explore further [my translation].

References

Adamopoulos, Spiridon 1989. La spécialisation en interprétation juridique. *Parallèles* 11, 67-70.

Adams, Willi Paul / Thelen, David 2000. *Roundtable on Translations of the Declaration of Independence.* <http://chnm.gmu.edu/declaration/foreword.html>.

Bach, Stanley 1996. *Voting and Quorum Procedures in the House of Representatives.* <http://www.house.gov/rules/crs_reports.htm>.

Boulton, Clifford (ed.) 1989. *Erskine May's Treatise on the Law, Privileges, Proceedings and Usage of Parliament*, London: Butterworths.

Cosentino, Francesco 1958. Note sui principi della procedura parlamentare [Principles of Parliamentary Procedure], *Studi sulla Costituzione*, Milano: Giuffré.

De Franchis, Francesco 1996. *Dizionario giuridico – Law dictionary.* Milano: Giuffré.

Eco, Umberto 2003. *Dire quasi la stessa cosa. Esperienze di traduzione* [Saying almost the same. Translation experiences]. Milano: Bompiani.

Frosini, Vittorio 1988. Il messaggio legislativo: tecnica e interpretazione [The Legislative Message. Techique and Interpretation].

Normative europee sulla tecnica legislativa, *Quaderni di documentazione*, 10, 3-62. Roma: Camera dei Deputati.

Frosini, Vittorio 1992. Traduzione e interpretazione dei testi giuridici [Translation and Interpretation of Legal Texts]. *La traduzione. Saggi e documenti (I)*. *Quaderni di Libri e riviste d'Italia* 28, 105-118. Roma: Ministero per i beni culturali e ambientali.

Galeotti, Ugo 1900. *Principi regolatori delle Assemblee,* Torino: Fratelli Bocca (Ristampa anastatica, 1997. Roma: Editore Colombo).

Gémar, Jean Claude 1988. La traduction juridique: art ou technique d'interprétation? *Meta* 33/2, 305-319.

Marrone, Stefano 1990. Is it Possible to Translate Institutional terms? A Pragmatic Approach. *The Interpreters' Newsletter* 3, 72-74.

Newmark, Peter 1982. The Translation of Authoritative Statements: A Discussion. In J.P. Gémar (Ed.) *Langage du droit et traduction.* Montreal: Linguatech.

Nord, Christiane 1997. *Translating as a Purposeful Activity.* Manchester: St. Jerome Publishing.

Pym, Anthony. (1998). *Translation and Text Transfer.* <http://www.fut.es/~apym/cover.html>.

Pym, Anthony 2004, *The Moving Text. Localization, Translation, and Distribution.* Amsterdam: Benjamins.

Sacco, Rodolfo 2000. Traduzione giuridica [Legal Translation]. *Digesto delle discipline privatistiche. Sezione civile. Aggiornamento.* Torino: UTET.

Šarčević, Susan 1997. *New Approach to Legal Translation.* The Hague: Kluwer Law International.

Schena, Leandro, Editor, 1997. *La lingua del diritto. Difficoltà traduttive. Applicazioni pratiche.* [The Language of Law. Translation Difficulties. Practical Applications]. Milano: CISU.

Slaughter, James 2000. *Introduction to Parliamentary Procedure.* <http://www.jimslaughter.com/Parliamentaryprocedure.htm>.

Snel Trampus, Rita 1989. *La traduzione e i linguaggi giuridici olandese e italiano: aspetti e problemi.* Trieste: Edizioni Italo Svevo.

Ulrych, Margherita 1992. *Translating Texts, From Theory to Practice.* Rapallo: CIDEB Editrice.

Viezzi, Maurizio 1994. Introduzione alle problematiche della traduzione giuridica con particolare riferimento alla traduzione di testi in lingua inglese. *Traduzione, società e cultura* 5, 1-48. Trieste: Edizioni LINT.

Parliamentary Documents and References

Conferenza dei Presidenti dei Parlamenti dell'Unione Europea, Atti e documenti del Gruppo di lavoro sulla qualità della legislazione. 2000. [Proceedings and Documents of the Working Group on the Quality of Legislation. Conference of EU Speakers]. Roma: Camera dei deputati.

House of Commons – Canada 1997. A Glossary of Parliamentary Procedure.<http://www.parl.gc.ca/information/about/process/house/glossary/gloss-e.htm>.

NATO Parliamentary Assembly, Rules of Procedure, 2005, <http://www.nato-pa.int/default.asp?SHORTCUT=346>.

Parliament of South Africa, Joint Rules, 1999, <http://www.Parliament.gov.za/pubs/jointrules.html>.

Houses of The Oireachtas, Rules of Procedure, 1999, <http://www.irlgov.ie/oireachtas/frame.htm>.

Lok Sabha, Rules of Procedure and Conduct of Business, 2001, <http://alfa.nic.in/rules/rules.html>.

European Parliament, Rules of Procedure, 1999, <http://www.europarl.eu.int/home/default_en.htm>.

House of Representatives of the United States, Rules, 1999, <http://clerkweb.house.gov/106/docs/rules/contents.htm>.

Senate of the United States, Standing Rules, 1999, <http://www.senate.gov/learning/learn_rules.html>.

Notes on Contributors

VIJAY BHATIA is a Visiting Professor in the Department of English and Communication at the City University of Hong Kong. He is also an Adjunct Professor at the Macquarie University, Sydney, Australia. His research interests include applied genre analysis of academic and professional discourse, including, legal, business, newspaper, advertising and other promotional genres; ESP and Professional Communication (Theory and Practice); cross-cultural and disciplinary variation in professional discourses. Some of his current research projects, include *Analysing Genre-bending in Corporate Disclosure Documents* and *International Arbitration Practice: A Discourse Analytical Study*, in which more than 20 countries are participating. His recent book *Worlds of Written Discourse: A Genre-based View* (2004) is published by Continuum in Advances in Applied Linguistics Series.

GIUDITTA CALIENDO, PhD (Naples), MA (Bath), is a researcher in English Language and Translation at the University of Naples Federico II. She has taught English for Law at the University of Naples Federico II and English Linguistics at the University of Naples 'l'Orientale'. Her research interests target the field of specialised translation and institutional discourse. She has published extensively on the legal language of the European Union institutions. Her recent publications include "Intercultural traits in legal translation" in M. Rogers and A. Khurshid (eds) *Evidence-based ESP* (2007); "The Interpretation of Community Documents in the European Court of Justice" in A. Duszak *et al.* (eds) *Langue, Droit et Société* (Dictionnaire des notions politiques et sociales des pays d'Europe centrale et orientale, 2006). Since 2007, she has been a member of the teaching Board for PhD candidates in English for Special Purposes, University of Naples Federico II.

CHRISTOPHER N. CANDLIN is Senior Research Professor in the Department of Linguistics at Macquarie University, Sydney. His research is in professional communication, primarily in the fields of law, healthcare and management, legal discourse and he has published widely in these fields. Current research focuses on the comparative analysis of the written discourses of arbitration and contract law across languages and legal systems, and on the discursive processes of international commercial arbitration.

PAOLA CATENACCIO attained a doctoral degree in English literature from the Catholic University of Milan and later an MA in Applied Linguistics from Birkbeck College, London. She holds a research and teaching position at the University of Milan, where she teaches English Linguistics courses for the degree programme in Linguistic and Cultural Mediation. Her research interests span from second language acquisition to translation and discourse analysis, especially in the context of LSP research. Her most recent contributions focus on the genre of the press release and, more in general, on linguistic aspects of corporate communication. Some of her latest publications are: "Dehumanising the alien: The construction of migrants' rights in EU legislation" (2007); "Constructing identities in the fashion industry: Building brand and customer image through press releases" (2007); "Press releases as a hybrid genre: Addressing the informative/promotional conundrum" (2008). She has also co-edited, with Giuliana Garzone and Gina Poncini, *Multimodality in Corporate Communication. Web Genres and Discursive Identity* (2007) and, with Giuliana Garzone, *Language and Bias in Specialised Discourse* (2008).

MARTA CHROMÁ, Head of the Foreign Language Department of the Charles University Law School in Prague, Czech Republic, has been teaching legal linguistics and legal translation for more than 20 years. Her research is based upon comparison between the Czech law and language and the Anglo-American system of law and legal English. She focuses on issues of equivalence, conceptual analysis and lexicography, as well as teaching legal English to students and legal professionals with different legal and linguistic background and needs.

MARINA DOSSENA is Professor of English Language and head of department at the Department of Comparative Languages, Literatures and Cultures at the University of Bergamo (Faculty of Foreign Languages and Literatures). Her research interests focus on the features and origins of British varieties of English and the history of specialized discourse. Recent publications include the proceedings of ICEHL 14 (3 vols., edited with Maurizio Gotti and Richard Dury; 2008), *Studies in Late Modern English Correspondence: Methodology and Data* (edited with Ingrid Tieken-Boon van Ostade; 2008) and a special issue of *Textus* on *(R)evolutions in Evaluation* (edited with Andreas H. Jucker). She is also the author of the monograph *Scotticisms in Grammar and Vocabulary* (2005); in co-operation with Richard Dury she is currently compiling a corpus of nineteenth-century Scottish correspondence.

PAOLA EVANGELISTI ALLORI is Professor of English at the Italian University for Sport and Human Movement- IUSM, Rome, Italy. Her main research interests are in the language/culture interaction in domain specific-discourse both academic and professional. She has published extensively on comparative analysis of specialized discourse in various disciplinary areas and fields of action (Economics, Psychology, Politics, History, Journalism), both cross-linguistically and cross-disciplinarily. Current research includes the comparative analysis of the legal discourse of international arbitration practice with special emphasis on Sports related Arbitration. Recent publications include *Academic Discourse in Europe. Thought processes and Linguistic Realisation.* (1998); *English in Academic and Professional Settings.* Textus XV, 2002 co-edited with Eija Ventola; "International Arbitration in Different Settings: Same or Different Practice?", In Bhatia V. K:, Candlin C. N., Gotti M. (eds) 2004. *Intercultural Aspects of Specialized Communication*; "Methaphors they report by. The Construction of National Identity through Sport Commentaries in different Cultural Communities", in Cortese G., Duszak A. (eds) 2005. *Identity, Community, Discourse: English in Intercultural Settings.* "Arbitration in Sport. Rules and Practices from two different codes", in Bhatia V. K., Candlin C. N., Engberg J. (eds) 2008. *Legal Discourse across Cultures and Systems.*

GIULIANA GARZONE is Full Professor of English Linguistics and Translation at the University of Milan, Italy. In the methodological perspective, she has explored the integration of micro- and macro-linguistic analysis in studying discourse, and in particular specialized discourse ("The Use of Discursive Features Expressing Causal Relations in Annual Company Reports", 2006), and the application of corpus linguistics to Critical Discourse Analysis ("What can corpus linguistics do for Critical Discourse Analysis?", 2004). Specialized discourse in its different domains is her main field of investigation, in which she has co-ordinated several research projects and published extensively. In particular, she has worked on legal language (*Performatività e linguaggio giuridico*, 1996), on scientific discourse (*Perspectives on ESP and popularization*, 2006) and on specialised communication (*The Role of English in Institutional and Organizational Settings: An intercultural Perspective*, 2007, edited with C. Ilie; *Discourse, Ideology and Specialized Communication*, edited with S. Sarangi). She has also authored or edited several works on translation (*L'italiano delle traduzioni*, 2005, with A. Cardinaletti; *Esperienze del tradurre*, 2005) and interpreting (*Perspectives on Interpreting*, with P. Mead and M. Viezzi; *Interpreting in the 21st Century: Challenges and Opportunities*, with M. Viezzi, 2002). Her other research interests include the phonology and the syntax of the English language. She is general editor (with A. Cardinaletti e F. Frasnedi) of the book series *Lingua, traduzione, didattica*.

MAURIZIO GOTTI is Professor of English Linguistics at the University of Bergamo. He is Director of CERLIS, the research centre on specialized languages based at the University of Bergamo. From 1999 to 2001 he was President of the Italian Association of English Studies. From 2000 to 2004 he was President of the European Confederation of University Language Centres. His main research areas are the features and origins of specialized discourse, both in a synchronic and diachronic perspective (*Robert Boyle and the Language of Science*, 1996; *Specialized Discourse: Linguistic Features and Changing Conventions*, 2003; *Investigating Specialized Discourse*, 2005) as well as English syntax (*English Diachronic Syntax* (ed.), 1993; *Variation in Central Modals* (co-author), 2002) and English lexicography (*The Language of Thieves and Vagabonds: 17th and 18th Century Canting Lexicography in England*, 1999). He is a member of the Editorial Board of national and international journals, and edits the *Linguistic Insights* series for Peter Lang.

STEFANO MARRONE has a Diploma in Conference Interpreting and has been Permanent interpreter at the European Parliament. He is a Member of the International Association of Conference Interpreters and since 1985 has been Head of the Interpreting and Translating Unit at the Lower House of the Italian Parliament. He has revised the English and German versions of the *Rules of Procedure of the Chamber of Deputies* and the *Italian Constitution*. Since 2001 he has been Professor of Consecutive Interpreting at Libera Università degli Studi S. Pio V, Rome. In 2005-2006 he taught Legal English for lawyers at the Master's Course on "Parliament and Public Policy" at LUISS University. More recently, he has been a Lecturer on legal English and legal translation at ESIT, Sorbonne III, Paris. He has been working as simultaneous and consecutive interpreter in meetings on comparative law and constitutional law, such as: Civil law harmonisation; Legislative simplification and harmonisation of anti-bribery regulations; Specific comparative issues (German, U.S., U.K. parliamentary and constitutional systems); European Central Bank meetings (Working Group of Legal Experts, harmonisation of financial regulations).

MICHELA MENGHINI is working on a research grant at IUSM, Italian University for Sport and Human Movement, Rome, as part of the research project PRIN 2005-2007 "Cultural identity in sport-related legal discourse. The interaction of cultural schemata and international socio-cultural constructs in the linguistic realisation of arbitral Awards" and specifically within the I.U.S.M. Unit topic: "Linguistic and Intercultural Aspects of Juridical Discourse: the case of International Sports Arbitration". She has studied computer science as well as foreign languages and is interested in corpus linguistics and the application and development of computer tools for language analysis in general. Among her publications, it is currently in print, with Alessandra Fazio, "Professional identity in sports-related arbitration discourse: building a bilingual database of key concepts and correspondences". In: Garzone, G. / Catenaccio, P. (eds), *Language and Bias in Specialised Discourse*, which was a product of her work within the project PRIN 2005-2007.

CRISTINA PENNAROLA is associate professor of English Language and Linguistics at the Faculty of Political Science, University of

Naples Federico II. She has published a book analysing advertising discourse in the light of nonsense strategies, *Nonsense in Advertising* (2003), and a number of short essays on various research topics ranging from language learning to war discourse. Her current research interests include political satire and institutional discourses.

GIGLIOLA SACERDOTI MARIANI is Professor of English at the University of Florence. She has published widely on English and American literature, including books and essays on the language of Spenser's *Shepheardes Calendar*, and on English lexicography. Her articles on G. Eliot, B. Disraeli, D. Abse, S. Bellow, B. Malamud, I. B. Singer, H. Miller, M. Rukeyser, A. Ostriker have appeared in a variety of volumes and journals. Recently authored/edited books include M. Camboni, G. Sacerdoti Mariani, B. Tedeschini Lalli (eds), *'Words at War': parole di guerra e culture di pace 'nel primo secolo delle guerre mondiali'*, 2005; *Guida alla Costituzione degli Stati Uniti d'America* (1985; 1999, 4th edition); *La guerra civile spagnola tra politica e letteratura* (1995); Il Federalista (1997). Her latest work explores ethical, social and political issues also within the framework of women's studies: "The Power of the Language in Delineating the Boundaries of Power: the US Constitution Interpreted by the First 'Federalist Community'" in Cortese G., Duszak A. (eds), *Identity, Community, Discourse: English in Intercultural Settings* (2005); "Fuller e Mazzini: tra fede e fato", in Salvo Mastellone (ed.), Mazzini e gli scrittori politici europei (1837-1857), 2005; "Words at War: testi e pre-testi di Muriel Rukeyser", in M. Camboni, G. Sacerdoti Mariani, B. Tedeschini Lalli (eds), *'Words at War': parole di guerra e culture di pace 'nel primo secolo delle guerre mondiali'*, 2005; "Joseph Mazzini & Company: il linguaggio dell'amicizia e dell'ideologia", in G. Angelini, M. Tesoro (eds), *De Amicitia. Saggi in onore di Arturo Colombo*, 2006; "Preghiera e arte ebraica a Forlì in un manoscritto del 1383", in Studi Romagnoli, LVII, 2007; "To be against war is not enough: it is hardly a beginning", in M. Petricioli, D. Cherubini (eds), *For Peace in Europe. Institutions and Civil Society between the World Wars*, 2008.

TARJA SALMI-TOLONEN is currently a full time researcher at the Corporate Contracting Capabilities Research Consortium funded by the

Academy of Finland. Her research interests are the linguistic manifestations of law in all its functions. She is an invited legal language expert for national bodies and government departments, and has instructed judges and lawyers on language issues. She has also been invited to speak on law and language at universities both in Europe and in the USA and worked as a visiting scholar at Cambridge University, UK. She is an international collaborator at an international research project concerning international commercial arbitration practice and has published extensively on law and language and lately on contracting.

MARTIN SOLLY is Associate Professor of English Language and Translation at the University of Florence. He holds a PhD in Applied Linguistics and his main research interests concern language learning in higher education and specialized discourse, currently in the domains of marine insurance, healthcare insurance and educational reform. His recent publications include "'Don't get caught out': pragmatic and discourse features of informative and promotional texts in international healthcare insurance" *Communication & Medicine* 4.1 (2007) and "Linguistic Choice in the Discourse of Contemporary Educational Reform" in Norman Fairclough *et al.* (eds) *Discourse and Contemporary Social Change* (2007). He is co-editor (with Sandra Campagna and Michelangelo Conoscenti) of *Verbal/Visual Narrative Texts in Higher Education* (2008).

GIROLAMO TESSUTO is Associate Professor of English Language and Translation. He teaches on English and Legal English courses in the Faculty of Law – Seconda Università degli Studi di Napoli and Università degli Studi di Napoli Federico II. He is a member of the *International Round Table for the Semiotics of Law*, *Plain English Movement Campaign*, and *DSFF/LSP Centre*. His current research interests are in the fields of English legal genre analysis in academic and professional settings, legal translation and applied terminology, and plain language issues. Besides a monograph on English criminal language, discourse, and terminology, he has published several research papers in English legal language in a variety of applications. His most recent publications are *Opinions of Counsel: An Exploratory Survey of Generic Features* (2006), *Discourse Systems in English*

Arbitration Awards (2008), *Drafting Laws in UK Settings: Implementing Plain Language and Discourse?* (2008), and others (forthcoming).

MARCO VENUTI received his doctorate in English for Specific Purposes from the University of Napoli 'Federico II', where he is currently a Research Associate (Ricercatore) in English language and linguistics at the Faculty of Economics. He is co-author of *La stampa britannica e la moneta unica. Le metafore dell'economia da una prospettiva di linguistica dei corpora* (2004). His main research interests are in the field of discourse analysis, corpus linguistics and English for Specific Purposes. He is a member of the *Media Linguists Working Group of the European Union Sixth Framework project* (2005-2009), 'Integrated and United? A quest for citizenship in an ever closer Europe'.

MARCHILIA VOLINI is currently contract lecturer of English at the University of Naples Federico II, Faculty of Biotechnology and has worked on ESP at the Faculty of Engineering for 3 years. She is also YLE, KET, PET, FCE and ILEC examiner for the British Council. She has published a number of short essays like "Web-listening Activities" in *Sperimentazione e Didattica nei Centri Linguistici di Ateneo* (edited by Gabriella Di Martino and Maurizio Gotti, 2007, pp. 437-447) and "The Sense of 'Europeanness' in New Generations" in *Atti del Seminario di Studi Identity and Culture in English Domain-Specific Discourse: Methodological Issues and Preliminary Studies* (forthcoming). Her current research interests include Legal English in International Contexts.

Linguistic Insights

Studies in Language and Communication

This series aims to promote specialist language studies in the fields of linguistic theory and applied linguistics, by publishing volumes that focus on specific aspects of language use in one or several languages and provide valuable insights into language and communication research. A cross-disciplinary approach is favoured and most European languages are accepted.

The series includes two types of books:

- **Monographs** – featuring in-depth studies on special aspects of language theory, language analysis or language teaching.
- **Collected papers** – assembling papers from workshops, conferences or symposia.

Each volume of the series is subjected to a double peer-reviewing process.

Vol. 1 Maurizio Gotti & Marina Dossena (eds)
Modality in Specialized Texts. Selected Papers of the 1st CERLIS Conference.
421 pages. 2001. ISBN 3-906767-10-8. US-ISBN 0-8204-5340-4

Vol. 2 Giuseppina Cortese & Philip Riley (eds)
Domain-specific English. Textual Practices across Communities and Classrooms.
420 pages. 2002. ISBN 3-906768-98-8. US-ISBN 0-8204-5884-8

Vol. 3 Maurizio Gotti, Dorothee Heller & Marina Dossena (eds)
Conflict and Negotiation in Specialized Texts. Selected Papers of the 2nd CERLIS Conference.
470 pages. 2002. ISBN 3-906769-12-7. US-ISBN 0-8204-5887-2

Editorial address:

Prof. Maurizio Gotti Università di Bergamo, Facoltà di Lingue e Letterature Straniere,
Via Salvecchio 19, 24129 Bergamo, Italy
Fax: 0039 035 2052789, E-Mail: m.gotti@unibg.it

Vol. 4 Maurizio Gotti, Marina Dossena, Richard Dury, Roberta Facchinetti & Maria Lima
Variation in Central Modals. A Repertoire of Forms and Types of Usage in Middle English and Early Modern English.
364 pages. 2002. ISBN 3-906769-84-4. US-ISBN 0-8204-5898-8

Vol. 5 Stefania Nuccorini (ed.)
Phrases and Phraseology. Data and Descriptions.
187 pages. 2002. ISBN 3-906770-08-7. US-ISBN 0-8204-5933-X

Vol. 6 Vijay Bhatia, Christopher N. Candlin & Maurizio Gotti (eds)
Legal Discourse in Multilingual and Multicultural Contexts. Arbitration Texts in Europe.
385 pages. 2003. ISBN 3-906770-85-0. US-ISBN 0-8204-6254-3

Vol. 7 Marina Dossena & Charles Jones (eds)
Insights into Late Modern English. 2nd edition.
378 pages. 2003, 2007.
ISBN 978-3-03911-257-9. US-ISBN 978-0-8204-8927-8

Vol. 8 Maurizio Gotti
Specialized Discourse. Linguistic Features and Changing Conventions.
351 pages. 2003, 2005.
ISBN 3-03910-606-6. US-ISBN 0-8204-7000-7

Vol. 9 Alan Partington, John Morley & Louann Haarman (eds)
Corpora and Discourse.
420 pages. 2004. ISBN 3-03910-026-2. US-ISBN 0-8204-6262-4

Vol. 10 Martina Möllering
The Acquisition of German Modal Particles. A Corpus-Based Approach.
290 pages. 2004. ISBN 3-03910-043-2. US-ISBN 0-8204-6273-X

Vol. 11 David Hart (ed.)
English Modality in Context. Diachronic Perspectives.
261 pages. 2003. ISBN 3-03910-046-7. US-ISBN 0-8204-6852-5

Vol. 12 Wendy Swanson
Modes of Co-reference as an Indicator of Genre.
430 pages. 2003. ISBN 3-03910-052-1. US-ISBN 0-8204-6855-X

Vol. 13 Gina Poncini
Discursive Strategies in Multicultural Business Meetings.
2nd edition. 338 pages. 2004, 2007.
ISBN 978-3-03911-296-8. US-ISBN 978-0-8204-8937-7

Vol. 14 Christopher N. Candlin & Maurizio Gotti (eds)
Intercultural Aspects of Specialized Communication.
2nd edition. 369 pages. 2004, 2007.
ISBN 978-3-03911-258-6. US-ISBN 978-0-8204-8926-1

Vol. 15 Gabriella Del Lungo Camiciotti & Elena Tognini Bonelli (eds)
Academic Discourse. New Insights into Evaluation.
234 pages. 2004. ISBN 3-03910-353-9. US-ISBN 0-8204-7016-3

Vol. 16 Marina Dossena & Roger Lass (eds)
Methods and Data in English Historical Dialectology.
405 pages. 2004. ISBN 3-03910-362-8. US-ISBN 0-8204-7018-X

Vol. 17 Judy Noguchi
The Science Review Article. An Opportune Genre in the Construction of Science.
274 pages. 2006. ISBN 3-03910-426-8. US-ISBN 0-8204-7034-1

Vol. 18 Giuseppina Cortese & Anna Duszak (eds)
Identity, Community, Discourse. English in Intercultural Settings.
495 pages. 2005. ISBN 3-03910-632-5. US-ISBN 0-8204-7163-1

Vol. 19 Anna Trosborg & Poul Erik Flyvholm Jørgensen (eds)
Business Discourse. Texts and Contexts.
250 pages. 2005. ISBN 3-03910-606-6. US-ISBN 0-8204-7000-7

Vol. 20 Christopher Williams
Tradition and Change in Legal English. Verbal Constructions in Prescriptive Texts.
2nd revised edition. 216 pages. 2005, 2007. ISBN 978-3-03911-444-3.

Vol. 21 Katarzyna Dziubalska-Kołaczyk & Joanna Przedlacka (eds)
English Pronunciation Models: A Changing Scene.
2nd printing. 476 pages. 2005, 2008. ISBN 978-3-03911-682-9.

Vol. 22 Christián Abello-Contesse, Rubén Chacón-Beltrán, M. Dolores López-Jiménez & M. Mar Torreblanca-López (eds)
Age in L2 Acquisition and Teaching.
214 pages. 2006. ISBN 3-03910-668-6. US-ISBN 0-8204-7174-7

Vol. 23 Vijay K. Bhatia, Maurizio Gotti, Jan Engberg & Dorothee Heller (eds)
Vagueness in Normative Texts.
474 pages. 2005. ISBN 3-03910-653-8. US-ISBN 0-8204-7169-0

Vol. 24 Paul Gillaerts & Maurizio Gotti (eds)
Genre Variation in Business Letters. 2nd printing.
407 pages. 2008. ISBN 978-3-03911-681-2.

Vol. 25 Ana María Hornero, María José Luzón & Silvia Murillo (eds)
Corpus Linguistics. Applications for the Study of English.
2nd printing. 526 pages. 2006, 2008. ISBN 978-3-03911-726-0

Vol. 26 J. Lachlan Mackenzie &
María de los Ángeles Gómez-González (eds)
Studies in Functional Discourse Grammar.
259 pages. 2005. ISBN 3-03910-696-1 / US-ISBN 0-8204-7558-0

Vol. 27 Debbie G.E. Ho
Classroom Talk. Exploring the Sociocultural Structure
of Formal ESL Learning. 2nd edition.
254 pages. 2006, 2007. ISBN 978-3-03911-434-4

Vol. 28 Javier Pérez-Guerra, Dolores González-Álvarez,
Jorge L. Bueno-Alonso & Esperanza Rama-Martínez (eds)
'Of Varying Language and Opposing Creed':
New Insights into Late Modern English.
455 pages. 2007. ISBN 978-3-03910-788-9

Vol. 29 Francesca Bargiela-Chiappini & Maurizio Gotti (eds)
Asian Business Discourse(s).
350 pages. 2005. ISBN 3-03910-804-2 / US-ISBN 0-8204-7574-2

Vol. 30 Nicholas Brownlees (ed.)
News Discourse in Early Modern Britain.
Selected Papers of CHINED 2004.
300 pages. 2006. ISBN 3-03910-805-0 / US-ISBN 0-8204-8025-8

Vol. 31 Roberta Facchinetti & Matti Rissanen (eds)
Corpus-based Studies of Diachronic English.
300 pages. 2006. ISBN 3-03910-851-4 / US-ISBN 0-8204-8040-1

Vol. 32 Marina Dossena & Susan M. Fitzmaurice (eds)
Business and Official Correspondence:
Historical Investigations.
209 pages. 2006. ISBN 3-03910-880-8 / US-ISBN 0-8204-8352-4

Vol. 33 Giuliana Garzone & Srikant Sarangi (eds)
Discourse, Ideology and Specialized Communication.
494 pages. 2007. ISBN 978-3-03910-888-6

Vol. 34 Giuliana Garzone & Cornelia Ilie (eds)
The Use of English in Institutional and Business Settings.
An Intercultural Perspective.
372 pages. 2007. ISBN 978-3-03910-889-3

Vol. 35 Vijay K. Bhatia & Maurizio Gotti (eds)
Explorations in Specialized Genres.
316 pages. 2006. ISBN 3-03910-995-2 / US-ISBN 0-8204-8372-9

Vol. 36 Heribert Picht (ed.)
Modern Approaches to Terminological Theories and Applications.
432 pages. 2006. ISBN 3-03911-156-6 / US-ISBN 0-8204-8380-X

Vol. 37 Anne Wagner & Sophie Cacciaguidi-Fahy (eds)
Legal Language and the Search for Clarity / Le langage juridique et la quête de clarté. Practice and Tools / Pratiques et instruments.
487 pages. 2006. ISBN 3-03911-169-8 / US-ISBN 0-8388-5

Vol. 38 Juan Carlos Palmer-Silveira, Miguel F. Ruiz-Garrido & Inmaculada Fortanet-Gómez (eds)
Intercultural and International Business Communication: Theory, Research and Teaching.
2nd edition. 343 pages. 2006, 2008. ISBN 978-3-03911-680-5

Vol. 39 Christiane Dalton-Puffer, Dieter Kastovsky, Nikolaus Ritt & Herbert Schendl (eds)
Syntax, Style and Grammatical Norms: English from 1500–2000.
250 pages. 2006. ISBN 3-03911-181-7 / US-ISBN 0-8204-8394-X

Vol. 40 Marina Dossena & Irma Taavitsainen (eds)
Diachronic Perspectives on Domain-Specific English.
280 pages. 2006. ISBN 3-03910-176-0 / US-ISBN 0-8204-8391-5

Vol. 41 John Flowerdew & Maurizio Gotti (eds)
Studies in Specialized Discourse.
293 pages. 2006. ISBN 3-03911-178-7 / US-ISBN 0-8204-8393-1

Vol. 42 Ken Hyland & Marina Bondi (eds)
Academic Discourse Across Disciplines.
320 pages. 2006. ISBN 3-03911-183-3 / US-ISBN 0-8204-8396-6

Vol. 43 Paul Gillaerts & Philip Shaw (eds)
The Map and the Landscape: Norms and Practices in Genre.
256 pages. 2006. ISBN 3-03911-182-5 / US-ISBN 0-8204-8395-4

Vol. 44 Maurizio Gotti & Davide Giannoni (eds)
New Trends in Specialized Discourse Analysis.
301 pages. 2006. ISBN 3-03911-184-1 / US-ISBN 0-8204-8381-8

Vol. 45 Maurizio Gotti & Françoise Salager-Meyer (eds)
Advances in Medical Discourse Analysis:
Oral and Written Contexts.
492 pages. 2006. ISBN 3-03911-185-X / US-ISBN 0-8204-8382-6

Vol. 46 Maurizio Gotti & Susan Šarcević (eds)
Insights into Specialized Translation.
396 pages. 2006. ISBN 3-03911-186-8 / US-ISBN 0-8204-8383-4

Vol. 47 Khurshid Ahmad & Margaret Rogers (eds)
Evidence-based LSP: Translation, Text and Terminology.
584 pages. 2007. ISBN 978-3-03911-187-9

Vol. 48 Hao Sun & Dániel Z. Kádár (eds)
It's the Dragon's Turn: Chinese Institutional Discourses.
262 pages. 2008. ISBN 978-3-03911-175-6

Vol. 49 Cristina Suárez-Gómez
Relativization in Early English (950-1250):
the Position of Relative Clauses.
149 pages. 2006. ISBN 3-03911-203-1 / US-ISBN 0-8204-8904-2

Vol. 50 Maria Vittoria Calvi & Luisa Chierichetti (eds)
Nuevas tendencias en el discurso de especialidad.
319 pages. 2006. ISBN 978-3-03911-261-6

Vol. 51 Mari Carmen Campoy & María José Luzón (eds)
Spoken Corpora in Applied Linguistics.
274 pages. 2008. ISBN 978-3-03911-275-3

Vol. 52 Konrad Ehlich & Dorothee Heller (Hrsg.)
Die Wissenschaft und ihre Sprachen.
323 pages. 2006. ISBN 978-3-03911-272-2

Vol. 53 Jingyu Zhang
The Semantic Salience Hierarchy Model:
The L2 Acquisition of Psych Predicates
273 pages. 2007. ISBN 978-3-03911-300-2

Vol. 54 Norman Fairclough, Giuseppina Cortese & Patrizia Ardizzone (eds)
Discourse and Contemporary Social Change.
555 pages. 2007. ISBN 978-3-03911-276-0

Vol. 55 Jan Engberg, Marianne Grove Ditlevsen, Peter Kastberg &
Martin Stegu (eds)
New Directions in LSP Teaching.
331 pages. 2007. ISBN 978-3-03911-433-7

Vol. 56 Dorothee Heller & Konrad Ehlich (Hrsg.)
Studien zur Rechtskommunikation.
322 pages. 2007. ISBN 978-3-03911-436-8

Vol. 57 Forthcoming.

Vol. 58 Carmen Frehner
Email – SMS – MMS
294 pages. 2008. ISBN 978-3-03911-451-1

Vol. 59 Isabel Balteiro
The Directionality of Conversion in English:
A Dia-Synchronic Study.
276 pages. 2007. ISBN 978-3-03911-241-8

Vol. 60 Maria Milagros Del Saz Rubio
English Discourse Markers of Reformulation.
237 pages. 2007. ISBN 978-3-03911-196-1

Vol. 61 Forthcoming.

Vol. 62 Sandrine Onillon
Pratiques et représentations de l'écrit.
458 pages. 2008. ISBN 978-3-03911-464-1

Vol. 63 Hugo Bowles & Paul Seedhouse (eds)
Conversation Analysis and Language for Specific Purposes.
334 pages. 2007. ISBN 978-3-03911-469-6

Vol. 64 Vijay K. Bhatia, Christopher N. Candlin &
Paola Evangelisti Allori (eds)
Language, Culture and the Law.
The Formulation of Legal Concepts across Systems and Cultures.
342 pages. 2008. ISBN 978-3-03911-470-2

Vol. 65–67 Forthcoming.

Vol. 68 Eva Alcón-Soler (ed.)
Learning How to Request in an Instructed
Language Learning Context.
260 pages. 2008. ISBN 978-3-03911-601-0

Vol. 69 Domenico Pezzini
The Translation of Religious Texts in the Middle Ages.
428 pages. 2008. ISBN 978-3-03911-600-3

Vol. 70 Tomoko Tode
Effects of frequency in classroom second language learning.
Quasi-experiment and stimulated-recall analysis.
195 pages. 2008. ISBN 978-3-03911-602-7

Vol. 71 Forthcoming.

Vol. 72 Cynthia J. Kellett Bidoli & Elana Ochse (eds)
English in International Deaf Communication.
444 pages. 2008. ISBN 978-3-03911-610-2

Vol. 73 Joan C. Beal, Carmela Nocera & Massimo Sturiale (eds)
Perspectives on Prescriptivism.
269 pages. 2008. ISBN 978-3-03911-632-4

Vol. 74–75 Forthcoming.

Vol. 76 Marina Dossena & Ingrid Tieken-Boon van Ostade (eds)
Studies in Late Modern English Correspondence.
Methodology and Data.
291 pages. 2008. ISBN 978-3-03911-658-4

Vol. 77-79 Forthcoming.

Vol. 80 Martin Solly, Michelangelo Conoscenti & Sandra Campagna (eds)
Verbal/Visual Narrative Texts in Higher Education.
384 pages. 2008. ISBN 978-3-03911-672-0

Vol. 81 Meiko Matsumoto
From Simple Verbs to Periphrastic Expressions:
The Historical Development of Composite Predicates, Phrasal Verbs, and Related Constructions in English.
235 pages. 2008. ISBN 978-3-03911-675-1

Vijay Bhatia / Jan Engberg /
Maurizio Gotti / Dorothee Heller (eds)

Vagueness in Normative Texts

Bern, Berlin, Bruxelles, Frankfurt am Main, New York, Oxford, Wien, 2005.
474 pp.
Linguistic Insights. Studies in Language and Communication. Vol. 23
Edited by Maurizio Gotti
ISBN 978-3-03910-653-0 / US-ISBN 978-0-8204-7169-3 pb.
sFr. 99.– / € 68.50 / €** 70.40 / € 64.– / £ 48.– / US-$ 99.95*

* includes VAT – valid for Germany ** includes VAT – valid for Austria

Normative texts are meant to be highly impersonal and decontextualised, yet at the same time they also deal with a range of human behaviour that is difficult to predict, which means they have to have a very high degree of determinacy on the one hand, and all-inclusiveness on the other. This poses a dilemma for the writer and interpreter of normative texts. The author of such texts must be determinate and vague at the same time, depending upon to what extent he or she can predict every conceivable contingency that may arise in the application of what he or she writes. The papers in this volume discuss important legal and linguistic aspects relating to the use of vagueness in legal drafting and demonstrate why such aspects are critical to our understanding of the way normative texts function.

With contributions by: Vijay Bhatia – Jan Engberg – Maurizio Gotti – Dorothee Heller – Timothy Endicott – Markus Nussbaumer – Lawrence M. Solan – Pierre A. Karrer – Peter M. Tiersma – Celina Frade – Ruth Vatvedt Fjeld – Anne Wagner – Christopher Williams – Giuseppina Cortese – Girolamo Tessuto – Martin Solly – Marta Chromá – Anna Giordano Ciancio – Davide Simone Giannoni.

«To summarize, 'Vagueness in Normative Texts' is a timely contribution to work on legal discourse and vague language in use. The volume's interdisciplinary perspectives and its range and breadth of contributions make it a valuable resource for linguists and researchers who focus on legal discourse as well as other areas of professional and specialized discourse.» (Gina Poncini, Multilingua)

PETER LANG
Bern · Berlin · Bruxelles · Frankfurt am Main · New York · Oxford · Wien

Anne Wagner / Sophie Cacciaguidi-Fahy (eds/éds)

Legal Language and the Search for Clarity

Practice and Tools

Le langage juridique et la quête de clarté

Pratiques et Instruments

Bern, Berlin, Bruxelles, Frankfurt am Main, New York, Oxford, Wien, 2006. 493 pp.
Linguistic Insights. Studies in Language and Communication. Vol. 37
Edited by Maurizio Gotti
ISBN 978-3-03911-169-5 / US-ISBN 978-0-8204-8388-7 pb.
sFr. 109.– / € 74.90 / €** 77.– / € 70.– / £ 52.50 / US-$ 108.95*

* includes VAT – valid for Germany ** includes VAT – valid for Austria

This interdisciplinary collection with contributions in English and French explores how the various disciplines of law and linguistics appreciate and work towards improving the nature of clarity and obscurity in legal language. For the first time, it brings together legal academics and practitioners, jurilinguists and linguists from the common law and civil law with the specific aim to understand the complex nature, practice and tools of clarity and obscurity in legal drafting. Topics addressed include how the Clarity framework has been put into practice through the use of plainer language, better comprehensibility, readability and access to legal or administrative texts. In an attempt to reflect the more recent development of the Clarity-Obscurity debate, the editors have also focused on the use of specific instruments to respond to the problems raised by obscurity to improve clarity.

Cette collection interdisciplinaire offrant des contributions en anglais et en français, explore comment les diverses disciplines du droit et de la linguistique appréhendent et visent à perfectionner la nature de la clarté et de l'opacité du discours juridique. Cet ouvrage rassemblant pour la première fois, des universitaires et professionnels du droit, des jurilinguistes et linguistes de la common law and et du droit civil, propose de découvrir la nature complexe, les pratiques et outils de la clarté et de l'opacité utilisés en rédaction juridique. Les questions abordées examinent la mise en pratique de la clarté juridique au travers de l'utilisation de la langue courante, une meilleure lisibilité, compréhensibilité et accès aux textes juridiques et administratifs. Dans le but de refléter l'actualité du débat Clarté-Opacité du discours juridique, les éditrices se sont également concentrées sur l'utilisation des outils et méthodes les plus récents et utilisés pour résoudre les difficultés soulevées par l'opacité des langues du droit et ainsi améliorer la transparence du discours juridique.

PETER LANG
Bern · Berlin · Bruxelles · Frankfurt am Main · New York · Oxford · Wien

www.ingramcontent.com/pod-product-compliance
Ingram Content Group UK Ltd.
Pitfield, Milton Keynes, MK11 3LW, UK
UKHW020201290926
15471UKWH00005B/1004

9 783039 11470